CPEC: A Precursor to Regional Economic Growth and Stability

Editor

Zafar Iqbal Cheema

STRATEGIC **V**ISION
I N S T I T U T E

**China Studies & Information Center (CSIC)
Strategic Vision Institute (SVI) Islamabad**

STRATEGIC VISION INSTITUTE (SVI)

Strategic Vision Institute (SVI) is a multidisciplinary and non-partisan institution established in 2013. It has since cultivated professional expertise to cope with the increasingly complex strategic environment for policy formulation and decision-making across multiple areas pertaining to national and international politics. SVI aims to project strategic foresights on issues of national and international import through dispassionate, impartial, and independent research, analyses, and studies. The current spotlight of the SVI is on regional and international peace, stability and security.

The SVI China Studies & Information Center (CSIC) was set up to provide a shared platform for Pakistani and Chinese scholars, as part of the burgeoning Pak-China bi-lateral framework to discuss and highlight key issues of interest such as CPEC.

Editor
Zafar Iqbal Cheema

Associate Editor
M. Waqas Jan

ISBN No. 978-969-9907-04-3

CONTACT DETAILS
E-Mail: info@thesvi.org
Web: www.thesvi.org
www.facebook.com/svicom
Tel: +92-51-8434973-75
Fax: +92-51-8431583

Disclaimer: The views and opinions expressed in this edition are those of the authors and do not necessarily reflect the policy or position of the Strategic Vision Institute

CONTENTS

Part III: Restructuring Pakistan's Economy via CPEC

Part IV: CPEC as Part of a New Global Paradigm

ACKNOWLEDGMENT

This book was made possible by the unwavering support of its learned contributors and experts from both China and Pakistan. Their tireless efforts and meticulous attention to detail is what has made this book possible.

The talented SVI Editorial team as part of the China Studies & Information Center (CSIC) has also played a leading role in its compilation and editing. This book would not have been what it is today without their unflinching dedication and commitment. Special thanks to Ms. S Sadia Kazmi, Dr. Anjum Sarfraz, Qura tul ain Hafeez and Beenish Altaf for their assistance in ensuring that the referencing, drafting and overall quality of this detailed work lived up to the strict standards maintained by them at the SVI.

The Editors would also like to extend their most heartfelt gratitude to the People's Republic of China for adding greater impetus to the importance of quality scholarship the world over. Their assistance in helping set up the China Studies & Information Center (CSIC) here at the SVI has played a crucial role in facilitating greater collaborations between scholars from both Pakistan and China. This book is evidence of these collaborations that also serves as a celebration of both countries' vision of promoting greater partnerships within academic discourse, as an extension of the long and storied relations between Pakistan and China. It is hoped that its continuing impact on students, teachers, policy-makers, administrators and people from all walks of life on both sides of the border carries on for many generations to come.

FOREWORD

Strategic Vision Institute (SVI) is pleased to announce the publication of its edited book titled: *CPEC – A Precursor to Regional Economic Growth and Stability* at the forum of SVI-China Studies & Information Center (SVI-CSIC). The idea for the SVI-CSIC was conceived in December 2016 and was announced on 19th June 2017. Based upon the recognition of a dire necessity of dedicated research, analyses and information on CPEC, the SVI-CSIC is devoted to the study of China-Pakistan Relations with special reference to the China-Pakistan Economic Corridor (CPEC) and the Belt and Road Initiative (BRI).

Producing an edited book in such a limited timeframe is indeed a great achievement. The prime objective which SVI has been striving for is to foster an academic discourse on economic development, regional connectivity and the promotion of investment (FDI) focusing on CPEC. CPEC is widely recognized as a 'flagship project' of the BRI and a 'game changer' and has attracted the establishment of many academic research institutes and teaching departments in both China and Pakistan. The SVI-CSIC and this book: *CPEC – A Precursor to Regional Economic Growth and Stability* is a complementary effort to reinforce the existing scholastic framework and discourse on the subject since SVI believes in promoting the spirit of national collaboration rather than acquisitive competition.

CPEC is an unparalleled project worth 63 billion US dollars and is bigger than the Post WW-II Marshall Plan in Europe. It aims to promote infra-structure development to boost regional connectivity and stimulate economic growth. While the CPEC is now a reality and holds a bright prospect and future for Pakistan, the problem it faces is the misconstrued criticism based upon the lack of objective understanding. The general public in Pakistan is still not fully aware of the facts, figures and realities about the CPEC. It is important to understand that CPEC is a vote of confidence in the future of Pakistan by its best friend, China.

Pakistan was supported by China at a time when neither any Western nor Muslim country seemed willing to come forward to help Pakistan. In this situation, China's trust in Pakistan is not only a tremendous morale booster but comprises of a substantial aid and investment project that would bring Pakistan out of economic instability and further strengthen this mostly friendly bilateral partnership.

CPEC merits a more informed narrative, which this book offers through objective analysis and well researched chapters contributed by established national and international scholars. It looks beyond the pedagogical debate on Sino-Pak relations and delves deeper into studying various dimensions of the CPEC not only vis-à-vis Pakistan and South Asia but beyond the regional settings in West and Central Asia as part of the BRI. It particularly explores the Chinese philosophy behind its phenomenally unprecedented development and the future vision reflected in the shape of the BRI of which CPEC is the flag-ship project.

CPEC carries profound impacts for the region's politics, economy, development and infrastructure. This is an exceptional milestone that has been achieved since the creation of Pakistan. Being the project of "connectivity" it has regional as well as global implications. It is extremely beneficial to Pakistan and equally favorable for China as well, although Pakistan is going to be the major beneficiary of CPEC. It provides a link between Western regions of China's Xinjiang Province and the Gwadar Port that lies in the Makran coast of Pakistan. This corridor will not only facilitate economic development, infrastructure, and communication but all kinds of transport between China, Pakistan and beyond. It is naturally assisted from both countries' peculiar geographical proximity where Pakistan provides direct links to Middle East and an easy access to Central Asia. So, CPEC shouldn't be looked at as an economic linkage just for China and Pakistan but as part of China's overall development strategy i.e. BRI which links three major regions of the world; Asia, Europe and Africa.

The book aims to promote an objective understanding about CPEC and further augmentation of friendly relations of China with Pakistan; a trustworthy all-weather friend, and how it aims at harnessing Pakistan's geostrategic significance into geo-economic enterprise through the CPEC, enhancing Pakistan's prospects for turning into a hub of regional connectivity, peace, and prosperity in due course of time.

This edited volume based on objective academic research and inquiry, establishes a positive perception about CPEC on which there are unmerited attempts to embroil it in controversies and polemic criticisms. It is a dedicated effort to bring forth impartial and dispassionate literature on the subject, highlighting the numerous opportunities and the potentials of the economic corridor. This is to mitigate the ambiguities and misgivings surrounding this project, while at the same time evaluating the impact of CPEC on Pakistan's national, regional as well as global politics, while highlighting the prospects of Pakistan undertaking the role of a key player in the region. This is exactly what this book has tried to establish.

The SVI-CSIC hopes to continue to further carry out an in-depth study of various dimensions of the CPEC and Sino-Pak relations, including development, geo-economics, and politics of the region, and beyond. Since its inception in 2013, SVI has been regularly contributing to the discourse on security, strategic and foreign policies through capacity-building workshops, in-house seminars / panel discussions, conferences, roundtables and opinion articles, covering a wide range of audience. SVI is equally dedicated to publishing analyses based academic literature in the form of books, policy papers, and journals. This edited volume is part of the same effort envisioned to develop a connection and dialogue between the content of its discourse and the audience / readership. It is hoped that this book will provide the readers with a comprehensive and impartial understanding of Sino-Pakistan relations through the lens of CPEC.

Zafar Iqbal Cheema

LIST OF ABBREVIATIONS

ACD	Asia Cooperation Dialogue
ADB	Asian Development Bank
AIIB	Asian Infrastructure Investment Bank
AJK	Azad Jammu and Kashmir
ANP	Awami National Party
APEC	Asia-Pacific Economic Cooperation
APTTA	Afghanistan-Pakistan Transit Trade Agreement
ASEAN	Association of South East Asian Nations
ASEM	Asia-Europe Meeting
BLA	Balochistan Liberation Army
BLF	Balochistan Liberation Front
BNP	Baloch Nationalist Party
BoI	Board of Investment
BoP	Balance of Payments
BRI	Belt and Road Initiative
BTC	Baku-Tbilisi-Ceyhan
CAR	Central Asian Republics
CAREC	Central Asia Regional Economic Cooperation
CASA	Central Asia South Asia
CASCF	China-Arab States Cooperation Forum
CCI	Council of Common Interests
CDB	China Development Bank
CDWP	Central Development Working Party
CENTO	Central Treaty Organization
CICA	Conference on Interaction and Confidence-Building Measures in Asia
CIS	Commonwealth of Independent States

CMEC	China Machinery Engineering Corporation
COD	Commercial Operation Date
COIN	Counter Insurgency
COPHC	China Overseas Ports Holding Company
CONUS	Contiguous United States
COSCO	China Ocean Shipping Company
CPC	Communist Party of China
CPEC	China-Pakistan Economic Corridor
CPIH	China Power International Holding Limited
CRI	China Radio International
CSNO	China Satellite Navigation Office
CSTO	Collective Security Treaty Organization
CTG	China Three Gorges Corporation
DTMB	Digital Terrestrial Multimedia Broadcast
DZ	Domestic Zones
EAD	Economic Affairs Division
ECNEC	Executive Committee of the National Economic Council
EEE	Economic, Energy Efficient and Eco Friendly
EEZ	Exclusive Economic Zone
EPZA	Export Processing Zones Authority
ETIM	East Turkestan Islamic Movement
EU	European Union
FATA	Federally Administrated Tribal Areas
FBR	Federal Board of Revenue
FC	Financial Close
FDI	Foreign Direct Investment
FTA	Free Trade Agreement
FPCCI	Federation of Pakistan Chambers of Commerce and Industry
FY	Fiscal Year

GATT	General Agreement on Tariff and Trade
GB	Gilgit-Baltistan
GCAP	Greater Central Asia Partnership
GCC	Gulf Cooperation Council
GDA	Gwadar Development Authority
GDP	Gross Domestic Product
GNP	Gross National Product
GMS	Greater Mekong Subregion
GSP	Generalized System of Preferences
HDPPL	Hydro China Dawood Power Limited
HUBCO	Hub Power Company Limited
HVDC	High Voltage Direct Current
IBRD	International Bank for Reconstruction and Development
ICBC	Industrial and Commercial Bank of China
ICT	Information and Communications Technology
IFC	International Finance Corporation
IFIs	International Financial Institutions
IMF	International Monetary Fund
IOR	Indian Ocean Region
ISIS	Islamic State of Iraq and Syria / (Daesh)
IT	Information Technology
JCC	Joint Coordination Committee
JWG	Joint Working Group
KCR	Karachi Circular Railway
KKH	Karakorum Highway
KPK	Khyber Pakhtunkhwa
LeJ	Lashkar-e-Jhangvi
LNG	Liquefied Natural Gas
ML	Main Line
MoPNR	Ministry of Petroleum and Natural Resources

MSR	Maritime Silk Road
Mta	Million Metric Tons Annually
NATO	North Atlantic Treaty Organization
NBC	National Broadcasting Company
NDN	Northern Distribution Network
NDRC	National Development and Reform Commission (China)
NEA	National Energy Administration
NEPRA	National Electric Power Regulatory Authority
NFC	National Finance Commission
NFCS	National Finance Commission Secretariat
NICE	NUML International Centre of Education
NUML	National University of Modern Languages
NWFP	North West Frontier Province
OBOR	One Belt One Road
ODI	Outward Direct Investment
OECD	Organization for Economic Co-operation and Development
OFC	Optical Fiber Cable
OPEC	Organization of the Petroleum Exporting Countries
PBC	Pakistan Broadcasting Corporation
PKR	Pakistani Rupees
PLA	People's Liberation Army
PPIB	Private Power and Infrastructure Board
PSA	Port of Singapore Authority
PSDP	Public Sector Development Program
POF	Pakistan Ordinance Factory
PPP	Pakistan Peoples Party
PTI	Pakistan Tehreek-e-Insaf
RAW	Research and Analysis Wing
RMB	Renminbi

SAARC	South Asian Association for Regional Cooperation
SASAC	State-owned Assets Supervision and Administration Commission
SCO	Shanghai Cooperation Organization
SCS	South China Sea
SDPI	Sustainable Development Policy Institute
SDR	Special Drawing Rights
SEATO	South East Asian Treaty Organization
SEC	Shanghai Electric Power Company
SEZ	Special Economic Zone
SMEs	Small and Medium Enterprises
SREB	Silk Road Economic Belt
SRF	Silk Road Fund
SSRL	Sino Sindh Resources Limited
SUPARCO	Space and Upper Atmospheric Research Commission
TAPI	Turkmenistan-Afghan-Pakistan-India
TPP	Trans-Pacific Partnership
TTIP	Transatlantic Trade and Investment Partnership
TTP	Tehreek-e-Taliban Pakistan
UEP	United Energy Pakistan
UNDP	United Nations Development Program
USD	United States Dollar
USGS	United States Geological Survey
USSR	Union of Soviet Socialist Republics
WB	World Bank
WOT	War on Terror
WTO	World Trade Organization
XUAR	Xinjiang Uyghur Autonomous Region

Introduction

Since its formal inception nearly five years ago, the China-Pakistan Economic Corridor has captured the imagination of millions across Pakistan and the wider region. It has done so in a manner unlike anything that has come before it in recent history. In fact it is hard to imagine any similar bilateral agreement achieving this much popularity amongst such a diverse audience. For quite some time now CPEC has remained the focus of countless diplomats, policy-makers, scholars, business-owners, journalists and observers from all sorts of backgrounds and walks of life. Each of whom, is in one way or another, deeply influenced by its development. This in itself testifies to the diverse and broad ranging ways in which CPEC has permeated through multiple spheres of Pakistan's body-politics. Touching across economics, politics, diplomacy, technology, defense and much of everyday society, CPEC in its overarching vision has brought with it both hope, as well as certain challenges for millions of Pakistanis.

Its massive scope and unrivalled ambition has led to its own set of expectations for the people of Pakistan. The promises of much needed socio-economic development, of international recognition and a key standing amidst the global comity of nations are all benefits well worth their proposed costs and required attention. However, with these promises have also come unique hurdles, both internal and external, that require a renewed sense of vigor and commitment if they are to be surpassed successfully. While there are immense benefits to be gained from CPEC, especially with regard to the long-term growth and development of the country, great care and vigilance is required to ensure that its eventual outcomes thus remain true to these objectives, and that all that is envisioned under CPEC for Pakistan and the wider region manifests into reality, ultimately for the benefit of its people.

Within this short span of time, much has been written on the expected outcomes of this massive initiative. This is in spite of the fact that while still being in its developmental stages, CPEC's immense popularity has led to the emergence of a thriving discourse on the many merits and challenges brought along by it. Much of this discourse however has drifted more towards CPEC's 'Geo-Strategic' implications on Pakistan and the wider region, despite its intentions to the contrary. The resulting connotations to the South Asian region's security dynamics are what such discussions on CPEC have been mostly contextualized. These include debates that have been restricted to the perhaps more rudimentary concepts explaining the South Asian region's power politics, from which many a Pakistani scholar seems unable to move beyond.

Instead, taking into account the broad contours of the overarching Belt and Road Initiative, (of which CPEC is a key component), this book aims to address this gap by offering a broader more inclusive framework from which to approach this important initiative. This includes taking into account the dramatic shifts in global economic growth and stability currently being witnessed the world over. Representing the most recent trends in international politics and the changing world financial system, these changes are a direct result of the rise of China as a global economic power, as it increasingly comes to challenge the US's global supremacy and unilateralism.

The Belt and Road Initiative which in essence serves as an extension of China's rise has itself polarized opinions across the world as to its purported merits, as well as to the potential dangers it poses to the current status-quo. Yet, considering the inescapable reality of China's rise as an economic power and its projected growth for the decades to come; it is evident that the BRI is to continue to re-shape major trends and key fault-lines the world over. This holds equally true for its impact on Pakistan, its long-standing ally.

Thus, keeping in mind the BRI's long term impact on global growth and stability, this book addresses the many issues surrounding CPEC with a clear view to its contribution within this wider international framework. By drawing on the long history of close ties between Pakistan and China, and the multi-faceted nature of their bi-lateral cooperation, the ensuing discussions provide a more holistic framework

2

from which to examine the purported effects of CPEC. This allows for a much broader evaluation of CPEC's impact on the region's economic growth and stability, thus adding greater value to the already saturated discourse on its security implications.

Drawing on the expertise of a diverse range of scholars and experts, this book has been divided into four distinct parts that deal with the relations between China, Pakistan, CPEC and the BRI. Each of these parts subsequently focuses on a select aspect of these relationships that are developed in further detail by the individual chapters comprising them.

Part I by defining CPEC within the Pak-China framework, discusses the history, current progress and overarching scope of CPEC within the current global context. Its opening chapter presents a brief overview of the historical development of Pak-China relations, placing CPEC as the historical culmination of these relations. The second chapter in defining the present scope and mandate of CPEC, positions it within the overarching BRI framework. It provides an updated snapshot on its current progress in relation to its envisioned targets. The third and final chapter of this section presents a detailed discussion on the newly developed port of Gwadar which it argues as forming the underlying blue-print for CPEC and its envisioned objectives. It contextualizes its development from a global standpoint in an attempt to provide a more innovative approach to the already immense body of work based on it.

Moving on from this introductory exposition of Pakistan and CPEC, Part II goes on to contextualize the emergence of the Belt & Road Initiative as a direct consequence of the economic rise of China. Based on this, Chapter 4 presents a historical overview of the numerous factors that contributed to China's unprecedented economic growth over the last few decades. It offers a detailed exposition of the Chinese development model, inviting questions as to whether it can be replicable within Pakistan. Chapter 5 while drawing on the success of China's development model presents a thorough overview of the Belt & Road Initiative from the perspective of Chinese policy-makers. It details the inner workings and rationale behind this important initiative including its overall objectives and the challenges faced in achieving them. Chapter 6 by further expanding on these objectives presents a comprehensive look into the impact of the Belt & Road Initiative on the global financial system. Taking into consideration China's emergence as a major economic power, it examines the numerous ways in which the BRI, and by extension CPEC, is to influence the international financial system for many years to come.

Part three while continuing this discussion on the economic and financial impacts of these initiatives, presents viable recommendations to the many ways CPEC can be used to restructure the Pakistani economy. This includes overcoming the myriad challenges currently limiting the socio-economic development and growth of Pakistan. Chapter 7 highlights these challenges specifically with regard to those being faced by Pakistan's export sector. Based on these, it offers pragmatic suggestions to help leverage the next phase of CPEC projects to the sector's advantage. Chapter 8 in a similar vein discusses the importance of Special Economic Zones, as part of these upcoming phases. By first defining and evaluating the impact setting up such zones has had on numerous countries across the world, the ensuing discussion highlights the importance of these zones for Pakistan as part of the next phase of developments under CPEC.

The fourth and final part of this book ties together the previous discussions on the key roles being played by CPEC and BRI, to the wider region's growth and development. Within this section, Chapter 9 does this by assessing the viability of these roles within the contemporary international security framework, while taking into account both local and external security constraints. Chapter 10 contextualizes this debate within the super-power politics pervading through the Asian region, citing the importance of regional connectivity as intersecting the fine line between geo-strategic and geo-economic advantage. Chapter 11 takes this discussion further and posits viable scenarios and recommendations that can be leveraged to Pakistan's advantage as part of a series of win-win partnerships with key states across the region. Chapter 12, the final chapter of this book provides a detailed progress report on CPEC projects, as of publication of this book.

By thus drawing together this diverse body of work, and highlighting the most salient implications emanating from CPEC and the BRI, this book aims to present an important point of departure for evaluating and assessing the purported impacts of CPEC on regional growth and stability. In doing so, this entire work attempts to fill the void left by the dearth of scholarship on the subject, with particular consideration of the fact that the initiative's long term outlook is still very much in its developmental stages. Nevertheless, it is hoped that the collected work of this book's contributors will go a long way in assisting scholars and researchers in studying the myriad possibilities regarding Pakistan's geo-economic and geo-strategic potential with regard to CPEC.

By advocating a wider more diverse perspective, it is hoped that this book presents a suitable point of departure for further scholarship, that takes into account the various themes and subjects this massive initiative continues to encompass and straddle across.

Zafar Iqbal Cheema

Part I:
CPEC within the Pak-China Framework

Chapter 1: CPEC as the Historic Culmination of Pak-China Relations

Qura tul Ain Hafeez[*]

Introduction

Throughout the region's history bilateral relations between China and Pakistan have been bound together by the shared hopes and challenges of both countries. Despite major political, cultural and socio-economic disparities both countries have continued to strengthen their relations, growing ever closer in terms of greater regional integration and cooperation. These relations were established not only on the basis of mutual interests, but shaped by the changing geo-political history of the region as well.

Pakistan has continued to prefer a more bilateral policy towards China and has remained a key strategic partner. As will be shown in this chapter, Pakistan has throughout its history served as a key bridge between China and the rest of the world in a number of ways.[1] Through a combination of political, economic and diplomatic support, Pakistan has as a result, played a key role in facilitating China's rise at both the regional and international levels.[2] Keeping in mind this historical context, this chapter discusses how Pakistan continues to play that role

---

[*] Ms. Qura tul Ain Hafeez is a Research Associate at the Strategic Vision Institute (SVI), Islamabad.
[1] Yafeng Xia, "The Cold War and Chinese Foreign Policy," *E-International Relations*, July 2008, http://www.e-ir.info/2008/07/16/the-cold-war-and-China/ (accessed May 15, 2017).
[2] Farrukh Kayani, Mumtaz Ahmed, Tahir Shah, and Umar Kayani, "China-Pakistan Economic Relations: Lessons for Pakistan," *Pakistan Journal of Commerce and Social Sciences* 7, no. 3 (2013): 454- 462.

under the renewed and accelerated impetus of CPEC as part of the greater Belt and Road Initiative.

Whereas, South Asia's regional politics have often been defined amidst the zero-sum nature of India-Pakistan relations and regional power politics, there have been several areas of mutual interest and cooperation between Pakistan and China. Both Countries have set a prime example of regional cooperation through their adherence to the principles of peaceful coexistence and non-interference, while respecting each other's sovereignty and territorial integrity. Hence, even amidst the constantly shifting dynamics of global power relations, the Pak-China bilateral frame work has forged ahead and prospered despite the numerous extraneous constraints and challenges imposed upon it. This shows the marked resilience and 'All-weather' nature of the Pak-China friendship that has remained a salient feature of the South Asian region throughout its history.

The Historic Foundations of the Pak-China Alliance

Formal diplomatic ties between China and Pakistan were first established on May 21, 1951. The following September, the first Chinese ambassador to Pakistan, Mr Han Nianlong took up his station in Karachi, the then capital of Pakistan. Two months later, his Pakistani counterpart Major Gen N.A.M Raza presented his credentials to Beijing on November 1st 1951. The establishment of these formal relations later paved the way for two barter trade agreements for cotton, jute and coal that were signed between China and Pakistan in 1952 and 1953.[3] This also marked the beginning of a rich history of mutually beneficial ties, which were to develop into one of the world's most cogent partnerships extending to even today.

Later, the Bandung Conference in 1955 was the first high level meeting between the two countries amidst a multilateral setting. In October and December of the following year, the Prime Ministers of Pakistan and China visited each other setting a bilateral precedent for

---

[3] Umbreen Javaid and Asifa Jahangir, "Pakistan-China Strategic Relationship: A Glorious Journey of 55 Years," *Journal of the Research Society of Pakistan* 52, no. 1 (2015): 157-183.

relations between both countries.[4] The same year Prime Minister Huseyn Shaheed Suhrawardy and Premier Zhou Enlai signed a Treaty of Friendship between China and Pakistan, further formalizing the basis of cordial relations for many years to come.

During its initial phases, the geo-political situation within the Cold War environment had more or less defined the framework within which Sino-Pakistan relations developed. In fact in their earliest phase, Pakistan-China relations were not as close to what they have now currently grown to be. During those initial years, a number of factors had contributed towards Pakistan's limitations in recognizing China as a potentially close ally.[5]

First and foremost was the security of Pakistani territory. During its formative years, key areas along Pakistan's Western and Eastern borders were still under dispute with its neighboring countries. As a result, Pakistan was not in a position to afford any conflicts that could further jeopardize its territorial integrity.[6]

Pakistan also feared that Soviet expansion to its North-West would further endanger its security. Communist China's alliance with the USSR had further added to this perception. Since Pakistan had sided with the Capitalist bloc through its participation in the South East Asian Treaty Organization (SEATO-1954) and the Central Treaty Organization (CENTO-1955)[7], it had to tread quite carefully in diplomatically maneuvering its interests during this troubled phase of international relations.

Yet, despite this complex web of Cold War alliances at the multi-lateral level, both China and Pakistan capitalized on a number of opportunities for developing positive relations within a bilateral framework. From the late 1950's onwards, Pak-China cooperation gained

---

[4] Hafeez-ur-Rahman Khan, "Pakistan's Relations with the People's Republic of China," *Pakistan Horizon* 14, no. 3 (1961): 212-232.

[5] Umbreen Javaid and Asifa Jahangir, "Pakistan-China Strategic Relationship: A Glorious Journey of 55 Years," *Journal of the Research Society of Pakistan* 52, no. 1 (2015):157-183.

[6] Ibid.

[7] Ibid.

considerable momentum forming much of the basis of their relationship for many years to come. This included the signing of a formal trade agreement in 1963 followed by a border agreement demarcating the frontier territories of both countries. An air transport agreement was also signed in the same year with a large proportion of air traffic to and from China being routed via Pakistan. In this way Pakistan served as a key bridge between China and the rest of the world during this important era of modernization within the region.

In fact, Pakistan served as a key intermediary between China and the rest of the world in numerous ways during this key phase of international relations. For instance, in 1971 US Secretary of State, Henry Kissinger's secret meeting with Premier Zhou Enlai in Beijing was facilitated to a large extent by the Pakistani government. This in turn paved the way for President Nixon's groundbreaking visit to China the following year, marking the normalization of China-US relations after more than two decades of Cold War antagonism.[8] This in itself was a historic move, which in retrospect offered perhaps the earliest glimpse of the shifting power dynamics within the international world order.

The following years, both China and Pakistan re-affirmed their desire for mutually beneficial relations embarking on a period of renewed cooperation. This included the signing of landmark agreements outlining military and economic assistance worth US $300 million in 1972. This further opened doors to closer cooperation in the fields of Science and Technology during an era when Pakistan was exploring possibilities of developing an indigenous nuclear energy program. In effect, the scope of Pak-China bilateral cooperation had begun to take on a significance of its own making a marked impact within a larger regional and global context.

The Karakoram Highway cutting through some of the world's most treacherous terrain was also built in 1978, serving as one of the most endearing examples of Pak-China cooperation. A marvel of modern

---

[8] Laurence Vandewalle, "In Depth Analysis Pakistan and China Iron Brothers Forever?," *European Union*, June, 2015, http://www.europarl.europa.eu/RegData/etudes/IDAN/2015/549052/EXPO_IDA(2015)549052 EN.pdf (accessed August 19, 2018).

engineering in and of itself, it was one of the earliest representations of how both Pakistan's and China's combined strategic, geo-political and socio-economic interests were manifested in a spectacular infrastructure project that had been setup quietly amidst the cold mountainous passes of the Karakoram. It is quite interesting when one surmises that this was when CPEC's very roots were laid almost 30 years ago. This marked yet another important and historic milestone within a fast expanding bilateral framework.

Growing Convergence on Economic and Trade Issues

Over the years, growing Pak-China ties have further led to increased economic development, investment and financial cooperation between the two countries. Even though during its formative years, trade relations were not as developed as they are today, Pakistan has always remained important for China partly due to its strategic location, geography and close proximity. Pakistan is located at the crossroads of three regions which include Central Asia, South Asia, the Middle East and West Asia. Moreover, Pakistan serves as a convenient and secure access point for China bridging the gap between the Persian Gulf and Central Asia. In effect Pakistan provides China with the shortest route for trade through its Gwadar and Port Qasim sea ports, as well as its major road networks along the Indus and Karakoram Highways.[9]

The full benefits of Pakistan's geo-strategic potential have yet to be fully realized with respect to economic cooperation between both countries. Nevertheless, considering their long history of shared progress, the last few years have presented a unique opportunity to address these gaps and take advantage of this vast potential across a broader regional platform.

In order to better contextualize the scope of this vast potential, it is important to first see how economic cooperation between both countries has unfolded throughout their shared history. If one simply takes the expansion of bilateral trade as an indicator, the continued and steady

---

[9] Umbreen Javaid and Asifa Jahangir, "Pakistan-China Strategic Relationship: A Glorious Journey of 55 Years," *Journal of the Research Society of Pakistan* 52, no. 1 (2015): 157-183.

growth in trade volume throughout the history of Pak-China ties is evidence of a burgeoning economic relationship, which has gained increasing momentum over the last few decades.

For instance, just in the period between 1970 and 1979, Pak-China bilateral trade almost tripled in terms of total volume. As described in the preceding section, this growth in trade was arguably one of the earliest manifest signs of the shared dividends flowing from the increasingly cordial relations during this period.[10]

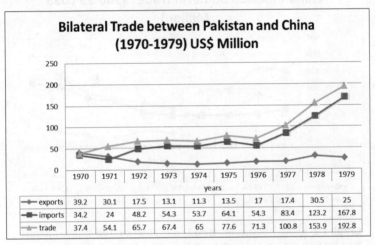

Bilateral Trade between Pakistan and China (1970-1979) US$ Million

years	1970	1971	1972	1973	1974	1975	1976	1977	1978	1979
exports	39.2	30.1	17.5	13.1	11.3	13.5	17	17.4	30.5	25
imports	34.2	24	48.2	54.3	53.7	64.1	54.3	83.4	123.2	167.8
trade	37.4	54.1	65.7	67.4	65	77.6	71.3	100.8	153.9	192.8

Graph 1.1- Bilateral Trade between Pakistan and China (1970-1979) US$ Million. Ahmed Rashid Malik, "The Pakistan-China Bilateral Trade: The Future Trajectory," Strategic *Studies* 37, no. 1 (2017): 66-89.

In the mid 1980's however this steady growth in trade experienced a sharp pull back owing to a number of internal and external factors. The most glaring reason was that Pakistan's economy at the time was still reeling from the loss of East Pakistan. Coupled with internal political turmoil as well as a sudden influx of immigrants, trade as well as economic development suffered immensely. Moreover, the withdrawal of the Soviet Union from Afghanistan and its subsequent collapse which even though was a great victory for the US, led to a number of challenges

---

[10] Ahmed Rashid Malik, "The Pakistan-China Bilateral Trade: The Future Trajectory," *Strategic Studies* 37, no. 1 (2017): 66-89.

for Pakistan. The ensuing instability in Afghanistan has resulted in a myriad range of security issues which have been compounded by the influx of refugees streaming in. In fact, the same challenges have continued to plague the country's development potential for decades since then, even today.[11] It was during this challenging period that the true significance of China's continuing 'all-weather' relationship with Pakistan was brought to the forefront.

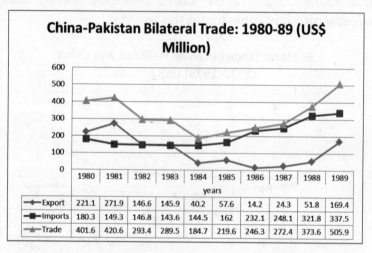

Graph 1.2- China-Pakistan Bilateral Trade: 1980-89 (US$ Million). Ahmed Rashid Malik, "The Pakistan-China Bilateral Trade: The Future Trajectory," *Strategic Studies* 37, no. 1 (2017): 66-89.

Continuing Pak-China Ties Amidst a Changing World Order

The 90's which presented a more or less unipolar world following the collapse of the Soviet Union, brought about a major shift in the economics and politics of the broader international system as well as for the South Asian region. The collapse of the Soviet Union had coincided with the end of the Soviet occupation of Afghanistan for which the US and Pakistan had worked closely together. With its end also came the end of US assistance under the Pressler Amendment sanctions which came into effect in 1990. As a result all American military support and economic aid to Pakistan were deferred in the US's attempts to contain

---

[11] Ibid.

Pakistan's nuclear ambitions. This was in spite of the decades of Pak-US cooperation built over the Cold War.

It was also during this phase that the first signs of China's economic successes had led to it being considered as a viable alternative to US assistance in the region. Hence, Pakistan-China economic cooperation entered an important phase of enhanced significance.[12] This was again evident in the sharp increase in trade volume between Pakistan and China, which again doubled in less than 10 years by 1994.[13]

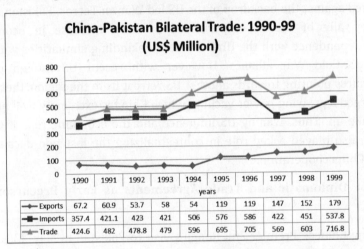

China-Pakistan Bilateral Trade: 1990-99 (US$ Million)

	1990	1991	1992	1993	1994	1995	1996	1997	1998	1999
Exports	67.2	60.9	53.7	58	54	119	119	147	152	179
Imports	357.4	421.1	423	421	506	576	586	422	451	537.8
Trade	424.6	482	478.8	479	596	695	705	569	603	716.8

Graph 1.3- China-Pakistan Bilateral Trade: 1990-99 (US$ Million). Ahmed Rashid Malik, "The Pakistan-China Bilateral Trade: The Future Trajectory," *Strategic Studies* 37, no. 1 (2017): 66-89.

It is important to point out here that China's rapid economic success over the last few decades has itself been hailed as a marvel of international economic development. It is the consequence of its economic growth that China has over the past several years emerged as a major global power. Currently standing as the world's second largest economy, China's GDP rose from US$50 Billion in 1978 to US$10.35

---

[12] Shahzad Akhtar, "Sino-Pakistani Relations: An Assessment," *Institute of Strategic Studies*, 2014, http://issi.org.pk/?p=1258 (accessed October 12, 2017).
[13] Ahmed Rashid Malik, "The Pakistan-China Bilateral Trade: The Future Trajectory," *Strategic Studies* 37, no. 1 (2017): 66-89.

trillion in 2015.[14] As a result, it currently contributes to 30% of the world's economic growth.[15] Hence, it is based on its immense influence on the global economy that China has contributed extensively to the recent multi-polarization of international relations.

On the other hand, waning US influence throughout the broader Asian, and more localized South Asian region has further amplified the impact of China's economic power. Since the start of the new millennium, both diplomatic and economic relations within the world order were framed against the backdrop of the US led War on Terror. Pakistan being a key ally of the US experienced a sharp increase in economic interdependence with the United States, rekindling similarities with the Pak-US Cold War alliance. However with recent US foreign policy measures pointing towards another US retreat from the region, there has emerged a growing power vacuum which China is extremely well poised to take up. Thus, waning US influence and the economic rise of China have also played a key role in contextualizing the last two decades of Pak-China cooperation.

Major Diplomatic and Trade Agreements as Early Precursors to CPEC

During Chinese Premier Zhu Rongji's visit to Pakistan in May 2001, key agreements were signed between Pakistan and China straddling across a number of different areas of economic and technical cooperation. These included partnerships in the energy, minerals, tourism, transport and IT sectors, all of which have remained under-developed throughout Pakistan's history despite their immense potential. The white oil pipeline running from Port Qasim to Multan, the Saindak Copper Gold project and the subsequent modernization of the Pakistan Railways all resulted from these agreements. These present one of the earliest precursors of China's interests in supporting Pakistan's economic development through large-scale infrastructural projects. Nearly US$1 billion were pledged for these

---

[14] S.M. Muneer, "Economic Relations between Pakistan and China," *Business Recorder*, December 15, 2016, https://fp.brecorder.com/2016/12/20161215113672/ (accessed July 7, 2018).
[15] Ibid.

projects along with assurances of completing the Gwadar Port and Coastal Highway.[16]

The following year (2002) Vice Premier Wu Bangguo visited Pakistan to attend the groundbreaking ceremony of the Gwadar deep-sea port, for which China had so far invested US$198 million. This served as a major landmark in Pak-China cooperation, serving as the logical successor to the Karakoram Highway that was developed nearly two decades earlier. Even before the China-Pakistan Economic Corridor (CPEC) was formalized a decade later, Gwadar had already stood as a key symbol of Pakistan and China's shared desire of establishing a major naval transit point along the Indian Ocean. While much has been made of both countries' strategic reasons for doing so, it is the immense potential for trade and greater economic development that has more recently led Gwadar to be termed as the 'Crown Jewel of CPEC'.[17]

While such mega infrastructural projects have stood as the most salient examples of Pak-China cooperation in recent years, the underlying work that has been put in by political leaders, diplomats, economists, and numerous other experts from both sides has often been under-represented within this vast history of Pak-China relations.

For instance, during the state visits of Presidents Pervez Musharraf and Hu Jintao in 2006 a number of landmark agreements were signed between both countries including an all-important Free Trade Agreement. This agreement was in a sense an extension of the previously inked 'Treaty of Friendship, Cooperation and Good Neighborly Relations signed the previous year.

Building on these precedents, this phase of Pak-China relations saw a renewed impetus in military and strategic cooperation. This was highlighted by the huge strides made by both countries in joint

---

[16] Jafar Riaz Kataria and Anum Naveed, "Pakistan-China Social and Economic Relations," *Journal of South Asian Studies* 29, no. 2 (2014): 395-410.

[17] Rajeev Ranjan Chaturvedy, "China's Strategic Access to Gwadar Port: Pivotal Position in Belt and Road," *S. Rajaratnam School of International Studies (RSIS)*, 2017, https://www.rsis.edu.sg/rsis-publication/rsis/co17005-chinas-strategic-access-to-gwadar-port-pivotal-position-in-belt-and-road/#.XFqQPlUzblV (accessed July 7, 2018).

technological development and research. The jointly developed JF-17 Thunder aircraft along with the expansion of Pakistan's Chashma Civilian Nuclear complex present some of the most salient aspects of these developments.

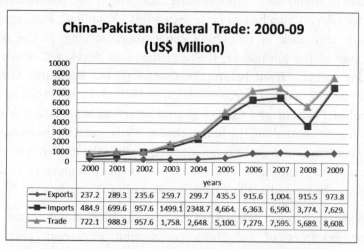

China-Pakistan Bilateral Trade: 2000-09 (US$ Million)

years	2000	2001	2002	2003	2004	2005	2006	2007	2008	2009
Exports	237.2	289.3	235.6	259.7	299.7	435.5	915.6	1,004.	915.5	973.8
Imports	484.9	699.6	957.6	1499.1	2348.7	4,664.	6,363.	6,590.	3,774.	7,629.
Trade	722.1	988.9	957.6	1,758.	2,648.	5,100.	7,279.	7,595.	5,689.	8,608.

Graph 1.4- China-Pakistan Bilateral Trade: 2000-09 (US$ Million). "IMF: Direction of Trade Statistics Year 2009," *International Monetary Fund*, October 28, 2009, https://www.imf.org/en/Publications/Search?series=Direction%20of%20 Trade%20Statistics&when=During&year=2009 (accessed July 7, 2018).

The vast strides made during this period are also evident in the total volume of Pak-China trade during this period. From nearly US$700 million in 2000, total trade between both countries stood at around US$7.6 billion in 2007 and US$8.6 billion by 2009; an increase of over a 1000%.

Not only had these and numerous other developments brought Pak-China ties to a defining moment in history, they had set a major precedent for a host of new opportunities to be pursued within this framework. As bilateral ties between both countries continued to excel even further, policy makers and planners on both sides have remained extremely keen on ensuring that these developments are taken forward to their logical conclusions. Based on these trends of shared progress and prosperity, both China and Pakistan continue to expand on the decades of goodwill straddling across political, socio-economic and technological boundaries.

Building on Six Decades of a Burgeoning Bilateral Relationship

On May 21st 2011, both China and Pakistan marked the 60th anniversary of Pak-China bilateral relations. With 2011 already marked as the Pak-China Friendship year, the idea was to reiterate this long history of shared ties, re-emphasizing the 'all weather' nature of their friendship. It was during this time that the narrative of this relationship was tinged with a sort of a poetic charm with leaders from both sides referring to the Pak-China relationship as "Higher than mountains, deeper than the ocean, stronger than steel and sweeter than honey".[18] This allowed the significance and long history of Pak-China relations to be imbibed within the popular mindset while also presenting a clear affirmation of the two countries' long-standing alliance at the international level.

However, political rhetoric aside, the significance of this move provided further evidence to the fact that building on this broad history of shared progress, the storied success of this alliance presented a platform for launching one of the world's most ambitious attempts at regional integration and connectivity. This in effect provided the perfect backdrop against which to formalize the US$48 billion China Pakistan Economic Corridor (CPEC) as part of China's overall Belt and Road Initiative. A historic framework agreement was signed between both countries on 5th July 2013 outlining how Pakistan's Gwadar Port would link the city of Kashgar situated in the Xinjiang province of North Western China, to the Arabian Sea.

In order to facilitate its implementation, a Joint Coordination Committee (JCC) was setup between key ministries and officials from both countries comprising largely of economists, administrators, lawyers, financial and development experts. The JCC has so far held eight annual meetings till the writing of this book, allowing Pak-China ties to

---

[18] "Pak-China Friendship is Higher than Mountains, Deeper than Ocean and Sweeter than Honey: PM," *The Nation*, December 9, 2010, https://nation.com.pk/19-Dec-2010/pakchina-friendship-is-higher-than-mountains-deeper-than-ocean-and-sweeter-than-honey-pm (accessed July 7, 2018).

expand across multiple levels of the state apparatus. These have included an in depth examination of all CPEC related projects comprising of detailed progress reports, shared feasibility studies and new project proposals to help jointly coordinate this massive initiative. In their second last meeting held in November 2017, the JCC finalized the CPEC Long Term Plan (LTP) outlining the scope, duration and targets of the entire CPEC initiative, thus marking a historic step in its implementation.[19]

Even in its early phases, the results of this targeted collaboration have made a marked impact on Pakistan's economy, offering a preview of the immense potential CPEC holds for years to come. Around the same time when the CPEC bilateral framework was finalized in 2013, China's net investment in Pakistan sharply rose to around US$700 million. By the end of 2017, this figure had more than doubled to around US$1.6 billion.

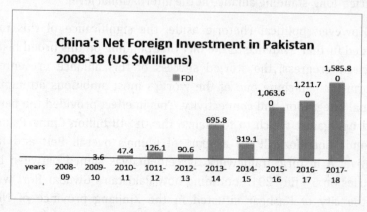

Graph 1.5- Net Foreign Investment in Pakistan ($Millions) "Net Foreign Investment in Pakistan ($Millions)," *Board of Investment Pakistan*, n.d., http://boi.gov.pk/ForeignInvestmentinPakistan.aspx (accessed July 7, 2018).

This rise in capital inflows has been steadily accompanied by growing investor confidence amidst a broad range of both public and private organizations from China. At present around 60 Chinese

[19] "Top Cooperation Body Okays CPEC Long-Term Plan," *Dawn*, November 22, 2017, https://www.dawn.com/news/1372079 (accessed July 7, 2018).

companies are involved in nearly 122 projects in Pakistan.[20] As a result more than 10,000 Chinese engineers and technical experts have arrived in the country and are actively contributing to the country's growth across a wide range of sectors. These include the IT & Communications, Construction, Energy, Transport and Oil & Gas sectors all of which have recently served as the primary engines of growth within the country.

Furthermore, this recent impetus towards fostering ever closer ties has also led to experts from both countries to make huge strides in the joint research and development of cutting edge technologies. This includes recent collaborations in expanding Pakistan's nuclear energy capabilities as well as its most recent forays into outer space. The latter for instance was evident in the launch of two indigenously developed Pakistani satellites in July 2018 aided by the Chinese Space Agency's launch facilities in China.[21]

Based on these developments, the results of this decades-old alliance with China while quite literally achieving new heights, has permeated through to vast sectors of Pakistan's politico-economic framework. Especially considering the ongoing CPEC initiative, the full impact of this collaboration will become even more apparent in the decades to come. However, taking stock of the most recent developments, the trajectory of this relationship remains steadfast in its direction of shared progress and prosperity through a widely positive and burgeoning bilateral framework.

A Shared Future for the People of Pakistan and China

Going back to the broader historical and global context that was outlined in the beginning of this chapter, it is important here to take a step back and gauge the enormity of all that has transpired throughout the history of the Pak-China bilateral framework. By surpassing often opposing cultural, political, geographical and economic divides, Pak-China relations stand as a true example of a historic partnership that has been

---

[20] See Appendices A- F
[21] "Pakistan Launches Remote Sensing Satellite in China," *Dawn*, July 9, 2018, https://www.dawn.com/news/1418966 (accessed August 10, 2018).

built on the principles of mutual respect and non-interference, all amidst a shared vision of peace and prosperity.

These principles have in turn also played a major role in allowing relations between these two countries to surpass the numerous challenges and constraints imposed upon by broader regional and international politics. Be it the tumultuous phases of the Cold War, the post 9/11 security paradigm, or the more recent multi-polarization of the international system; Pak-China relations have forged ahead and to this day, have continued to define the 'all weather' nature of their bilateral relations.

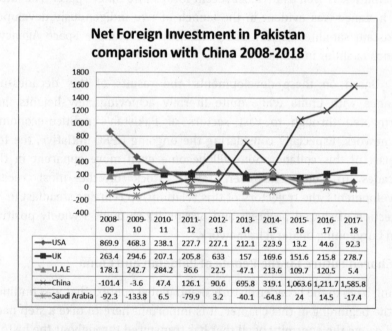

Net Foreign Investment in Pakistan comparision with China 2008-2018

	2008-09	2009-10	2010-11	2011-12	2012-13	2013-14	2014-15	2015-16	2016-17	2017-18
USA	869.9	468.3	238.1	227.7	227.1	212.1	223.9	13.2	44.6	92.3
UK	263.4	294.6	207.1	205.8	633	157	169.6	151.6	215.8	278.7
U.A.E	178.1	242.7	284.2	36.6	22.5	-47.1	213.6	109.7	120.5	5.4
China	-101.4	-3.6	47.4	126.1	90.6	695.8	319.1	1,063.6	1,211.7	1,585.8
Saudi Arabia	-92.3	-133.8	6.5	-79.9	3.2	-40.1	-64.8	24	14.5	-17.4

Graph 1.6- Net Foreign Investment in Pakistan Comparison with China (US $Millions) "Net Foreign Investment in Pakistan ($Millions)," *Board of Investment Pakistan*, n.d., http://boi.gov.pk/ForeignInvestmentinPakistan.aspx (accessed July 7, 2018).

The discussion thus far has attempted to depict the implications of this partnership on Pakistan's economic progress and development. This has been highlighted by the key role this relationship has played in enhancing trade and investment within the Pak-China bilateral framework. It is worth noting here that the scale of China's investment and its subsequent stake in Pakistan's progress assumes even greater significance when compared against the more recent investment figures of Pakistan's other major allies. As evident in the following graph, the most salient trend one is faced with is that of rising inflows from China against declining capital from the US. This again bears evidence of the direct impact of waning US influence, exacerbated by the economic rise of China as discussed earlier in the chapter.

Yet, beyond this rudimentary comparison of numbers, it is the way that the Pak-China relationship has taken hold of the popular imagination that has defined the true culmination of its rich history. After being forged amidst the highest echelons of the two countries' leadership, the very essence of this relationship has in turn permeated through to the people living in both China and Pakistan. Passed on from the sturdy hands of numerous diplomats and statesmen, it is now up to the numerous students, professionals, entrepreneurs, artists and innovators of future generations to come, and further build on this rich history of Pak-China relations.

Chapter 2: CPEC - From Geo-Strategic to Geo-Economic Advantage

Hassan Daud Butt*

Contextualizing CPEC's Objectives

In recent years, the international monetary landscape has transformed immensely. The driving factors of this transformation are technological advancements, trade liberalization, the free movement of capital, improvements in various means of communication, transportation infrastructure, and the formation of trans-frontier supply chains. Recently, collaborative agreements in the Asian region have further proliferated and reinforced these phenomena of global transformation, further accelerating this process.

Pakistan and China in particular are keenly focusing on global economic cooperation with the objective of attaining peace, prosperity and the well-being of the people of countries, the region, and the world. While the West is moving towards protectionism, the two all-weather friends; China and Pakistan, have enjoyed the steady development of bilateral ties ever since the establishment of formal diplomatic relations. Over the last few years, these cordial relations between the two historic allies have culminated into the development and implementation of the China Pakistan Economic Corridor (CPEC); one the world's most ambitious attempts at economic and socio-cultural integration.

A recent report by Price Water House Coopers' (PwC) Economic Outlook forecasts Pakistan to be the 16th largest economy of the world.[1]

---

* Mr. Hassan Daud Butt is the Coordinator and Project Director of CPEC at the Ministry of Planning, Development & Reform, Govt. of Pakistan.

The report states that as a result of CPEC, Pakistan has the potential of gaining up to 2% of incremental GDP growth. This is based on the expected returns emanating from reduced manufacturing costs, cheaper electricity, a wider choice of quality goods and services, increased foreign investment, and increased access to global markets for its exporters.

The China-Pakistan Economic Corridor (CPEC) stretches from Kashgar in Western China to Gwadar in South West Pakistan. It traverses through the entirety of Pakistan providing China with a direct link to the Arabian Sea. Aimed at serving as a key conduit for regional integration, CPEC is further geared towards promoting broader links between Central Asia, the Middle East and South Asia greatly boosting inter-regional connectivity. Thus, based on this frame work of mutual cooperation on the basis of economic connectivity and regional integration, CPEC is aimed at creating far reaching opportunities for both Pakistan and China, as well as the surrounding region.[2]

While there has been considerable emphasis on infrastructural development under CPEC, it is not just a network of roads and bridges. Rather it is a wide-ranging platform which provides a whole host of opportunities for mutual collaboration and joint ventures. The development plans of CPEC envisage regional and cross regional connectivity, communication and infrastructure networks, energy security, industrial modernization, agricultural development, poverty alleviation, tourism, and greater people to people contacts. It also intends to raise living standards by facilitating the general population with core necessities such as basic municipal infrastructure, education, public health, and socio-economic development. Eventually all these projects are aimed at developing new opportunities and millions of jobs across the country and region.[3]

---

[1] Dilawar Hussain, "Pakistan could become 16th largest economy by 2050: PwC," *Dawn*, February 9, 2017, https://www.dawn.com/news/1313636 (accessed July 13, 2017).
[2] Akber Ali, "China Pakistan Economic Corridor: Prospects and Challenges for Regional Integration," *Arts and Social Science Journal* 7, no. 4 (July 2016): 1-5.
[3] Ibid.

Furthermore, CPEC would enable both Pakistan and China to unleash each other's comparative advantages, and strengthen all-round cooperation in a bid to upgrade their level of economic cooperation. Once the Corridor is fully operationalized it would bring Pakistan into a new era of progress and prosperity greatly accelerating national economic growth. Not only would it create greater economic and trade opportunities for Pakistan, it would also immensely benefit its neighboring countries including Afghanistan, Iran, India as well as Central Asian States such as Tajikistan, Uzbekistan, Kazakhstan and Turkmenistan.[4]

Against this broader regional context, the "Belt and Road Initiative" (BRI) formerly known as the "One Belt, One Road" (OBOR), aims to usher in a new era of international relationships. By building a community of common development partners, it is aimed at promoting the globalization of the world economy while remaining wholly cognizant of the needs of developing nations. It would in essence serve as a sort of reincarnation of the ancient Silk Road in the modern era, allowing the 21st century to be better defined as the 'Asian Century'.[5] This would create a win-win position for China as well as its regional partners in the BRI. While the entire initiative comprises of several large investment projects, they can be broadly grouped under the following two programs:

i.   The 21st Century Maritime Silk Road (MSR)
ii.   The Silk Road Economic Belt (SREB).[6]

The former relates to the maritime component of this initiative, focusing on the development of new ports and sea-faring routes for regional trade. The latter is based more on linking land routes that connect China with Europe, Russia, South Asia, the Middle East and Africa. Thus since being officially announced in 2013, China's Belt and

---

[4] Ibid.
[5] Aleem Shahid, "Gateways along Border Planned," *Dawn,* December 14, 2006, https://www.dawn.com/news/223351/gateways-along-border-planned (accessed July 13, 2017).
[6] Hans-Peter Brunner, "What is Economic Corridor Development and What Can It Achieve in Asia's Sub- regions ?," *Asian Development Bank,* July 2013, https://www.adb.org/publications/economic-corridor-development-and-what-it-can-achieve-in-asia-subregions (accessed July 13, 2017).

Road Initiative has attracted considerable international attention due to its all-encompassing potential. According to the most recent estimates, the BRI is slated to involve nearly 80 countries, comprising 68 percent of the world's population and 40 percent of global GDP. Its final investment cost is expected to stand between US$4 trillion and US$8 trillion. If Pakistan caters to harness just 2% of China's total trade within the BRI, billions worth of goods would be transiting through Pakistan.[7]

CPEC is the centerpiece of China's BRI vision and it is worth mentioning here that it is one of the most important, game-changing projects ever undertaken in the history of Pakistan. As of writing, it has achieved record completion times with respect to its numerous phases due to the coordination and hard work of officials straddling across Pakistan and China. It is their enduring work and careful attention to detail that is highlighted in this chapter, presenting a brief overview of the most salient features and projects under CPEC that have been so far completed or are currently underway.

Policy and Implementation Framework

China and Pakistan are jointly collaborating towards the unified development of CPEC projects for the economic and social development of some of their most underserved regions.[8] The CPEC Development Plan subsequently emphasizes this commonality of interests and is primed towards benefitting the diverse populations of the entire region. It also manifests a collective politico-economic future for both China and Pakistan, highlighting the prospects of a shared destiny. It thus generates a new frame of cooperation based on economic connectivity and cross

---

[7] James Griffiths, "Just What is This One Belt, One Road Thing Anyway?," *CNN*, May 12, 2017, https://edition.cnn.com/2017/05/11/asia/china-one-belt-one-road-explainer/index.html (accessed July 13, 2017).
[8] "CPEC has Brought Many Positive Changes to Pakistan's Economy: Imran Khan," *China Pakistan Economic Corridor*, July 24, 2018, http://www.cpecinfo.com/news/cpec-has-brought-many-positive-changes-to-pakistan-economy-imran-khan/NTYyMw (accessed August 13, 2017).

border collaboration that is to benefit not only China and Pakistan, but the wider region as well.[9]

As part of its ensuing policy and implementation framework, both countries have developed a bilateral cooperative mechanism to plan and execute this massive initiative. This comprises of a Long Term Plan, Transport Monographic Study and their respective MoUs that all serve as the overarching policy guides for the entire CPEC initiative.[10] Specific breakdowns of CPEC projects can be seen in Appendix (A).[11]

For the effective implementation of these numerous CPEC projects, both China and Pakistan have designated respective departments to ensure that these projects are carried out based on the agreed upon policies and guidelines, as part of a continuous process of monitoring and evaluation. The National Development and Reform Commission (NDRC) and Ministry of Planning, Development and Reform serve as the focal points for the coordination and monitoring of the CPEC initiative from the Chinese and Pakistani sides respectively. The NDRC along with the Ministry of Planning, Development & Reform have constituted subsidiary Working Groups of the Joint Coordination Committee (JCC). The JCC itself serves as the apex governing body of this initiative at the ministerial level as outlined in the MoU signed between both countries. The subsidiary Working Groups within the JCC thus comprise of various experts in charge of Planning, Transport Infrastructure, Energy, Gwadar and Industrial Cooperation for which they have been nominated by their respective lead agencies. Accordingly, numerous Joint Working Groups (JWG) along similar lines of expertise, have also been constituted on the Pakistani side.[12] These include sub-groups in the fields of Agriculture, Oil and Gas and Education that are also currently in the process of being formed.

---

[9] "Long Term Plan for China-Pakistan Economic Corridor (2017-2030)," *Government of Pakistan, Ministry of Planning Development and Reform,* 2017, https://www.pc.gov.pk/uploads/cpec/LTP.pdf (accessed July 13, 2017).
[10] "CPEC Infrastructure Projects," *China Pakistan Economic Corridor,* n.d., http://cpec.gov.pk/infrastructure/ (accessed July 13, 2017).
[11] See Appendix "A." at page 265.
[12] "Pakistan, China Sign CPEC Agreements, MoUs," *ARY News,* May 14, 2017, https://arynews.tv/en/pakistan-china-sign-cpec-agreements-mous/ (accessed July 13, 2017).

Since the signing of the MoU formalizing the CPEC bilateral framework in July 2013, eight meetings of the Joint Coordination Committee (JCC) have been held aside from numerous other subsidiary visits and meetings.

It is worth noting here that during the 6th and 7th JCC meeting, a much wider national consensus was observed as all the Chief Ministers and representatives of Pakistan's diverse political milieu participated in a unanimous appraisal of CPEC. During this meeting, a number of new Projects and Economic Zones were proposed. The finalized Long Term Plan was also approved with clear targets and objectives for CPEC being set for up to 2030.[13]

Overview of the Approval Process of Projects

A robust project approval process has so far led to the planning and implementation of numerous MoUs on paper towards developing a portfolio worth around US$46 billion by 2018. As per the approved process, the Planning Commission's Guidelines for project management are followed for securing the external financing for these projects. Foreign funding is secured (agreements signed) only for projects approved from competent forums such as the Central Development Working Party (CDWP) and the Executive Committee of the National Economic Council (ECNEC) etc. After approval of PC-I and the frame work agreement, the Chinese Government recommends 3 or more state owned enterprises with which the bidding process is carried out.

After the signing of the commercial contract with Chinese contractors, the Economic Affairs Division (EAD) writes a formal loan/grant request to the Chinese government (Ministry of Commerce, China). After consent of the Chinese side, loan negotiations are held between the EAD and Chinese Banks (after clearance of terms and conditions from Finance Division and relevant stake holders). After agreement on the loan terms, the formal loan agreement is signed

---

[13] "6th JCC on CPEC Held in Beijing," *China Daily,* December 30, 2016, http://www.chinadaily.com.cn/world/2016-12/30/content_27820740.htm (accessed July 13, 2017).

between both sides. Other sources of funding however may also be explored in cases of urgency where concept clearance is available.

Long Term Plan

The CPEC Long Term Plan was approved in the 7th JCC held on 21st November 2017 after extensive rounds of discussions and negotiations between experts on both sides. Laying down the overarching blueprint for the entire initiative, the Long Term Plan defines and specifies the vast scope and vision of CPEC. It specifies the targets and timelines for the development of the economic corridor, highlighting the plan's overall vision and development goals.[14] Appendix (B) provides a detailed breakdown of the CPEC Long Term Plan and its accompanying Social Sector Development Projects respectively.[15]

Energy Projects

Recognizing the growing energy needs of Pakistan and to overcome existing deficits, CPEC has allocated a major proportion of its funds to energy generation and transmission. The projects mentioned are a key part of the CPEC framework as they would contribute towards the sustainable growth of industry while offering unhindered electricity for domestic consumption in Pakistan. At present nearly 15 energy projects are in various stages of implementation while 4 are being actively developed.[16] Details of these projects are attached in Appendix (C).[17]

Transport Infrastructure Projects

As part of CPEC's transport infrastructure projects, a 1,100 kilometer extended motorway is to be built between the cities of Karachi and Lahore. By more efficiently linking two of the country's largest cities, this highway would play a crucial role in boosting trade and commerce between two already established commercial hubs. Similarly, the

---

[14] "7th Meeting of Joint Coordination Committee (JCC) of Pakistan China Economic Corridor (CPEC)," *China Pakistan Economic Corridor*, November 1, 2017, http://cpec.gov.pk/news/74 (accessed November 29, 2017).

[15] See Appendix "B" at page 266.

[16] "CPEC Projects Update," *China Pakistan Economic Corridor*, n.d., http://cpec.gov.pk/progress-update/ (accessed July 13, 2017).

[17] See Appendix "C" at page 267-270.

Karakoram Highway between Rawalpindi and the Chinese border would also be entirely rebuilt and overhauled. The Karachi–Peshawar main railway line-1 will also be improved to permit train travel at up to 160 kilometers per hour.[18] Discussions on the cost and technical scope of this project are in progress and have entered the final stages of planning. Similarly, the Karachi Circular Railway (KCR) is also being viewed as a feasible project by China with discussions on its implementation currently underway.[19]

Table 2.1: Transport Infrastructure Projects Motorways

Name of project	Status
KKH Phase II (Thakot-Havelian Section) KPK	• (Length:120 Km) • Contractor mobilized. Work commenced in September, 2016. To be completed by March, 2020
Karachi - Peshawar Motorway (Multan - Sukkur Section) PUNJAB-SINDH	• (Length:392 Km) • Contractor mobilized • Construction works commenced in August, 2016 • Multan-Shujabad section inaugurated by Prime Minister on May 2018 • Completion planned in August 2019

Source: "CPEC Infrastructure Projects," *China Pakistan Economic Corridor*, n.d., http://cpec.gov.pk/infrastructure (accessed February 19, 2018).

Experts on both sides are also exploring new avenues to strengthen cooperation in providing vocational and technical education in major cities alongside the various CPEC routes. This would help Pakistan train local technical talent and fulfill the wide gap in quality human resource currently required for the timely execution of CPEC.

---

[18] "CPEC Infrastructure Projects," *China Pakistan Economic Corridor*, http://cpec.gov.pk/infrastructure (accessed February 19, 2018).
[19] Ibid.

Figure 2.1- An Overview of Infrastructure Projects under CPEC. "CPEC improves local infrastructure, people's life," *SAMMA*, April, 2017, https://www.samaa.tv/pakistan/2017/04/cpec-improves-local-infrastructure-peoples-life-report/ (accessed July 13, 2017).

At the time of writing, both of CPEC's Western and Eastern routes are being developed simultaneously with 2019 as the expected date of completion.[20] Work on the Western route is being carried out through the Public Sector Development Program (PSDP) and is currently on fast track. The speed with which its development is nearing completion is evident in the movement of the first trade caravan in 2016.[21] Details of these Western route projects, new infrastructural projects pertaining to railways, and the proposed mass transit system are all attached in Appendices (D) and (E).[22]

Gwadar Deep Sea Port

The city of Gwadar, which is situated along the South Western coast of Pakistan, is uniquely positioned to play an immense role within CPEC

---

[20] "Eastern, Western Routes of CPEC to be Completed by 2019," *Mattis Global Link News*, June 29, 2017, 2018, https://mettisglobal.news/eastern-western-routes-of-cpec-to-be-completed-by-2019-hassan-daud/ (accessed February 19).

[21] Sharif Khan, "Gwadar Launches CPEC Trade Today," *The Nation*, November 13, 2016, https://nation.com.pk/13-Nov-2016/gwadar-launches-cpec-trade-today (accessed March 19, 2018).

[22] See Appendices "D" and "E." at pages 271 and 272 respectively.

owing to its strategic location and the recent development of its deep water port. Due to its strategic and geographical significance, it has the potential to surpass neighboring ports in terms of trade activity. President Xi Jinping's vision of connecting Asia with a new Maritime trade route as part of the Belt and Road Initiative is being realized to a significant extent just via Gwadar. It is thus, the gateway and jewel of CPEC which is presently witnessing the most rapid development it has ever experienced in its history. By bringing about such immense development in Gwadar, there has been at present a sustained and positive improvement in the lives of the people of Balochistan.

Figure 2.2- A Scenic View Of Gwadar Port and Gwadar Free Zone Facilitation Center, "A Scenic View of Gwadar Port and Gwadar Free Zone Facilitation Center," *Gwadar Port Authority*, n.d., http://www.gwadarport.gov.pk/Picture%20Gallery2.aspx (accessed July 13, 2017,).

The development of Gwadar port is slated to positively transform the very basis of trade and commerce throughout the South-Asian and Central Asian regions. The inauguration of the SEZ in Gwadar and the ensuing shipping service by the China Ocean Shipping Company (COSCO) have heralded this new era of prosperity. Keeping in view its long-term prospects, current development projects being carried out in Gwadar are geared towards expanding its capabilities for oil refining, shipbuilding and repairs, the transport, storage and processing of chemicals, nonferrous metals, logistics, port, services and in-land transportation. These would serve as a catalyst for providing a diverse array of industrial goods and services, laying the foundations for the success of the entire CPEC initiative. This would also ensure the socio-economic development of the country's less developed South-Western region providing much needed job opportunities in Baluchistan and its surrounding areas.[23] A detailed breakdown of the projects currently underway at Gwadar port is provided in Appendix (F).[24]

Designated Special Economic Zones (SEZs)

China's experience in the development and success of Special Economic Zones as part of their robust industrial development serves as an important example that is worth learning from and emulating in Pakistan. Building on the massive scale of industrial cooperation between China and Pakistan, these SEZs are geared towards greatly incentivizing both local and foreign investors to take advantage of the shared vision of growth and prosperity under CPEC.

This would in turn provide an excellent opportunity for Pakistan to strengthen its industrial capability leading to the much needed structural rebalancing of its economy. It is hoped that with the help of these SEZs, Pakistan can help bring about a sustainable impetus towards poverty alleviation, both within these SEZs and their surrounding areas.

In the 6th Joint Cooperation Committee (JCC) meeting held in Beijing on 29th December 2016, 9 Special Economic Zones (SEZs) were agreed to be developed in Pakistan as part of the overall CPEC initiative.[25] Each economic zone is aimed at specializing in a particular product and/or service, depending upon on the availability of indigenous raw materials, local labor expertise and various other factors. The proposed composition for these SEZs include a large number of environment friendly industries including textiles, light engineering, electronics,

---

[23] "CPEC Gwadar Projects," *China Pakistan Economic Corridor*, http://cpec.gov.pk/gwader/ (accessed July 13, 2017).
[24] See Appendix "F" at page 275.
[25] Naveed Butt, "Special Economic Zones: Chinese Seek New Trade Avenues," *Business Recorder*, October 17, 2017, https://fp.brecorder.com/2017/10/20171017226751/ (accessed February, 2018).

pharmaceuticals, chemicals, food processing, automobiles, manufacturing, minerals processing, agriculture, logistics and various research and science parks etc. Through these Economic Zones Pakistan can bolster its reputation as a strong destination for investment helping greatly accelerate the pace of its overall economic development.[26]

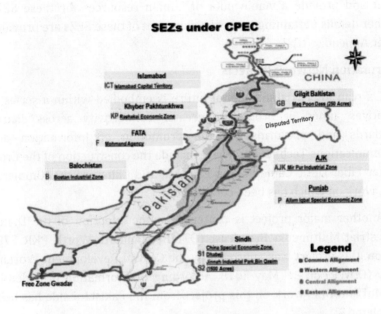

Figure 2.3- An Overview of Special Economic Zones at Stretch of Pakistan.∴ "Highway Network of CPEC," *China Pakistan Economic Corridor*, n.d., http://cpec.gov.pk/map-single/1 (accessed August 17, 2018).

Currently, efforts are underway to optimize the top-level design and layout of the proposed industrial parks, their structure, cooperation patterns and service platforms. Experts on both sides are also actively engaged in developing various incentive packages formulating an overall policy framework to expedite such an unprecedented scale of industrial development in Pakistan. These include careful deliberations on how to better formulate polices that would have an equal and binding force on federal and local governments; in the areas of industrial access

---

[26] Khaleeq Kiani, "Special Economic Zones Take Centre Stage as CPEC Talks Advance," *Dawn,* November 21, 2017, https://www.dawn.com/news/1371792 (accessed February 20, 2018).

thresholds, financial support, taxation policy, land acquisition and environmental protection. Experts overseeing the implementation of these SEZs are also exploring ways in which they can strengthen cooperation in providing vocational and technical education in major cities alongside CPEC's various routes. This would train local technical talent and provide a viable pool of human resources for these SEZs. Further details pertaining to the development of these SEZs are provided under Appendix (G)[27].

Information Network Projects

CPEC's plan for Pakistan's digital future is embodied within a series of initiatives aimed at promoting greater connectivity across shared standards and platforms for the promotion of Information and Communications Technology. These include the construction of the Cross Border Fiber Optic Cable linking Pakistan and China via the Khunjerab Pass, work on which has been completed.[28]

Another major project is centered on the adoption of the Digital Terrestrial Multimedia Broadcast (DTMB) standard. Worth PKR 2789 million, this project was approved by the Central Development Working Party (CDWP) on 2nd May 2018. According to information provided by the MoI and BLE, work on this project from the Pakistani side has been completed.[29]

From Geo-Strategic to Geo-Economic Advantages

The construction of the CPEC corridor is a strategic consolidation of the rich history of bilateral ties between Pakistan and China. CPEC provides Pakistan with an enormous opportunity to serve as a key stakeholder in the region's prosperity as it provides a platform for connecting more than three billion people across Central, West and South Asia, the Middle East and African regions. The projected growth in trade, investment, and

---

[27] See Appendix "G" at page 277.
[28] "Cross Border Optical Fiber Cable," *China Pakistan Economic Corridor*, n.d., http://cpec.gov.pk/project-details/40 (accessed February 1, 2018).
[29] Fawad Yousafzai, "CDWP Approves 31 Projects of Rs.713b," *The Nation*, May 3, 2018, https://nation.com.pk/03-May-2018/cdwp-approves-31-projects-of-rs713b (accessed September 13, 2017).

fiscal flows would promote greater harmony, eliminate poverty and lead to a broad improvement in living standards throughout the region. Moreover, it will reduce interstate differences, societal disparity and increase the rate of life expectancy greatly improving the overall quality of life within the broader region.[30]

Through CPEC, Pakistan will be able to fully harness its geostrategic location into geo-economic advantage. When combined with the new Eurasian Continental Bridge, other proposed corridors (i.e China-Mongolia-Russia, China-Central Asia-West Asia and China-Indo China Peninsula corridors), and the safety and efficiency of the New Maritime Silk Road, CPEC as part of the BRI presents a new vision for global trade and harmony. It is in effect a crucial component of the "Belt & Road" Initiative.[31]

For the Pakistani economy, its projected monetary inflows are slated to positively increase the investment to GDP ratio by 20%.[32] Such an increment in investment would in turn help spur commercial activity and is projected to create around 2 million new jobs.[33] The new and improved infrastructure along with enhanced power generation capacity would add 2 percentage points to annual GDP over the medium and long term. Thus, by giving full play to China's industrial, capital and institutional advantages and effectively integrating these with Pakistan's market and comparative advantages in trade, Pakistan can achieve a sustainable and inclusive yearly growth of over 7%.[34]

---

[30] "CPEC to Benefit Entire Region," *Dawn*, August 31, 2015, https://www.dawn.com/news/1203965 (accessed September 13, 2017).

[31] "Repaving the Ancient Silk Routes," *PWC Global*, n.d., https://www.pwc.com/gx/en/issues/growth-markets-centre/publications/repaving-the-ancient-silk-routes.html (accessed August 17, 2018).

[32] Junaid Ashraf, "CPEC Key to Economic Success of China's Belt and Road Initiative," *Asia Times*, August 25, 2017, http://www.atimes.com/cpec-key-economic-ripening-belt-road-initiative/ (accessed August 17, 2018).

[33] Saif Ur Rahman and Zhao Shurong, "Analysis of Chinese Economic and National Security Interests in China-Pakistan Economic Corridor (CPEC) under the Framework of One Belt One Road (OBOR) Initiative," *Arts and Social Science Journal* 8, no. 284 (2017): 2.

[34] Nadeem Omar Tarar, "Cementing the Friendship Bond: Pak-China Cultural Ties," *Hilal Magazine*, October, 2015, http://hilal.gov.pk/index.php/layouts/item/1672-cementing-the-friendship-bond-pak-china-cultural-ties (accessed September 13, 2017).

To support the above targets Pakistan needs to focus on sound macro-economic policies, optimum utilization of the country's physical and human resources and full exploitation of the technological potential of its industry, agriculture and services.[35]

In summary, CPEC is expected to bring about improvements in six major areas:

i. US$62 billion would boost GDP growth rate to 6-8 percent.[36]
ii. Ensure energy security while overcoming the prevailing energy crisis.
iii. Bolster Pakistan's industrial capacity.
iv. Link Pakistan's rural and remote areas with its urban centers.
v. Strengthen Pakistan domestically bringing in prosperity.[37]
vi. Enable the transfer of knowledge and technology through widespread interaction with Chinese and other international experts.[38]

Conclusion

Pakistan's macroeconomic performance has shown that key improvements in certain areas can lead to a widely favorable growth outlook if long-term policies are pursued with diligence and an eye to the future. At present the government is striving to achieve sustainable growth to overcome inadequate infrastructure, limited domestic public resources, declining exports and competitiveness, and a low level of tax revenues, savings and investments. The state needs to urgently address these challenges to improve economic development across a number of sectors and provinces and enhance connectivity with global trade and production networks.

---

[35] Ibid.
[36] "CPEC to Boost Pakistan GDP Growth To 7.5%," *The Nation*, October 8, 2016, https://nation.com.pk/08-Oct-2016/cpec-to-boost-pakistan-gdp-growth-to-7-5 (accessed August 17, 2018).
[37] Mansoor Ahmad, "CPEC to Benefit Pakistan in Both Short- and Long-Term," *The News International*, February 4, 2017, https://www.thenews.com.pk/print/183809-CPEC-to-benefit-Pakistan-in-both-short-and-long-term (accessed August 17, 2018).
[38] Ibid.

It is envisaged that through CPEC, Pakistan has the potential of entering into an era of political and socio-economic stability which would greatly help in realizing the goals set in Pakistan's Vision 2025. It is hoped that this large-scale industrial cooperation between China and Pakistan serves as the main contributor towards the transformation of this trade corridor into an economic corridor, by producing new growth centers under a unified framework of industrial and urban development. This would help reinvigorate Pakistan's industry through joint ventures with Chinese enterprises in manufacturing, agriculture, light engineering and the services sectors providing a significant boost to Pakistan's exports throughout the world. It would also help the country evolve from an agrarian to an industrialized, and finally to a knowledge based economy. The subsequent upsurge in trade, investment and financial flows is expected to directly translate to economic development and poverty alleviation.

Considering the overall context of the BRI, the overarching vision of CPEC not only includes Pakistan's economic well-being through regional trade but also allows it to position itself as a key regional hub for connecting diverse cultures and societies. Promising peace and sustainable development, CPEC truly presents a pragmatic and wholly realistic solution to much of what ails the region across a broader level. It is hoped that carrying forward its current momentum project by project, the true goal and vision of CPEC can be finally realized in terms of the vast benefits that are to be reaped by the people of this historically underserved region.

Chapter 3: Gwadar - The Crown Jewel of CPEC

*M Waqas Jan**

Introduction

Situated on the South-Western tip of Pakistan, the port city of Gwadar has come to herald a new era of development for not just Pakistan but for the wider region as well. Known as a mere fishing village not too long ago, the sudden surge of funds and attention being poured into Gwadar over the last couple of decades, highlights the city's growing importance as part of Pakistan's economic and strategic plans for the future.

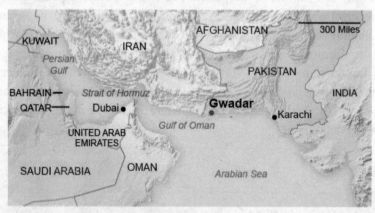

Figure 3.1- Map Highlighting Gwadar. Declan Walsh, "Chinese Firm Will Run Strategic Pakistani Port at Gwadar," *New York Times,* Jan 31, 2013, www.nytimes.com/2013/02/01/world/asia/chinese-firm-will-run-strategic-pakistani-port-at-gwadar.html?_r=0 (accessed October 19, 2018).

---

* Mr. M Waqas Jan is the Program Coordinator for the China Studies & Information Center (CSIC) at the Strategic Vision Institute, Islamabad.

This includes Pakistan's potential of serving as a key conduit for regional trade between Asia, the Middle East, and Africa while also creating a unique strategic vantage point overlooking the Arabian Sea. All of these developments have in turn allowed Gwadar to serve as a catalyst for reinvigorating the surrounding areas of the historically under-served Balochistan province, greatly contributing to Pakistan's overall human development.

Fueled largely by Chinese funding, Gwadar and its recently developed sea port form a crucial component of the US$62 billion China Pakistan Economic Corridor (CPEC). This is because, as a key potential transit point along one of the world's busiest shipping lanes, the Gwadar sea port holds immense importance to both Pakistan's and China's plans for economic growth and infrastructure development for the future. For China, Gwadar serves as a key link between the Silk Road Economic Belt (SRB) and the 21st Century Maritime Silk Road being envisioned as part of the overarching Belt and Road Initiative (BRI). As one of CPEC's most important components, it provides a crucial link between the land-based and maritime components of the overall BRI framework. Its untapped potential offers a whole host of opportunities to help build a broader regional framework centered on enhanced trade, mutually beneficial infrastructure and greater people to people linkages; all contributing to greater peace, stability and prosperity across the wider region. Hence, over the last two decades, Gwadar has increasingly served as a major focal point within the Pak-China bi-lateral framework.

Numerous projects, some completed and some underway have since testified to these growing levels of strategic and economic cooperation between the two countries. These include the development of the Gwadar sea-port, construction of rail and road networks, the establishment of key industrial and special economic zones, as well as numerous other projects centered on social and human development. The added emphasis on poverty reduction and the economic mobilization of the local population has significantly come to define both Pakistan's and China's shared vision of mutual development and prosperity across the wider region.

Highlighting Gwadar's importance within this framework, this chapter aims to show how Gwadar's development serves as the underlying blueprint for the China Pakistan Economic Corridor. Representing some of the most significant objectives of the entire CPEC initiative, the ensuing discussion examines the extent to which Gwadar's development is directly related to the future development plans of Pakistan and China, from both an economic and strategic perspective. In its essence, this chapter thus aims to provide an answer to why Gwadar is widely considered as the 'Crown Jewel of CPEC.'

From Ancient Maritime Trade to Modern Supply Chains

This significance of Gwadar as a key port city has carried on to this day in its very name. In the local Balochi language, the word *Gwat* translates to 'Gateway' and the word *'Dar'* as 'the wind'. Hence Gwadar, being the 'Gateway to the Wind',[1] has served countless generations of rulers with access to the burgeoning trade routes linking Asia, the Mediterranean, Africa and the Persian Gulf along the Arabian Sea.

Its importance as a key port city can be traced back to antiquity where it served as part of the Eastern frontier of Alexander's vast empire during the Hellenistic era. Referred to by historians as *Gedrosia,*[2] Gwadar and its adjacent port has long served as a key transit point for the historic flow of trade, linking together vital supply lines across the region. Based on its geo-strategic importance the city and its surrounding regions have been since ruled by a succession of Persian, Mauryan and Arabic rulers, all of which contributed to its diversely rich historical background. As a result, Gwadar and its surrounding region comprises of a unique and often under-represented local culture and population. This testifies to its rich heritage from being at the cross-roads of a diverse range of civilizations since time immemorial.

---

[1] Zahid Anwar, "Gwadar Deep Sea Port's Emergence as Regional Trade and Transportation Hub: Prospects and Problems," *Journal of Political Studies*1, no. 2 (June 2011): 97.
[2] Aurel Stein, "On Alexander's Route into Gedrosia: an Archaeological Tour in Las Bela," *The Geographical Journal* 102, no. 5/6 (Nov - Dec 1943): 193-227.

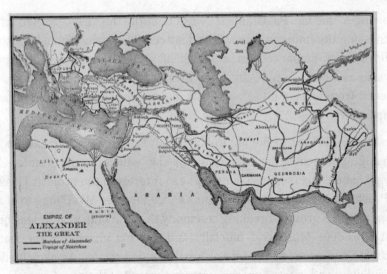

Figure 3.2- Empire of Alexander Circa 326 BCE. George Willis Botsford, *A History of the Ancient World* (London: The MacMillan Company, 1913), 5.

This diversity is evident for instance in the significant influence of Arabic amongst its local population even today. This is due to the fact that as recently as 1958, Gwadar was under the suzerainty of the Omani Kingdom which it had been a part of for the last two hundred years.[3] As part of a major maritime power within the Arabian Sea, Gwadar had represented one end of the Omani kingdom's sprawling maritime empire, stretching across the horn of Africa all the way to Madagascar.

Its economic and strategic importance for a recently independent Pakistan however wasn't realized until 1954 when it engaged the United States Geological Survey (USGS) to carry out a detailed survey of its coastline. It was based on this survey that Worth Condrick, the surveyor deputed by the USGS, identified Gwadar as a potential site for a deep water port.[4] After four years of negotiations, Gwadar was bought by Pakistan from Oman for reportedly UK£3 million.

Yet despite its obvious potential, Gwadar remained undeveloped for nearly half a century owing to a myriad of economic and geo-political

---

[3] "Gwadar Port: 'History-Making Milestones," *Dawn,* April 14, 2008, www.dawn.com/news/297994/gwadar-port (accessed October 19, 2018).
[4] Ibid.

challenges facing Pakistan. It wasn't until the 1990's that after witnessing the immense growth and success of nearby Dubai, Pakistani policymakers embarked on a series of efforts aimed at developing Gwadar as a modern port city. Even then with limited funds and a lack of interest from foreign investors, plans to develop the port started to take shape slowly.

During his visit to Beijing in May 2001, President Pervez Musharraf directly approached the subject of Gwadar with Chinese Premier Zhu Rongji, who expressed his country's keen interest in the project. This led to President Musharraf hosting China's Vice Premier, Wu Bangguo at the Gwadar port's ground-breaking ceremony the following year. It was here that President Musharraf officially laid out his vision for the port's strategic and economic potential for the wider region. As explained in the following oft-quoted passage from his speech at the occasion:

> "If we see this whole region, it is like a funnel. The top of the funnel is this wide area of Central Asia and also China's Western region. And this funnel gets narrowed on through Afghanistan and Pakistan and the end of this funnel is Gwadar port. So this funnel, futuristically, is the economic funnel of this whole region" (Former President of Pakistan Pervez Musharraf, 2002: 22nd March).[5]

President Musharraf's above statement has since laid out the underlying rationale for Pakistan's and China's joint interests in the development of Gwadar. By envisioning Gwadar as a viable port city for the landlocked Central Asian region, the idea of establishing a burgeoning regional trade corridor was thus put forth. This was based on the historic role Gwadar has already played for centuries over the Arabian Sea. Hence, the proposed trade corridor would provide Pakistan, China and Central Asia with a direct maritime link with the Middle East and Africa, significantly contributing to the future economic development of the entire region.

---

[5] Hasan Yaser Malik, "Strategic Importance of Gwadar Port," *Journal of Political Studies* 19, no.2 (2012): 57.

This emphasis on development was evident in how in the very same speech, President Musharraf had directly linked the construction of the port with the human development of the Baluchistan province.[6] This has since served as a major driving force considering how the province has been historically marred by under-development and insecurity for decades. This aspect was also evident in the references made to Afghanistan and Western China, where similar conditions have prevailed owing to a broad range of economic and security related issues. By equating infrastructure development with economic development, and subsequently economic development with human development, the idea has since been to leverage regional partnerships based on mutual interests at the state level for the betterment of the general population.

Even though President Musharraf had injected new impetus into Gwadar with China's assistance, construction and development remained stifled by delays for a number of years. This was evident during the first phase of the port's construction, which slated for completion in 2005 remained nonoperational till 2008.[7] It was also during this phase that the Pakistani government invited bids from port operators the world over to set up operations in Gwadar and take charge of the port's management. This was carried out in 2006, based on which the contract was awarded to a consortium led by the Port of Singapore Authority (PSA) as the highest bidder.[8] Within a few months the PSA was granted a 40 year operational lease starting from 2007, during which it was exempted from corporate taxes. To spur investment and rapid development, Pakistan had also abolished import duties on all port-related equipment and machinery that was to be used as part of its growth.

Speaking at the signing ceremony between the Pakistani government and the PSA, Pakistani Prime Minister Shaukat Aziz laid out his expectations from Gwadar port's new operators and managers.

---

[6] Saleem Shahid, "Gwadar Project Launched: Musharraf Lauds China's Assistance," *Dawn*, March 23, 2002, www.dawn.com/news/27285 (accessed October 19, 2018).

[7] "Gwadar Port: 'History-Making Milestones," *Dawn*, April 14, 2008, www.dawn.com/news/297994/gwadar-port (accessed October 20, 2018).

[8] Faisal Aziz, "Singapore's PSA Takes over Pakistan's Gwadar Port," *Reuters*, February 6, 2007, https://uk.reuters.com/article/singapore-pakistan/update-1-singapores-psa-takes-over-pakistans-gwadar-port-idUKISL16944320070206 (accessed October 20, 2018).

Emphasizing the long-term prospects of the port, he had stated that: "With the PSA running this port, down the road this can be a regional hub for sea transport and trade...we hope this will be the beginning of an era which will change the map of shipping in the world."[9]

Emphasizing the port's geo-economic and geo-strategic prospects, he had further explained that:

> "This can also be a potential energy port for the region. We are also looking at Gwadar as a major refining point as it is located near the largest hydrocarbon reserves of the world."[10]

This emphasis on energy was to subsequently propel Gwadar into the international spotlight, due to the complex web of intersecting national interests permeating through the region. Hence, as Gwadar's unique potential started to gain widespread attention, its growing importance within the Pak-China bi-lateral framework also became a site of contention amongst key regional players. For instance, it was widely reported that despite China paying around 75% of the port's US$248 million construction costs, President Musharraf was unwilling to hand over direct control of the port over to China.[11] This was out of concern for Washington, with whom Pakistan was unwilling to risk upsetting ties, especially during a key phase of cooperation on the Global War on Terror.

Washington's concerns during this phase were primarily informed by what it referred to as China's 'String of Pearls' strategy. Outlined in a US Department of Defense report titled 'Energy Futures in Asia',[12] the concept was based on the argument that:

---

[9] Ibid.

[10] Ibid.

[11] Declan Walsh, "Chinese Firm Will Run Strategic Pakistani Port at Gwadar," *New York Times*, January 31, 2013, www.nytimes.com/2013/02/01/world/asia/chinese-firm-will-run-strategic-pakistani-port-at-gwadar.html?_r=0 (accessed October 23, 2018).

[12] "China Builds up Strategic Sea Lanes," *Washington Times,* January 17, 2005, www.washingtontimes.com/news/2005/jan/17/20050117-115550-1929r/ (accessed October 23, 2018).

"China is building strategic relationships along the sea lanes from the Middle East to the South China Sea in ways that suggest defensive and offensive positioning to protect China's energy interests, but also to serve broad security objectives."[13]

The report, while citing Gwadar also referred to growing Chinese interests in key ports located in Bangladesh, Burma, Cambodia, Thailand and Sri Lanka. This emphasis on strategic over commercial interests is what subsequently prompted India to also raise its suspicions over growing Chinese influence across the region's ports and shipping lanes. Not to mention India's long-standing animosity towards Pakistan, the idea of a Chinese funded port in Pakistan has since stoked Indian concerns with regard to the increasing securitization of the Indian Ocean.

Nevertheless, in early 2013 a combination of factors led to Pakistan finally granting authority over the port's management operations to the China Overseas Ports Holding Company (COPHC).[14] Out of these factors; the Pakistani government's growing dissatisfaction with the PSA over the port's management, the growing friction in Pak-US ties, and the burgeoning growth of Pak-China cooperation proved crucial in Pakistan's decision to hand over control of the port's operations to China. This in turn sparked fresh reservations from the Indian Defense Minister, A.K Antony who marked the development as 'concerning' for India.[15]

---

[13] Ibid.

[14] Declan Walsh, "Chinese Firm Will Run Strategic Pakistani Port at Gwadar," *New York Times*, January 31, 2013, www.nytimes.com/2013/02/01/world/asia/chinese-firm-will-run-strategic-pakistani-port-at-gwadar.html?_r=0_ (accessed October 23, 2018).

[15] Anurag Kotoky and A Ananthalakshmi, "India 'Concerned' by China Role in Pakistan Port," *Reuters*, February 6, 2013, www.reuters.com/article/us-india-airshow-china-idUSBRE9150BX20130206 (accessed October 23, 2018).

Figure 3.3- Overview of CPEC Projects. Hernandez, Marco, Et Al, "China's Super Link to Gwadar Port - A Visual Explainer," *South China Morning Post*, May 12, 2017, https://multimedia.scmp.com/news/china/article/One-Belt-One-Road/pakistan.html (accessed October 23, 2018).

Despite these reservations, the accelerating pace of Pak-China cooperation that had been building up for the last few years culminated in the signing of the historical framework agreement outlining the China-Pakistan Economic Corridor (CPEC). Signed in July the same year, the agreement formalized the initiation of an economic corridor that would link Pakistan's Gwadar port on the Arabian Sea with Kashgar city in North Western China.[16] This marked a key phase in the inclusion of Gwadar as part of a wider initiative between Pakistan and China incorporating both countries' commercial and strategic interests. Two years later during his visit to Pakistan, President Xi Jinping pledged

---

[16] Nick Macfie, "Li Keqiang Urges Development of 'China-Pakistan Economic Corridor'," *South China Morning Post*, May 23, 2013, www.scmp.com/news/china/article/1244267/li-keqiang-urges-development-china-pakistan-economic-corridor (accessed October 18, 2018).

nearly US$46 billion for the entire CPEC initiative, which involved a number of projects straddling across energy, communications, manufacturing, agriculture, and trade and transport infrastructure.[17] It was also during his 2015 visit that President Xi emphasized CPEC's unique importance as part of China's overarching Belt & Road Initiative, particularly within the evolving international context.

In November the following year, Gwadar port handled its first shipment of Chinese goods transported via the CPEC land route between China and Pakistan.[18] The shipment that was headed towards the Middle East and Africa marked the operationalization of Gwadar port as a key component of CPEC, finally realizing the envisioned trade link between Western China and the Arabian Sea. As the port and the surrounding area further develop, a number of planned projects are slated to build on these beginnings and transform the port into a burgeoning regional hub. These include planned rail and air links, the development of a thriving special economic zone as well as key ancillary industries related to energy storage and transport, as well as state of the art ship-building and repair services. These would help the port city fulfill its potential as part of a major supply corridor catering towards the trans-continental flow of trade and energy in the 21st century.

Hence, while Gwadar has historically remained at the cross-roads of a diverse range of cultures and civilizations for centuries, recent developments have positioned it to uniquely impact an even wider range of people. As a key port that had for ages linked maritime trade routes along the Arabian Sea, Gwadar's importance as a key geo-strategic port has assumed even greater relevance today with respect to the growing energy requirements of fast developing economies. Its proximity to the critically important Strait of Hormuz on one end and the world's fastest growing economies such as China and India on the other end, allows it to

---

[17] "China Builds up Strategic Sea Lanes," *Washington Times,* January 17, 2005, www.washingtontimes.com/news/2005/jan/17/20050117-115550-1929r/ (accessed October 23, 2018).
[18] Kay Johnson, "Pakistani PM Welcomes First Large Chinese Shipment to Gwadar Port," *Reuters*, November 30, 2016, www.reuters.com/article/us-pakistan-china-port/pakistani-pm-welcomes-first-large-chinese-shipment-to-gwadar-port-idUSKBN1380LU (accessed October 23, 2018).

play a key role in shaping the trajectory of international trade and politics in the 21st century. It is however, also because of these broad ranging impacts that Gwadar has become a site of contestation with numerous countries vying for control and influence across the surrounding region. Yet, despite these challenges, Gwadar, by serving as a crucial gateway for the people of Central Asia, Western China and South Asia, remains well poised to determine the future trajectory of the wider region.

Gwadar as Part of a Vital New Energy Corridor

The above overview has so far presented a brief background to the key geo-strategic and geo-economic role that the port city of Gwadar has historically played in the Arabian Sea. Building on its growing importance within the current Pak-China framework however, Gwadar's prominence within CPEC and by extension the entire BRI framework is worth examining in further detail.

The following discussion provides a pointed exposition of Gwadar's potential as part of an emerging regional supply chain with far-reaching impacts the world over. Set to cater to the surging economies of key developing regions, Gwadar as a result holds tremendous influence in shaping the wider region's politics and development potential.

This potential as mentioned in the previous section is directly related to Gwadar port's close proximity to key energy supply lines fueling the world economy. This is because around two-thirds of the world's oil is currently transported by sea through various chokepoints such as the Strait of Hormuz, the Strait of Malacca, the Suez Canal, the Bab el-Mandeb Strait, and the Bosphorus.[19]

---

[19] Jean-Paul Rodrigue, "Straits, Passages and Chokepoints: A Maritime Geostrategic of Petroleum Distribution," *Cahiers De Géographie Du Québec* 48, no. 135 (Dec 2004): 364.

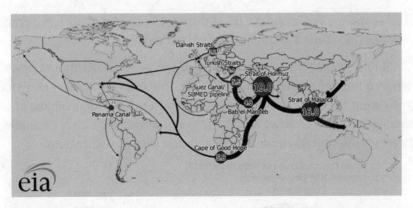

Figure 3.4- World Oil Transit Chokepoints [All estimates in million barrels per day. [Includes crude oil and petroleum liquids, Based on 2016 data] "World Oil Transit Chokepoints," *U.S Energy Information Administration (EIA)*, July 22, 2017, www.eia.gov/beta/international/regions-topics.php?RegionTopicID=WOTC (accessed October 23, 2018).

For the economies of Asia, the Strait of Hormuz and the Strait of Malacca serve as key chokepoints considering how nearly 19 million and 16 million barrels of oil pass through them respectively every day.[20] The most critical of these chokepoints, the Strait of Hormuz, is situated less than 400km away from Gwadar. It caters to about 88% of all oil outbound from the Persian Gulf to countries in Asia, Western Europe and the United States.[21] Based on last year's estimates, about 80% of the crude oil that moved through this chokepoint was headed to Asian markets comprising of China, Japan, India, South Korea and Singapore.[22] Considering how nearly 60% of the entire world's known oil reserves are concentrated in the Middle East and Persian Gulf regions,[23] the long-term geo-strategic importance of this chokepoint is likely to remain crucial for the world's key developing economies such as China. This is evident in the fact that just last year, China; owing to the rising demands

---

[20] Ibid.

[21] Ibid.

[22] "World Oil Transit Chokepoints," *U.S Energy Information Administration (EIA)*, July 25, 2017, www.eia.gov/beta/international/regions-topics.php?RegionTopicID=WOTC (accessed October 19, 2018).

[23] Eshita Gupta, "Oil Vulnerability Index of Oil-Importing Countries," *Energy Policy* 36, no. 3 (March 2008): 1195–1211.

of its economy, surpassed the US as the world's largest importer of crude oil importing around 8.4 million barrels per day.[24]

Similarly, the Strait of Malacca which serves as the maritime gateway between the Indian Ocean and the South China Sea also serves as a vital chokepoint for China's energy supply lines. Out of the total volume of oil passing through the Strait around 42% is destined for China, emanating directly from sources in the Middle East and Persian Gulf regions.

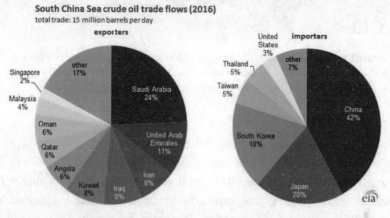

Figure 3.5- South China Sea Crude Oil Trade flows 2016. "More than 30% of Global Maritime Crude Oil Trade Moves through the South China Sea," *Today in energy-U.S. Energy Information Administration (EIA)*, August 27, 2018, www.eia.gov/todayinenergy/detail.php?id=36952 (accessed October 23, 2018).

This over-reliance on the South China Sea for its energy supplies is widely referred to as China's 'Malacca Dilemma'.[25] Considering how nearly 60% of the Oil consumed by China is transported from the Middle East and 80% of its total oil imports pass through the Malacca Strait,[26] China is in dire need of diversifying its energy supply lines to mitigate any potential risks to its current economy as well as future growth potential. This holds particular importance with respect to rising

---

[24] "China Surpassed the United States as the World's Largest Crude Oil Importer in 2017," Today *in Energy - U.S. Energy Information Administration (EIA)*, February 5, 2018, www.eia.gov/todayinenergy/detail.php?id=34812 (accessed October 19, 2018).

[25] Raja M Khan and M. Saif ur Rehman Khan, "Gwadar Port: An Economic Hub or a Military Outpost," *Journal of Contemporary Studies* 2, no. 1(2013): 51.

[26] S. Afzal, & Naseem A, "China Pakistan Economic Corridor (CPEC): Challenges and Prospects, Pakistan," *Administrative Review* 2, no. 1(2018): 209-222.

tensions in the South China Sea, which has come to increasingly serve as a potential flashpoint between the United States and China. The increasing securitization of the region has been highlighted by the growing presence of both US and Chinese naval assets, amidst the backdrop of rising tensions between China, Japan and a number of ASEAN states over the disputed nature of key islands and territories. These tensions subsequently pose immense risks to global stability owing to the complex web of strategic and commercial relations that have characterized the region.

Gwadar however, owing to its unique location and the long history of Pak-China bi-lateral relations offers a viable solution to China's Malacca Dilemma. As a key component of the China Pakistan Economic Corridor (CPEC), Gwadar port has the potential of creating a new supply corridor by linking an over-land route to Western China with the maritime supply lines passing through the Arabian Sea. As depicted in figure 3.6, China currently imports around 80% of its oil supplies through the Strait of Malacca.

This equates to a voyage of about 12,900 km, which takes around 45 days to complete.[27] The same journey would alternatively comprise of 2400 km via CPEC (400 km from the Strait of Hormuz to Gwadar, and 2000 km from Gwadar to Kashgar). With the total distance reduced by more than 80%, the entire journey is expected to take less than 10 days all the way from the Persian Gulf to Western China.[28]

In addition to being a faster and shorter supply route, energy shipments via Gwadar as part of CPEC would also reduce the risks associated with the increasing securitization of the maritime routes passing through the Indian Ocean and South China Sea. This would in turn nullify the risks to China's energy supplies as enshrined within its Malacca Dilemma.

---

[27] Khalid Manzoor Butt and Anam Abid But, "Impact of CPEC on Regional and Extra Regional Actors," *Journal of Political Science* 33 (January 2015): 23-44.
[28] Ibid.

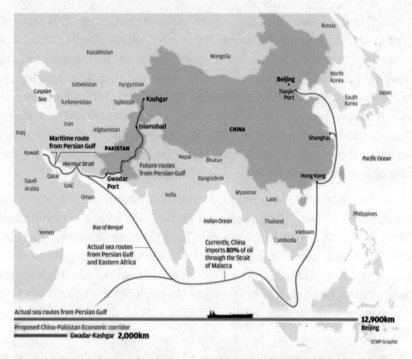

Figure 3.6- Proposed trade route under CPEC. Debasish R Chowdhury, "Pakistan Happy to Aid in China's Quest for Land Route to the West; India, Not so Much," *South China Morning Post,* Nov 19, 2013, www.scmp.com/business/commodities/article/1359761/pakistan-happy-aid-chinas-quest-land-route-west-india-not-so (accessed October 19, 2018).

In addition to serving as a viable inlet for China's energy imports, Gwadar also holds immense potential for serving as a key outlet for Central Asian energy exports. According to EU estimates; Kazakhstan, Turkmenistan and Uzbekistan together with Russia comprise of the world's second largest reserves of Oil and Gas.[29] Kazakhstan alone for instance accounts for double the oil reserves of the North Sea (the government estimates total reserves to be three times higher). Similarly Turkmenistan and Uzbekistan are estimated as holding the 5th and 8th largest gas reserves in the world. Kazakhstan and Uzbekistan are also

---

[29] "Central Asia - Energy - International Cooperation and Development - European Commission," *International Cooperation and Development, European Union*, July 1, 2014, https://ec.europa.eu/europeaid/regions/central-asia/eu-central-asia-energy-cooperationen (accessed October 23, 2018).

endowed with significant quantities of Uranium, with the former being the world's third largest producer of this key resource.[30]

Despite such vast natural endowments, these landlocked Central Asian states have for decades struggled to develop a robust energy infrastructure. They have been unable to develop these reserves into exportable surplus, and have been restricted to supplying a limited number of markets in Russia and Eastern Europe.[31] The lack of an adequate transport and delivery infrastructure has further restricted these states in unleashing their vast untapped potential.

However, more recent developments characterized by Chinese assistance have led to the development of key infrastructure projects that are directly focused on addressing these limitations.[32] The construction of key oil and gas pipelines, rail and road networks, and much needed refineries and storage facilities are all geared towards creating new energy supply chains capable of tapping into the Central Asian region's unutilized energy potential. These projects, most of which fall under the umbrella of the Belt and Road Initiative (BRI), are to work directly in tandem with CPEC; providing the Central Asian region with a direct overland route to the maritime sea lanes passing through the Arabian Sea. This would thus allow CPEC to serve as a viable delivery infrastructure that can be used to export Central Asian energy commodities to key markets the world over. With Gwadar playing a central role within this new supply chain, it holds the potential of linking Central Asian energy reserves with more immediate energy hungry markets in South Asia such as India; as well as markets farther off in South America, South Africa, South-East and Far-East Asia.

Hence, as a key component of CPEC and the BRI, Gwadar is set to play an undeniably crucial role in re-shaping the global flow of energy for decades to come. As a port that is directly geared towards serving some of the world's fastest developing emerging markets, its importance

---

[30] Ibid.

[31] Michael Hart, "Central Asia's Oil and Gas Now Flows to the East," *The Diplomat*, August 19, 2016, https://thediplomat.com/2016/08/central-asias-oil-and-gas-now-flows-to-the-east/ (accessed October 23, 2018).

[32] Ibid.

as a strategic economic hub for the region cannot be understated. Be it as the most efficient solution to the Malacca Dilemma, or as a key maritime outlet to landlocked Central Asia, Gwadar's immense potential as a regional energy hub holds wide-ranging implications radically re-shaping international politics and the growth trajectory of the world economy.

Gwadar as Part of a New Global Status-Quo

It is thus no wonder that owing to its far reaching implications Gwadar presents a whole host of strategic and security related issues with respect to the Indian Ocean Region (IOR). As mentioned earlier in this chapter, it forms a key portion of the 'String of Pearls'[33] theory subscribed to by the US, India and other regional powers.

This theory is premised on China's growing commercial interests at key geo-strategic ports throughout the world, many of which are characterized by a significant Chinese naval presence. These include a number of ports dotting the South China Sea, the Andaman Sea, the Bay of Bengal, the Laccadive Sea and the Arabian Sea surrounding India. In addition to Pakistan, China has helped fund and develop a number of strategic ports in Sri Lanka, Bangladesh, Myanmar, Thailand, Cambodia and a handful of islands that were reclaimed and developed within the contested waters of the South China Sea.

Considering how these ports are strategically located alongside vital maritime trade routes, China's growing influence along these locations is framed by the United States and India as a threat to the prevailing status quo within the region. The recent formation of the Quadrilateral Security Dialogue, (also known as the 'Quad') between the United States, Japan, India and Australia has more recently highlighted this issue as a key development specifically with respect to the Indian Ocean Region (IOR).[34] This was stated by senior officials of Australia, India, Japan, and

---

[33] "China Builds up Strategic Sea Lanes," *Washington Times,* January 17, 2005, https://www.washingtontimes.com/news/2005/jan/17/20050117-115550-1929r/ (accessed October 23, 2018).
[34] Gurmeet Kanwal, "Pakistan's Gwadar Port: A New Naval Base in China's String of Pearls in the Indo-Pacific," *Center for Strategic and International Studies (CSIS)*, April 2, 2018,

the United States in November 2017 at a meeting held on the sidelines of the East Asia Summit in the Philippines. During this meeting it was agreed that a "free, open, prosperous and inclusive Indo-Pacific region serves the long-term interests of all countries in the region and of the world at large."[35]

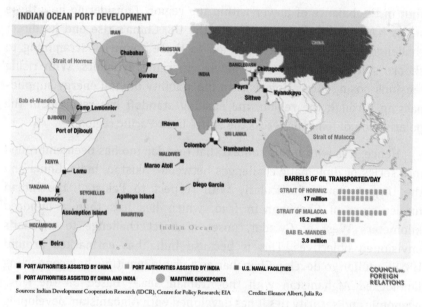

Figure 3.7- Key Geo-Strategic Ports Along the Indian Ocean Region. Eleanor Albert, "Competition in the Indian Ocean, Backgrounder - The New Geopolitics of China, India, and Pakistan," *Council on Foreign Relations*, May 19, 2016, www.cfr.org/backgrounder/competition-indian-ocean (accessed October 23, 2018).

The formation of this quadrilateral alliance is thus widely perceived as an attempt to contain China's growing maritime influence within the region. For the US, the alliance represents part of a broader strategy aimed at containing the rise of China, as evident in the series of escalating tensions between these two global powers. For India, the alliance represents a viable counter-weight against an increasingly assertive China with whom India has been competing for economic and

---

www.csis.org/analysis/pakistans-gwadar-port-new-naval-base-chinas-string-pearls-indo-pacific (accessed October 23, 2018).
[35] Ibid.

strategic supremacy within the region. Furthermore, China's long-standing strategic partnership with Pakistan further complicates Sino-Indian relations despite significant trade linkages between the world's two fastest developing economies. For Japan, Australia and a host of ASEAN Nations, China's growing maritime influence represents a major shift in the balance of power within the region. Considering how these states have traditionally allied with the US, China's rise and its direct challenge to US supremacy, has led to these countries scrambling to choose sides as part of these newly emerging dynamics. With rising tensions posing increasing risks to the stability of vital energy supplies passing through the region, the ensuing standoff has resulted in the polarization of tensions across the entire Indo-Pacific region.

Hence, it is within this context that Gwadar too has been embroiled in a series of diplomatic challenges between Pakistan, India, China and the United States. Particularly with respect to Pakistan, the Indian funded port of Chabahar in Iran, which lies less than a hundred kilometers West of Gwadar, poses a direct challenge to Gwadar's envisioned objectives. This is because India has earmarked around US$85 million to develop Chabahar as a viable maritime link connecting landlocked Afghanistan with the Arabian Sea.[36] Based on the close economic and security ties it has developed with Afghanistan, developing Chabahar would allow India to circumvent Pakistan and provide a direct link to the Central Asian Region. This in turn would provide it with unfettered access to the region's vast energy reserves discussed earlier in this chapter. Furthermore, a significant foothold in Chabahar, close to both Gwadar and the vital Strait of Hormuz, would also allow India to directly challenge Chinese naval presence within the region. This is likely to further contribute to the securitization and polarization of tensions within the wider region, exacerbated by the fact that China, Pakistan and India are all nuclear powers.

However, a number of observers have pointed out that based on the precedents that it has set across the world, China's interests in the

---

[36] Khalid Manzoor Butt and Anam Abid But, "Impact of CPEC on Regional and Extra Regional Actors," *Journal of Political Science* 32 (2015):23-44.

world's key ports and shipping routes are borne primarily out of commercial reasons.[37] Based on the extremely long-term nature of these investments, it has been argued that any strategic benefits that are to be accrued from these stakes, are more likely to be derived from whatever economic leverage China may be able to muster within these regions.

China's global port investment

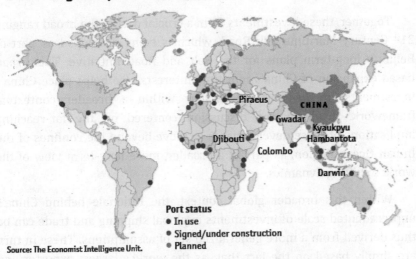

Source: The Economist Intelligence Unit.

Figure 3.8- Ports Developed and/or Partly Owned or Funded by China. "China's Expanding Investment in Global Ports," *The Economist Group,* October 11, 2017, https://www.google.com.pk/search?q=%E2%80%9CChina%E2%80%99s+Expanding+Investm ent+in+Global+Ports&rlz=1C1CHBD_enPK813PK813&oq=%E2%80%9CChina%E2%80%99 s+Expanding+Investment+in+Global+Ports&aqs=chrome..69i57j0.1216j0j4&sourceid=chrome &ie=UTF-8 (accessed October 20, 2018).

This is evident from the fact that in 2016, China had invested over $20 billion in a number of seaports all across the world. This was almost double of what China had spent on developing and acquiring stakes in key seaports the previous year.[38] As of September 2017, Chinese

[37] Wade Shepard, "China's Seaport Shopping Spree: What China is Winning by Buying up the World's Ports," *Forbes*, September 6, 2017, www.forbes.com/sites/wadeshepard/2017/09/06/chinas-seaport-shopping-spree-whats-happening-as-the-worlds-ports-keep-going-to-china/#4e66f9ae4e9d (accessed October 20, 2018).
[38] Ibid.

companies led by its state owned COSCO shipping company had confirmed investments or ownership stakes in 34 countries with 12 planned investments in another 8 countries.[39] These comprise of significant investments in port operations across a number of diverse regions in mostly developed countries. These have subsequently included countries such as Greece, the Netherlands, Spain, Australia and Brazil, among numerous other key locations.

Together, these investments form a crucial part of the broad ranging 21st Century Maritime Silk Road, which is being developed as part of Beijing's long-term plans for the Belt and Road Initiative. This broad based expansion of China's maritime interests also helps place China's investments in the port of Gwadar within a broader contextual framework. It allows the discussion centered on the far-reaching implications of these developments to move beyond the confines of the Indian Ocean Region, as part of a broader, more long-term view of the world's shifting dynamics.

Within this broader global context, the rationale behind China's unprecedented scale of investments in global shipping and trade can be thus derived from a more generalized set of assumptions. These in turn are simply based on the fact that; as the world's largest exporter and second largest importer, China's economy is deeply intertwined with global trade. While concepts such as the 'String of Pearls' may characterize China's maritime interests as being offensive in nature, it is here argued that China's stakes in global shipping are instead inherently defensive.

The argument thus follows that:

> "By owning and operating a complex network of key logistical nodes across Asia, Europe, and Africa, China can essentially control a huge portion of its inbound supply chain for essential commodities --

---

[39] "China's Expanding Investment in Global Ports," *The Economist Group*, October 11, 2017, https://www.google.com.pk/search?q=%E2%80%9CChina%E2%80%99s+Expanding+Investment+in+Global+Ports&rlz=1C1CHBD_enPK813PK813&oq=%E2%80%9CChina%E2%80%99s+Expanding+Investment+in+Global+Ports&aqs=chrome..69i57j0.1216j0j4&sourceid=chrome&ie=UTF-8 (accessed October 20, 2018).

like energy resources from the Middle East -- and
outbound trade routes for its exports. They provide
China with a higher degree of self-reliance, while
decreasing the amount of political and economic
leverage that other countries can apply."[40]

Hence, based on a holistic more broad ranging perspective, the above
argument allows China's overseas interests to be viewed from a more
trade-orientated and commercial standpoint than what they are often
otherwise made out to be. China has always maintained that its motives
for greater maritime expansion are based on securing vulnerable
shipping lanes through key maritime chokepoints that are instead
plagued by piracy and/or geo-political rivalries. By ensuring a more
robust and diversified global trade network (in the form of the 21st
Century Maritime Silk Road) China's primary objectives can be thus seen
as ensuring the stability of the global economy, on which its own growth
and prosperity are directly derived from.

This aspect is also clearly evident in the planned energy corridor
being built around Gwadar. While the Gwadar-Kashgar route presents a
viable alternative to the existing energy routes passing through the Strait
of Malacca, it also presents an opportunity to de-escalate tensions
currently pervading through the South China Sea. Furthermore, these
new supply chains in addition to benefitting China, are to directly benefit
the wider South Asian and Central Asian region which is in dire need of
economic and infrastructure development. Building on this surge of
investments, the subsequent growth and economic development is thus
expected to directly promote greater stability and prosperity across the
entire region.

It is therefore, this emphasis on global economic growth and stability
that China has time and again referred to as the primary objective and
outcome of its expanding influence. As part of its overall policy

---

[40] Wade Shepard, "China's Seaport Shopping Spree: What China is Winning by Buying up the
World's Ports," *Forbes*, September 6, 2017,
www.forbes.com/sites/wadeshepard/2017/09/06/chinas-seaport-shopping-spree-whats-
happening-as-the-worlds-ports-keep-going-to-china/#4e66f9ae4e9d (accessed October 23,
2018).

framework for the Belt and Road Initiative, China has repeatedly called to attention the notion of establishing pragmatic win-win partnerships, across the world. These partnerships have further been characterized as being all-inclusive and non-discriminatory in nature with China respecting the individual policy constraints, economic limitations and even cultural differences of its development partners. As is evident in numerous cases, the positive impact of Chinese investments on the economic growth and development of its partner countries has subsequently remained undeniable.

COSCO's recently acquired majority stake in the Greek port of Piraeus for instance testifies to the successes borne out of China's overseas investment strategy. Since setting up operations in 2009, China's influence on Piraeus has been widely credited as having transformed the once stagnant port into a major transport hub for the wider region.[41]

Similarly, China's investments aimed at expanding the aging Colombo Port in Sri Lanka have seen the port's capacity doubled in less than 30 months.[42] Its recently acquired controlling stake in the nearby Hambantota port, which has been cited as an example of its 'predatory debt trap diplomacy',[43] instead now testifies to China's long-term commitment and unchanging vision of the port's potential. This is evident in how beyond the construction of the deep sea port, China has helped develop an entirely new economic ecosystem comprising of a burgeoning industrial zone, a Liquefied Natural Gas Plant, a convention center, a stadium, a tourism area built on reclaimed land, and a

---

[41] Costas Paris and Alkman Granitsas, "Chinese Transform Greek Port, Winning over Critics," *Wall Street Journal*, November 20, 2014, www.wsj.com/articles/chinese-transform-greek-port-winning-over-critics-1416516560 (accessed October 23, 2018).

[42] "The New Masters and Commanders," *The Economist,* June 8, 2013, www.economist.com/international/2013/06/08/the-new-masters-and-commanders (accessed October 23, 2018).

[43] Maria Abi-habib, "How China Got Sri Lanka to Cough up a Port," *New York Times,* June 25, 2018, www.nytimes.com/2018/06/25/world/asia/china-sri-lanka-port.html (accessed October 23, 2018).

sprawling airport all of which was built keeping in mind its long-term potential.[44]

All of these developments bear striking similarity to what China is presently undertaking at Gwadar. The planned Special Economic Zone, the envisioned road and rail links, the planned state of the art airport and a dedicated technical and vocational training center all point towards China's long-term commitment and vision for the port's potential as a sprawling economic hub for the region. In addition to the development of the deep sea port's infrastructure and related industries, China has also helped fund a number of social development initiatives, the most salient of which are the recently set up desalination plant providing fresh water to the city, as well as the expansion of a major hospital.

Hence, taking into account China's vision for its long-term growth in relation to the growth and stability of the global economy; the Pakistani port city of Gwadar represents one of many components (albeit a crucial component) of China's overall strategy. Viewed from this wider perspective of the Belt and Road Initiative, Gwadar's relevance within the discourse on the securitization of the Indian Ocean Region thus pales in comparison to its broader economic potential for global growth and stability. It is in this way that moving beyond the perhaps more short-term geo-political confines of the Indian Ocean, Gwadar's geo-economic potential for the wider region and the world represents a more long-term view of the future trajectory of international relations. It is thus Gwadar's Geo-Economic, rather than Geo-Strategic impact that makes it a key part of a new global status quo in the long run.

Conclusion – Gwadar as Part of a Community of Shared Destiny

This chapter has placed the growing international interest around Gwadar within a series of historical, geographical, political and economic perspectives in an attempt to better understand its potential for Pakistan

---

[44] Wade Shepard, "China's Seaport Shopping Spree: What China is Winning by Buying up the World's Ports," *Forbes*, September 6, 2017, www.forbes.com/sites/wadeshepard/2017/09/06/chinas-seaport-shopping-spree-whats-happening-as-the-worlds-ports-keep-going-to-china/#4e66f9ae4e9d (accessed October 18, 2018).

and the wider region. In doing so it has discussed Gwadar's potential as a key conduit between the Mediterranean, Central Asian, African, and South and South-East Asian regions based on its historic inheritance of centuries old trade and supply routes. This was presented as forming the basis of an emerging energy corridor, based on the economic realities and requirements of the 21st Century. Laying particular emphasis on Gwadar's potential impact on the world's fast developing economies; the discourse on Gwadar's impact on the securitization of the region based on its geo-strategic significance, was shown as being secondary to its geo-economic significance for global growth and stability in the long run. This was done by contextualizing Gwadar as a key component of the China Pakistan Economic Corridor, and by extension the entire Belt & Road Initiative.

Yet, coming back to the rocky shores of Gwadar, where nearly thousands of fishermen still follow the centuries old techniques and practices handed down to them by their ancestors; the socio-economic impact that the above developments are likely to have on the city's residents is to more likely serve as the most significant outcome of this entire initiative for them. It is projected that over the next 8-10 years, development activities in Gwadar are expected to create around two million new jobs for the city's residents.[45] This, coupled with a vibrant economy comprising of a diverse range of products and services, state of the art education and healthcare facilities and a vibrant tourism sector built around the city's pristine beauty is to exponentially multiply the quality of life in the city and its surrounding regions. Local authorities estimate that based on these opportunities, nearly 1.7 million people are expected to migrate to the city within the coming thirty years.[46]

Based on its immense potential, it is often argued that without Gwadar, it is unlikely that the underlying rationale and impetus for the entire CPEC initiative would be justified as it does today. The strategic

---

[45] Dr. Azhar Ahmad, "Report on Gwadar Port: Potentials and Prospects," *Pakistan Institute for Conflict and Security Studies*, January 29, 2015, https://www.picss.net/wp-content/uploads/2015/02/Dr-Azhar-Gwadar-Potential-Prospects.pdf (accessed October 10, 2018).
[46] Ibid.

location of the port with respect to its vast potential for contributing to global economic growth is what many have cited as the primary reasons behind Gwadar being termed as the crown jewel of CPEC. However, there is no denying that Gwadar holds immense potential in uplifting the socio-economic conditions of a once stagnant region. Arguably, it is the purported human development which these projects are to lead to, that are of significant importance. In effect, it is this very opportunity which allows for one of the world's most marginalized communities to be able to play a leading role in the world' economic growth and development. This in fact is what truly places Gwadar as the Crown Jewel of CPEC.

Part II: The BRI & the Economic Rise of China

Chapter 4: The Age of China - Lessons in Economic Development for Pakistan

Ambassador (Retired) Syed Hasan Javed*

Developing countries can emulate China's speed, quality and sustainability of economic growth if they are able to muster a few things. These include having a fresh look on Economic Theory, a collectively honest leadership, a more inclusive society, and perhaps most importantly the willingness to employ 'Chinese characteristics'. These include, the ability of the highest leadership to admit one's mistakes, a readiness to reform, innovate or 'change the course' when necessary, the ability to think small before thinking big, to review every step before taking the next one, to be realistic and not delusional, and to focus more on results instead of the process. These characteristics work equally well in capitalistic, socialistic and market economy templates. They require the ability to think long term, and to often take decisions against the conventional norms of economics, diplomacy and statecraft.

It is worth noting that most, if not all Chinese characteristics are in fact universal human values which the Chinese state holds on to, and harnesses as part of their overall approach to governance. As will be shown in this chapter, these characteristics have formed the basis for China's tremendous economic development and its subsequent rise as a global power. They have served as the guiding principles of Deng Xiaoping's theory laid out over the last quarter of the previous century and continue to inspire President Xi Jinping's vision for China as a future global leader. The following discussion thus provides a unique insight

---
* *Ambassador (Retired)* Syed Hasan Javed is the Director of the Chinese Studies Centre at the School of Social Sciences and Humanities (S3H), NUST, Islamabad.

into the historical dimensions, as well as the guiding principles underlying China's Belt & Road Initiative within the context of CPEC.

Charting New Global Paradigms

Since the end of the Second World War and the 'Decolonization of the World', students of economics have been taught theories based on the experiences of the Great Depression (1933-1937) and the economic realities of largely Western societies. These theories subsequently draw inspiration from the writings of Malthus, Keynes, Marshall, Myrdal and Friedman.[1]As a result, the ascendance of America in the 20th century took the limelight away from the intellectual bastion of Britannica, across the Atlantic. It was theorized that this economic growth, was based on the 'Four Factors of Production' i.e. Land, Labor, Capital and Organization. It was also argued that this growth trajectory followed a growth percentage in single digits and decimal terms, given the constraints of natural resource endowments (both physical and non-physical), depending on a country's relative position in terms of 'Comparative Advantage'.

The decades following the Second World War were consumed by the intellectual debate on Capitalism versus Socialism, State ownership versus the Individual ownership of the means of production, and the differences between a Centralized Planned Economy versus a Free Enterprise Market Economy. The emergence of the International Financial Institutions (IFIs) as a result of the establishment of the Bretton Woods System was all meant to sustain this neatly drafted (or crafted) 'New International Economic Order'. These included the World Bank (known first as the International Bank of Reconstruction and Development), the International Monetary Fund (IMF) and the Private Sector Lender International Finance Corporation (IFC). The objectives of this entire system were to be further implemented by crafting political institutions of 'Liberal Democracy' and having the above mentioned IFIs

---

[1] "The History of Economic Thought," *Economic Realms*, January 4, 2013, http://theeconomicrealms.blogspot.com/2013/01/the-history-of-economic-thought-deals.html (accessed September 14, 2018).

ensure the maintenance of elitist rule and macroeconomic book keeping; all under the ironic guise of political and economic freedom

As they say, 'beggars have no choice, and that slaves even less; the subsequent wave of decolonization that spread through Asia and Africa immediately after the Second World War, represented more of a change on the surface of things as opposed to the deep rooted transformation that it was being hailed as. Policy-makers and the intellectual elite governing these newly decolonized states were still indebted to their former colonial masters as they had simply inherited their exalted power and privilege from them. Hence, the former colonial powers by virtue of their position as such were still hailed as the 'know-it-alls' of Economic growth, whose growth models simply needed to be replicated within these newly de-colonized societies.

The implementation of their economic theories and growth templates were thus monitored closely by the IFIs. But even that was not the end of this emerging global order. In order to ensure that these newly independent countries remained at the mercy of their former colonial masters, trade and investment were further regulated through the 'General Agreement on Tariff and Trade' (GATT), which saw extreme polarization in debates between the growing inequality between developed and developing countries. This carried on through to the 1990s, as the GATT metamorphosed into the 'World Trade Organization' (WTO), continuing even to this day. The recent questions of market access for agricultural goods and other issues underpinning the stalled 'Doha Development Agenda' continue to evoke strong sentiments across all sides.[2]

The inefficiencies of this Post War Global order are further argued to have permeated through the much acclaimed process of Globalization. This is evident from the 'Brain Drain' of talent and the sustained flight of capital from the developing to the developed world, for almost seven decades as part of this process.

---

[2] "Briefing Notes on some of the Main Issues of the Doha Round," *World Trade Organization*, n.d., https://www.wto.org/english/tratop_e/dda_e/status_e/brief00e.htm (accessed September 14, 2018).

However, running parallel to this process is a growing realization of how this imbalance can be overcome through a series of pragmatic solutions that have been implemented across a diverse range of policy measures. These are perhaps best evident in the economic growth models implemented by the East Asian developing countries which have quietly mastered the Western secrets of 'Wealth Creation', coupling them with their own socio-cultural frameworks. This is evident from the sustained economic growth experienced by countries such as Japan, Hong Kong, Republic of South Korea, Singapore, Malaysia, China, Vietnam and many others. Over the past seventy decades, the 'frog leaping growth trajectory' of these countries has led many economists to observe that economic power has shifted considerably from the Atlantic towards Asia with a lot more to follow.

Within this framework, the most significant challenge to the prevailing Western backed economic order has come from the rise of the People's Republic of China that has been critical to this power shift. China's rise in particular offers vital lessons not only in development per se, but in the need to look afresh into the underlying framework and principles of economic theory. It is important that as Economics as a discipline keeps evolving, the world built around it also evolves in tandem, in recognition of these profound changes.

Contextualizing the Rise of China

According to the American Central Intelligence Agency's (CIA) World Fact book, China's GDP alone in terms of Purchasing Power Parity exceeded US $ 23.12 trillion in 2017, as compared to US $ 20.2 trillion for the United States of America. Because of its large population and territory, allocation of economic resources, active diaspora, resource rich hinterland, growing social capital and overall worldview the Asian century looks more likely to be defined as China's century. China presently comprises a fifth of the world's population with pockets of flourishing communities in Hong Kong, Taiwan, Singapore, Malaysia, Indonesia and Thailand.[3] The Chinese community also owns a fifth of the

---

[3] Matt Schiavenza, "A Surprising Map of the World Shows Just How Big China's Population Is?," *The Atlantic*, August 14, 2013, https://www.theatlantic.com/china/archive/2013/08/a-

World's GDP and sits on roughly US $5 trillion of foreign exchange reserves.[4]

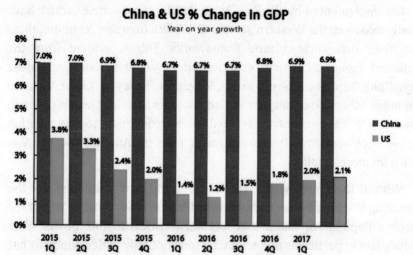

China & US % Change in GDP
Year on year growth

Source: Calculated from US Bureau of Economic Analysis NIPA Table 1.1.3, Trading Economics

Graph 4.1- China Growing Three Time Faster Than US. "China Growing Three Time Faster than US," *Learning from China*, n.d., https://www.learningfromchina.net/chinas-economy-is-growing-three-times-as-fast-as-the-us.html (accessed August 13, 2018).

Back in 1980, China was ranked as 32nd in global trade with a per capita income of US $180 (thirty percent less than the per capita income of US $250 in Pakistan, in 1980).[5] There were virtually no foreign exchange reserves and its stock market was largely unheard of. Since then China had taken out all but 7% of its population below the poverty line of US $1 per day by the year 2015. This is the largest number of

surprising-map-of-the-world-shows-just-how-big-chinas-population-is/278691/ (accessed August 13, 2018).

[4] "China's Choice: Capturing the $5 Trillion Productivity Opportunity," *Mckinsey Global Institute*, June 2016, https://www.mckinsey.com/~/media/mckinsey/featured%20insights/Employment%20and%20Growth/Capturing%20Chinas%205%20trillion%20productivity%20opportunity/Chinas-choice-capturing-the-5-trillion-productivity-opportunity-Executive-summary.ashx (accessed August 13, 2018).

[5] "China's Foreign Trade," *The State Council of Peoples Republic of China*, December 11, 2014, http://english.gov.cn/archive/white_paper/2014/08/23/content_281474983043184.htm (accessed August 13, 2018).

people in human history that have been taken out of poverty in the shortest possible time.[6]

In less than 30 years, China's exports increased from US$ 11 billion in 1979-80 to US$ 2.1 trillion in 2017[7]and imports from US$21 billion to US$1.7 trillion during the same period.[8] The Chinese economy has also diversified its foreign trade linkages away from dependence on the US market. From a high of 31 percent of exports in 2000, China's exports to the US fell to 18.2 percent in 2017.[9] On the other hand China's exports to the developing world accounted for more than half of its total exports in 2014.[10] China has already become the largest trading partner of more than 142 countries. Foreign firms account for nearly two third of all Chinese exports and almost four fifths of its exports of high tech items.

Foreign Direct Investment (FDI) has also thus played a key role in China's success with a cumulative total of 7.9% as of 2017.[11] Prior to 1979, Foreign Direct Investment (FDI) was unknown in China.[12] Based on lessons learnt from the success of neighboring East and South East Asian nations, the reforms carried out by China under Deng Xiaoping's leadership took the country on the path towards prolonged growth in its FDI.[13] China made stellar success in attracting FDI, mostly by the Overseas Chinese Diaspora. Today the outbound investment by the

---

[6] "Eradicate Extreme Hunger and Poverty Where we are," *UNDP China,* 2015, http://www.cn.undp.org/content/china/en/home/post-2015/mdgoverview/overview/mdg1.html (accessed August 13, 2018).

[7] "China Imports," *Trading Economics,* https://tradingeconomics.com/china/imports (accessed August 13, 2018).

[8] Ibid.

[9] Kimberly Amadeo, "China's Economy Facts and Effect on the U.S. Economy how much China Really Affects the U.S. Economy," August, 2018, https://www.thebalance.com/china-economy-facts-effect-on-us-economy-3306345 (accessed August 14, 2018).

[10] Joong Shik Kang and Wei Liao, "Chinese Imports: What's Behind the Slowdown?," *International Monetary Fund,* 2016, https://www.imf.org/external/pubs/ft/wp/2016/wp16106.pdf (accessed August 13, 2018).

[11] "China Says Foreign Direct Investment Up 7.9% in 2017," *China Daily,* January 16, 2018, http://www.chinadaily.com.cn/a/201801/16/WS5a5db178a3102c394518f986.html (accessed August 13, 2018).

[12] Shang-Jin Wei, "Foreign Direct Investment in China: Sources and Consequences," in *Financial Deregulation and Integration in East Asia,* ed. Takatoshi Ito and Anne O. Krueger (US: University of Chicago Press, 1996),77-105.

[13] Clem Tisdell, "Economic Reform and Openness in China: China's Development Policies in the Last 30 Years," *Economic Analysis and Policy* 39, no. 2 (September 2009): 271-294.

Chinese companies is competing with inward inflows. This has further allowed China to build up its foreign exchange reserves which stood at a whopping US $ 3.2 trillion as of 2016.[14] This has bestowed stability to the Chinese Yuan, which continues to be the envy of many developed nations who feel that it is still 'undervalued', making China's exports remarkably competitive. The success stories in China's economic reforms such as poverty alleviation, human resource development, agriculture modernization, mass industrialization, advancements in science and technology and space exploration have very few parallels in contemporary history.

Foreign investors have also been increasingly drawn to China's seemingly endless supply of cheap, skilled, disciplined and abundant manpower due to the widespread migration of rural labor to urban centers. This has been made possible by a strict emphasis on training and education at the policy level over the last few decades, the dividends of which have been apparent for the world to see.

'Crossing the River by Feeling Stones'

China's success can be attributed to a series of planned transitions, which were carried out with a clear direction and goal in mind. The vision of its leaders was based on overcoming incremental challenges which laid out a clear path to achieving what is now considered as historic levels of economic growth and development. It is thus argued that, China has hard earned its achievements which, in the words of the reformist leader Deng Xiaoping, was made possible by 'crossing the river by feeling the stones'.[15] This meant that the process of 'crossing' was gradual, exploratory, pragmatic, focused, and mission oriented.

The ensuing policy of "Economic Reforms" and "Open Doors" to the outside world was thus implemented by the Chinese state along these

---

[14] "China December Forex Reserves Rise To $3.14 Trillion, Highest since September 2016," *Reuters*, January 7, 2018, https://www.reuters.com/article/us-china-economy-forex-reserves/china-december-forex-reserves-rise-to-3-14-trillion-highest-since-september-2016-idUSKBN1EW061 (accessed August 14, 2018).

[15] "Crossing the River by Feeling the Stones," *South China Morning Post*, July 22, 2002, https://www.scmp.com/article/385907/crossing-river-feeling-stones (accessed September 1, 2018).

lines of thought. Set in motion in the Third Plenum of the 11th Congress of the Communist Party in December 1978[16], this Policy reversed some of the most salient aspects of the centrally planned economy that had been spearheaded by Chairman Mao Zedong. The new changes that were introduced permeated all aspects of Chinese life across its society, economy, politics, defense and diplomacy.

Deng Xiaoping 1904-1997

Figure: 4.3. Deng Xiaoping. "Deng Xiaoping Architect of Modern China," *China's Daily*, http://www.chinadaily.com.cn/opinion/deng xiaoping.html (accessed March 25, 2018).

On the political level, the main initiatives included the establishment of rule of law, greater freedom, more emphasis on basic individual rights, investment in higher education, avoidance of conflicts and disputes, improvement of relations with neighboring countries, normalization of relations with the Western nations and Japan, and so on. On the economic level, the new policies included implementing a four point modernization program, promoting free enterprise, removing nepotism, mobilizing the overseas Chinese diaspora, providing incentives to foreigners, establishment of a household responsibility system, restrictions on rural-urban migration, the one child family policy, industrial townships and the building of Special Economic Zones.

---

[16] Clem Tisdell, "Economic Reform and Openness in China: China's Development Policies in the Last 30 Years," *Economic Analysis and Policy* 39, no. 2 (September 2009): 271-294.

The role of the dedicated and honest leadership of Deng Xiaoping, his stalwarts, and able successors served as one of the primary factors behind the spectacular rise of China. These leaders showed a readiness for reform and change, believed in collective leadership, team work, ruled by consensus, forged a united front, and groomed generational leadership. This conceptual journey began with the end of the so-called Cultural Revolution, dealing a soft blow to Ultra Leftism and Factionalism. By de-mystifying ideology and ideologues, promoting mass education, cultivating a widespread change in mindset and emphasizing self- criticism, they laid the ground-work for a new economic direction for China, instilling a sense of pride and ownership amongst its people. These included tough decisions that involved reforming the Communist Party first for generating trust and prioritizing merit and professionalism instead of ideology, all while assigning a more professional role to the country's various institutions.

The government committed itself whole heartedly to the achievement of the 'Four Points Modernization Program'. This entailed the Uplift of Agriculture, Industry, Science and Technology and National Defence. It adopted policies encouraging 'reverse-engineering technology', a robust resource mobilization strategy, widespread investment in Human Resources and a more active role to be played by the Overseas Chinese Diaspora. This was geared at putting an end to the state of security paranoia, the adoption of modernization and moderation as state creed and restoring overall public confidence, trust and credibility in the state's public policies.

In the field of governance reforms, the Communist party and the Central government took momentous decisions on the devolution of power to the provinces, the autonomous regions and various municipalities. Effective reforms were introduced to improve the performance of the bureaucracy by reducing the size of the government, restructuring ministries, streamlining the system of transfers and promotions, rooting out corruption, and reducing wastage through stiff punishments. These reforms were also focused on the establishment of sound law and order by establishing effective border controls, setting up advanced surveillance measures grounded in technological innovation, the establishment of neighborhood committees, a more positive role by electronic and print media, and the imposition of legal reforms centered on the use of 'mediation courts.'

In tandem with their 'Economic Reforms', Deng Xiaoping and his team unleashed a soft power revolution which focused exclusively on laying the socio-cultural foundations for China's rapid rise as a global power. By incorporating the energy and spirit of private entrepreneurship, ensuring full participation of women in economy and society, the focus was on bringing about a widespread change in the mindset of the general population through the use of education and the media. These efforts, while drawing from traditional aspects of Confucian principles, emphasized maintaining a balance between change and permanence, and between material pursuits (*Wuzhiwenming)* and spiritual needs (*jingshenwenming*). On the political front this change in mindset was geared towards ending security paranoia and the adoption of a more inclusive political culture free of mudslinging, scapegoating and the victimization of political rivals.

In the arena of foreign relations, the guiding policy of the Communist Party and the Central Government was inspired by the slogan: 'Thousand friends, zero enemies, aim for global markets not global leadership'. Hence, the resulting foreign policy initiatives included the postponement of territorial disputes, relaxation of tensions, normalization of relations with neighbors, resumption of ties with the Western world and Japan, encouraging Western nations to have greater stakes in China's development, to build a world of balance and harmony, and to follow a policy paradigm of optimism with a win-win outcome.

In the initial days of the Economic Reforms and Open Door Policies of 1978, China was confronted with a ghastly set of conditions. Almost 80 percent of the country's population was below the poverty line. There were widespread shortages and rationing of essential consumer items was common. The fact that these challenges were so readily overcome does in no way point towards a 'Midas' Touch' or Magic Lamp. In fact, in order to achieve such historic levels of growth, the Chinese economy went through three mega structural phases of reforms including numerous sub-structural phases. These transitions ranged from a predominantly agricultural economy becoming the industrial workshop of the world; from state ownership to private ownership, and from a subsistence economy to one with an open door policy that greatly benefited from globalization. In China, these transitions promoted growth which in turn led to even further transformation. Considering the vast dynamics that came in to play, it is somewhat difficult to easily pinpoint the exact factors that acted as the major catalyst or the trigger for this chain reaction to take place. However, it is evident that all of these factors combined together to enable China to achieve an average GDP growth rate of 9-10 percent for more than three decades since 1978.

Consolidating Gains and Accelerating Growth

The economic restructuring exercise was the most challenging and yet most successful of Deng Xiaoping's policies. The open door policy to the outside world had begun with reversing the socialist model of egalitarianism, codified in the principle of 'eating from the same iron rice bowl'. Instead in breaking socialist taboos, Deng Xiaoping propagated the notion of: "let some people get rich and the coastal region get richer first".[17] The adoption of this new development paradigm thus entailed wholly welcoming foreign investment, capital, technology and knowledge. Coupled with the promotion of export culture and the simplification of rules and procedures for foreign investors these measures greatly improved the ease of doing business in China. These policies were further complimented by the deputation of 'study teams' to selected countries for imitating success stories, full hiring and firing powers in jobs, yes to private income, increased employment opportunities, the promotion of free enterprise and market de-regulation and emphasizing the importance of individual entrepreneurship. These were further supported by building industrial townships as new growth points, greatly promoting small and medium

---

[17] C. Cindy Fan, *Uneven Development and Beyond: Regional Development Theory in Post-Mao China* (Oxford UK: Blackwell Publisher, 1997), 623.

enterprises and setting up 'Special Economic Zones (SEZs) and Central Business Districts' (CBDs).

Even the People's Liberation Army, (PLA) was diligently employed in building key infrastructure projects by utilizing the excess capacity in military industries for civilian goods. This was part of a sustained push towards increased diversification in industrial production and innovation, technological up-gradation, greater investment in R&D, and learning and assimilating advanced technologies. By employing corporate knowledge and global best practices, and utilizing the country's immense demographic advantage in the form of competitive labor costs; China was able to leverage its strengths and eliminate its weaknesses across a grand scale of reform and development of its Economy.

Figure 4.4- Shanghai Skyline. "Modern Shanghai Skyline - Futuristic District of Pudong," *A China Family adventure*, n.d., https://www.china-family-adventure.com/shanghai-skyline.html (accessed March 8, 2018).

As stated previously, the end product of the Socialist centralized planning model that was followed by China from 1949 to 1979 had left it in an impoverished state with more than three fourths of the population under the poverty line.[18] Based on this experience the Chinese leadership which had toppled the 'Gang of Four' and assumed power

---

[18] Shujie Yao, "Economic Development and Poverty Reduction in China Over 20 Years of Reforms," *Economic Development and Cultural Change* 48, no. 3 (April 2000): 447- 474.

after the death of Chairman Mao Zedong in 1976 had decided on a wholesale transformation of China.[19] The subsequent reforms among other policy initiatives gave utmost importance to investment in human capital by deputing thousands of Chinese students and experts for higher education. These initially included universities in Western Europe and Japan and were subsequently followed by universities in the United States, Canada and Australia after these countries liberalized their student visa rules. This number kept increasing from a few thousand students in the early eighties to more than half a million by 2015. Initially a majority did not return, but gradually as the economy and the living conditions improved, a majority of those who traveled for higher education abroad, returned to China.[20]

As a result, the widespread availability of educated, disciplined and cheap human resource has been China's greatest boon for its double digit growth for more than three decades. This has impacted the development of the science and technology sectors the most. China's achievements and success in producing medium to high tech goods would not have been possible without the potent knowledge and embodied technology that was acquired abroad, brought back and re-engineered at home to produce the hybrid products which China has excelled in exporting, and creating its own brands around. Due to advances in science and technology, Chinese universities and R&D departments/institutions contributed 243,500 global patent applications in 2017.[21] Thus it is evident that at its present stage of development, China is no longer known as a cheap quality producer, as it was known in the early years of its economic transformation. China has gradually moved up the technological chain and continues to make new advances every day.

---

[19] "Gang of Four Chinese Politicians," *Encyclopedia Britannica*, n.d., https://www.britannica.com/topic/Gang-of-Four (accessed August 14, 2018).

[20] Kenneth Rapoza, "China's 'Best and Brightest' Leaving U.S. Universities and Returning Home," *Forbes*, April 17, 2017, https://www.forbes.com/sites/kenrapoza/2017/04/17/chinas-best-and-brightest-leaving-u-s-universities-and-returning-home/#152eb66d1d41 (accessed September 14, 2018).

[21] "China Drives International Patent Applications to Record Heights; Demand Rising for Trademark and Industrial Design Protection," *World Intellectual Property Organization (WIPO)*, March 21, 2018, http://www.wipo.int/pressroom/en/articles/2018/article_0002.html (accessed October 14, 2018).

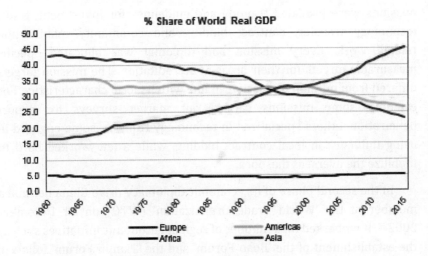

% Share of World Real GDP

Graph 4.2- Share of World GDP in % (1960-2015). "The Global Economic Revolution," *World Future Fund*," n.d., http://www.worldfuturefund.org/Charts/Economy/revolution.htm (accessed August 14, 2018).

Table 4.1: Real GDP Growth by Continent and Decade

	'61-70	'71-80	'81-90	'91-00	'01-10	'61-15
Asia Pacific	7.9	4.9	5.1	4.8	6.1	5.7
Americas	4.7	4.2	2.7	3.3	2.1	3.3
Europe	5.3	3.2	2.5	1.0	2.2	2.7
Africa	4.1	4.2	2.4	2.7	5.5	3.8

Source: "Real GDP Growth by Continent and Decade," *World Economics*, n.d., www.worldeconomics.com (accessed March 14, 2018).

The Chinese leadership in the wake of the widespread adoption of the economic reforms and open door policies of the 1980s[22] also emphasized the importance of using diplomacy to further its economic development. In order to achieve this objective a massive exercise to re-orient the work of economic ministries, departments and diplomatic missions abroad was undertaken. The revenue generation and regulatory functions of the ministries were separated. The diplomatic

---

[22] "Gang of Four Chinese Politicians," *Encyclopedia Britannica*, n.d., https://www.britannica.com/topic/Gang-of-Four (accessed August 14, 2018).

missions were provided training and guidelines for investment, trade, technology transfer, contract bidding and community mobilization related work. Every mission and diplomat was allocated specific measurable targets for their areas of accreditation. The mission targets differed from mission to mission, in line with its local characteristics. For example, some missions carried out market surveys for export penetration, others specialized in technology transfer, some engaged in using influence in local contract bidding, while a few worked hard to mobilize the overseas diaspora.

In the second phase of its economic diplomacy drive China became a member of the 'World Trade Organization' (WTO) on 11 December 2002[23]. It embarked on a number of regional economic initiatives such as the establishment of the 'Boao Forum' and the 'Tianjin Forum' followed by the founding of the Asian Infrastructure Investment Bank (AIIB) in January 2016.[24] China also built on its regional trading ties with its East Asian and South East Asian neighbors under arrangements comprising of the East Asia Summit and the FTA with ASEAN states, while also playing a more active role in numerous trans-continental and global arrangements namely Asia-Europe Meeting (ASEM) and Asia Pacific Economic Community.

China's Development as a Series of Key Transitions

In order to better understand the massive scale of these changes, it is important to realize how each stage of development fed into its subsequent stages, compounding the effects of growth and progress. This is evident in the way certain institutions and policies evolved in response to and in succession to each phase of economic governance along a series of varying initiatives. For example, when one phase of economic life was reformed, the subsequent advantages made reforms necessary in related sectors as a mutually complementary process. Thus, beginning from steps taken towards farm privatization, the fixation of farm tenure, farm goods pricing, the reduction of farm subsidies and the development of

---

[23] "China and the WTO," *World Trade Organization*, n.d., https://www.wto.org/english/thewto_e/countries_e/china_e.htm (accessed August 14, 201).
[24] "Introduction," *Asian Infrastructure Investment Bank*, n.d., https://www.aiib.org/en/about-aiib/ (accessed August 14, 2018).

the required markets, intermediaries and credit lines, the country was able to move towards achieving certain levels of rural industrialization. This in turn was characterized by the establishment of township village enterprises, urban wage adjustments and the adoption of planned urbanization. Continuing this trajectory of growth and development these further gave way to greater innovation, increased adoption of advanced technology and subsequent reforms in the financial and banking sectors, thus setting the foundations for the next phase of large-scale industrialization and trade.

China utilized all of its inherent and created advantages in a methodical self-complementing strategy, to become the world's largest Industrial Workshop. As global multinationals moved in throngs to take advantage of this solid base, they further benefited from being able to tap into its massive and rapidly growing market. This in turn fueled growing demand for Chinese goods both within and outside of China serving as a catalyst for a prolonged and sustained phase of rapid economic growth. Furthermore, even though China kept a tight control over population planning through its One-Child policy, it still had the supply of 270 million migrant workers moving in from its rural areas, who continued to push forward its high growth trajectory.[25] Thus with growing demand and increasing supply of capital and labor, the Chinese economy was able to sustain its high rates of growth for decades to come.

As a result of its rapid ascension as a global economic power, China is now everywhere. Its policies directly impact the world's consumers, employees and citizens across far-reaching regions. No other country has ever achieved such levels of economic development in such a short period of time.

Thus, while the economics of China's rise as discussed above may seem like a textbook case of economic growth, the essential question that then arises is why has China succeeded, while other developing countries have failed?

---

[25] Xiaoyi Shao & Umesh Desai, "China Challenge: Getting Poor Migrant Workers to Buy Vacant Homes," *Reuters,* January 4, 2016, https://www.reuters.com/article/china-property-idUSKBN0UI08220160104 (accessed August 14, 2018).

This can be attributed to the fact that in any socially unequal society, the privileged elite are favored by the government due to the prevailing exigencies and ground realities of electoral, dynastic, tribal, ethnic and regional politics. This is referred to by economists as a system of 'Exclusive Extractive Economics'.[26]

China on the other hand is a 'Socially Equal Society'.[27] The class wars of the Cultural Revolution were buried in 1978. Successive generations of the reformist leadership have learnt the art of effectively managing change for ensuring balance, harmony, stability and prosperity. During the various phases of China's reform program, Western observers predicted that this growth would soon run out of steam. Instead, China's economic boom has continued almost uninterrupted well in to the new millennium.

Conclusion

In short, China's success is courtesy of more than a hundred factors. Based on the discussion laid out in this chapter, these can be summarized under the following points which stand out as some the most salient factors contributing to its growth. These include the presence of a dedicated collective leadership; mindset change; agriculture household responsibility system, establishment of township village enterprises (TVEs); focus on Small and Medium Enterprises (SMEs); civil service reforms; mobilization of overseas Chinese; promotion of export culture; development of special Economic Zone (SEZs); investment in human capital; learning from global best practices; simplification of rules and procedures; end of security paranoia; restoration of individual rights and freedoms; rule of law, merit and justice; promotion of individual entrepreneurship; research and development; harnessing of social capital and soft power; grooming of

---

[26] "The Question of Extractive Elites," *The Economist*, April 14, 2012, https://www.economist.com/finance-and-economics/2012/04/14/the-question-of-extractive-elites (accessed August 14, 2018).

[27] Elizabeth Stuart, "China Has Almost Wiped Out Urban Poverty. Now It Must Tackle Inequality," *The Guardian*, August 19, 2015, https://www.theguardian.com/business/economics-blog/2015/aug/19/china-poverty-inequality-development-goals (accessed August 14, 2018).

future generations of leadership, and a more congenial external environment for greater peace and security.

Gleaning from these measures it becomes evident that China's rise has truly been most spectacular within contemporary history. It has converted its national power profile of relative inferiority and vulnerability to the West, into one of opportunity and strength for itself and others. It has lifted a billion people out of poverty in just three and half decades. From a mere 40 kilometer bullet train network in 2007, it has built 20,000 kilometers as of 2017.[28]

China's exponential rise brings opportunities for all Euro-Asiatic nations, particularly Pakistan, as both countries have enjoyed an all-weather strategic Partnership built over decades. With the announcement of 'China-Pakistan Economic Corridor' (CPEC) or *Zhong Ba Jingji Zuolang*,[29] Pakistan-China relations have been elevated to yet another higher level. For Pakistan and the region, the CPEC is a 'Game Changer', which if properly planned, monitored, and implemented will enable Pakistan to join the ranks of the top ten largest economies of the world by 2050. There is an ancient Chinese metaphor that says 'when the sea rises, all boats are lifted'. The fortunes of Central Asia, West Asia and South Asia will be elevated together, with the rise of China.

---

[28] "China has Built the World's Largest Bullet-Train Network," *The Economist*, January 13, 2017, https://www.economist.com/china/2017/01/13/china-has-built-the-worlds-largest-bullet-train-network (accessed August 14, 2018).

[29] "China's US$1.4 Trillion 'One Belt, One Road' Set to Make Bigger Impact than US' Marshall Plan to Rebuild Post-War Europe," *South China Morning Post*, August 8 , 2016, https://www.scmp.com/news/china/policies-politics/article/2000835/chinas-us14-trillion-one-belt-one-road-extends-beijings (accessed August 14, 2018).

Chapter 5: The Belt & Road Initiative - China's Grand Vision of Regional Connectivity

Song Guoyou[*]

What is the BRI?

In 2013, when Chinese President Xi Jinping visited Kazakhstan and Indonesia, he formally put forward the Belt and Road Initiative, outlining its basic tenets of enhanced regional connectivity. These tenets were namely, policy coordination, integration of infrastructure unimpeded trade, financial integration and greater people-to-people bonds. In May 2017, at the Belt and Road Forum for International Cooperation held in Beijing, the Belt and Road Initiative entered yet another historical phase in its development, further building on these principles.

In light of the weak global economic growth seen in recent years, the BRI has gained increasing credibility in providing a new impetus to the prosperity and progress of not only China, but Asia and the rest of the world as well. Slated to considerably expand China's ties with neighboring countries and regions, it would provide greater choices for regional economic development and social progress as part of a broader trend of greater international cooperation across multiple levels of International Relations.

---

[*]Professor Song Guoyou is the Director of Economic Diplomacy and Deputy Director for American Studies at the Fudan University in Shanghai, China.

This chapter aims to present a broad overview of the goals, assumptions and various mechanisms that are part of this overall vision for the Belt & Road Initiative. It presents a unique view directly from the perspective of Chinese policy-makers, and outlines the key opportunities and challenges being faced by them. By contextualizing these aspects within the current international framework, it attempts to dispel certain notions and misgivings surrounding the project, and aims to present an authentic take on the true scale and vision of China's Belt & Road Initiative.

The Essence of the BRI's Vision lies in 'Connectivity'

Contrary to the traditional viewpoint that connectivity is akin to better transport links, the Belt and Road Initiative imbibes 'Connectivity' with a much greater meaning. From the perspective of China, this idea of 'Connectivity' is a systematic project, based on five guiding principles that are aimed at formalizing cooperation with partner countries. These include:

   i.   Policy Coordination
   ii.   Facilities Connectivity
   iii.   Unimpeded Trade
   iv.   Financial Integration
   v.   People to People Bonds

The rationale and details underpinning these principles are further explained as follows.

Policy Coordination

Prior to the actual construction of the BRI, all partner countries are to put forth joint economic development strategies and policies, contributing extensively to the formulation of plans and measures outlining the scale of regional cooperation. This helps in laying down the legal and policy frameworks for this initiative. The reason why policy coordination comes first is mainly because it serves as the underlying premise to carry out all ensuing aspects of such large scale economic cooperation, while also helping secure important guarantees for building the actual Belt and Road.

Indeed, the outside world has had certain misgivings about the Belt and Road Initiative. For example, some think that the Belt and Road Initiative is China's "Marshall Plan", or that the Belt and Road Initiative is proof of China's new colonialism. These misunderstandings however, stand in direct contrast to the spirit of the Belt and Road Initiative, which is being planned and implemented through direct consultations and extensive policy coordination with all partner countries and international organizations.

Facilities Connectivity

At the outset, the Chinese government perhaps highlighted 'Road Connectivity' more than 'Facilities Connectivity'. However, in the later official documents, this emphasis on 'Road Connectivity' was adjusted to 'Facilities Connectivity' to better incorporate the regional scale of infrastructure integration being envisioned by the BRI. Compared to just road connectivity, the idea of facilities connectivity extends beyond just roads and transport to include information systems, energy transmission, entire supply chains and so on. This coincides more closely with the BRI's goal of strengthening overall infrastructure development and promoting cross-border and inter-regional interconnection.[1] The Chinese government encourages reputable enterprises with extensive experience to carry out the required infrastructure development comprising of railways, highways, ports, electricity and information and communication systems across multiple levels of regional integration. The construction of a cross-border transport infrastructure would in turn further complement this proposed sprawling regional industrial complex connecting East Asia, West Asia and South Asia to facilitate greater economic development and people to people exchanges.

Unimpeded Trade

The total population of the countries along the Belt and Road Initiative is nearly 3 billion. The market size and potential economy of the area constituting these countries is also unique. All these countries thus hold

---

[1] "Vision and Actions on Jointly Building Silk Road Economic Belt and 21st-Century Maritime Silk Road," *National Development and Reform Commission, Ministry of Foreign Affairs, and Ministry of Commerce of the People's Republic of China*, n.d., https://eng.yidaiyilu.gov.cn/qwyw/qwfb/1084.htm (accessed March 23, 2015).

immense potential for greater cooperation on trade and investment. The Chinese government believes that all partner countries should explore the issue of trade and investment facilitation, and make appropriate arrangements to eliminate trade barriers, reduce trade and investment costs, improve the regional economic cycle's speed and quality, and achieve mutual benefits all leading towards a win-win situation.

The idea of unimpeded trade also includes bilateral and multilateral cooperation regarding inspection and quarantine issues, certification and accreditation standards, having in place standardized measurements, and sharing statistical information and other aspects. This would in effect lead to more simplified customs clearance procedures while helping place low tariff and non-tariff measures to eliminate cross-border trade barriers.[2]

The above mentioned initiatives have all been placed to improve trade policy coordination and to achieve greater trade and investment facilitation, all while improving the living standards of people along the Belt and Road. In the contexts of anti-globalization and trade protectionism, such unimpeded trade helps to strengthen globalization and promote confidence in trade liberalism.

Financial Integration
Considering its massive scale and vision, implementation of the Belt and Road Initiative requires a significant level of funding from diverse sources. However, for the countries along the Belt and Road, shortage of capital has led to major bottlenecks. Therefore, the issue of capital supply has been given great importance by Chinese policymakers. China has taken numerous measures to make full use of the Chinese government's official development assistance funds, drawing from developmental finance budgets, policy finance budgets, commercial finance budgets and other domestic capital resources, jointly promoting the financing mechanism. All participating countries have also been advised to follow market economy principles guided by international rules and norms making full use of various types of enterprises. This

---

[2] Ibid.

would help secure greater participation and ownership while greatly diversifying the available pool of funds being implemented.

People-To-People Bonds

The strategic partnerships, institutional developments, enhanced policy coordination and greater physical connectivity through the Belt and Road Initiative are all inseparable from the understanding, support and cooperation amongst the people of all partner countries. The traditional friendships and mutual understanding between the peoples of each country form the social basis for carrying out this entire initiative. The construction of material dimensions alone is not enough to support the systematic project of connectivity. The establishment and maintenance of positive interaction between the people of all countries is just as important. People-to-people bonds here would include greater cooperation and sharing of ideas in the fields of education, culture, sports, health care, , tourism, social security, science and technology and other aspects, aimed at deepening mutual understanding.[3] Through books, movies, television, art festivals, exhibitions, cooperative schools and other different forms of communication, greater people-to-people bonds can all help promote greater understanding of all the different cultures permeating through the Belt and Road Initiative. At the same time, greater people to people bonds would give birth to new ideas and traditions providing a whole host of new opportunities, as these countries excel economically.

Regional Connectivity and its Impact on the International System

The Belt and Road Initiative and regional connectivity are of great significance in terms of the (i) Economics, (ii) Politics and (iii) Stability of the International System. In order to achieve better regional integration, Chinese policymakers have put in considerable thought and care in figuring out how to contribute effectively to the challenges facing the prevailing international system. These aspects along with their significance are outlined as follows:

---

[3] Ibid.

The Economic Significance of Regional Connectivity

The move towards higher economies of scale at the regional level has long been blocked by two obstacles; institutional barriers and natural barriers. Only by eliminating the above two obstacles can higher economies of scale arise from greater regional cooperation.[4] Based on these two aspects, the goal here is to establish resilient institutions that break through these barriers, while emphasizing the importance of infrastructure connectivity, both of which further help break infrastructure bottlenecks that limit regional integration.

Such level of integration at the regional level would further boost infrastructure development in Asia and Europe and drive trade and investment among countries along the Belt and Road. Infrastructure development here would also have a positive impact on trade and investment directly reducing the costs and time taken by transaction processes, reducing the risk of damage to transported goods (reduced insurance costs), and enhancing the access level of enterprise to a diverse range of markets.[5] The infrastructure advocated by this principle of connectivity, including the up gradation of transport routes would thus provide greater freedom in implementing the related trade and investment policies, particularly with respect to the comparative advantages of various regions, thus greatly expanding benefits from greater trade.

Within the context of the weak global economic growth of recent times and the weakening effect of its more traditional growth engines, the above mentioned trade facilitation measures would thus greatly improve trade efficiency at a global level. By directly addressing the lack of adequate infrastructure in most countries, the BRI can help boost development through economic integration across largely underserved regions of the world economy. This would in effect greatly improve the global trade and investment system, and gradually promote a mutually

---

[4] Wang Yuzhu, "The Connectivity Economics in Regional Integration," *Frontiers* 77, (May 2015): 21.
[5] Wu Zelin, "Connectivity of Regional Cooperation in Asia: A Preliminary Analytical Framework," *World Economics and Politics*, no. 430 (2016): 83.

beneficial win-win global value chain; all while eliminating developmental bottlenecks within these regions.

The Geo-Political Significance of Regional Connectivity

The political significance of this initiative is underlined by the importance of achieving greater policy coordination at the regional and international levels, through enhanced Sino-foreign national policy communication.[6] This is to be achieved by building a multi-level intergovernmental macro policy exchange and communication mechanism, making full use of existing forums such as the Shanghai Cooperation Organization (SCO), ASEAN Plus China (10+1), Asia-Pacific Economic Cooperation (APEC), Asia-Europe Meeting (ASEM), Asia Cooperation Dialogue (ACD), Conference on Interaction and Confidence Building Measures in Asia (CICA), China-Arab States Cooperation Forum (CASCF), China-Gulf Cooperation Council Strategic Dialogue, Greater Mekong Sub-region (GMS) Economic Cooperation, Central Asia Regional Economic Cooperation (CAREC) and various other multilateral forums and platforms. This is to ensure that all policies are conducive to the full exchange of the shared development strategy, while providing a common ground to clarify any potential misunderstandings and/or bias.

This process of policy coordination and resolution follows the principles of seeking a common ground, providing a platform for partner countries to put forward their unique developmental and regional concerns and to better communicate, coordinate and seek consensus on emerging issues. This entire process forms a decision-making model that is based on mutual participation and consensus. Within this model, it thus becomes easier to more efficiently discuss and enact policies that can be mutually agreed upon, and collectively implemented.

Overall, greater policy coordination at such a macro level helps eliminate institutional barriers to connectivity, while taking into account the many intricacies associated with such large-scale regional development. In its essence it provides a common platform for all

---

[6] "Vision and Actions on Jointly Building Silk Road Economic Belt and 21st-Century Maritime Silk Road," *Belt and Road Portal,* March 30, 2015, https://eng.yidaiyilu.gov.cn/qwyw/qwfb/1084.htm (accessed March, 2015).

partners to work together and collectively address other important regional issues such as cross-border crime, environmental pollution, border demarcation issues, etc.

The Stabilizing Influence of Regional Connectivity
From an international security perspective, the overall vision for greater regional connectivity is in its essence, to bridge the gap between different peoples and cultures for the promotion of greater peace and prosperity.

The idea is that through rapid economic and social development, relations based on self-interests between countries would instead give way to closer ties built on greater regional economic interdependence and cooperation. Building the Belt and Road with this spirit of equal inclusion and practice, reflects the common interests of all countries, allowing all to work together and collectively deal with the challenges that shape the international system.

Building on its dramatic rates of growth and development, China has taken the initiative for greater regional integration in its pursuit of new ideas and norms that are complementary to the current international order. Combined with the developmental will and comparative advantages of all countries, China views the Belt and Road Initiative as an important opportunity and cooperation platform to promote national economic policy coordination, improve regional integration, and promote cooperation on a broader, much deeper level to create an open, inclusive, balanced and commonly beneficial cooperative structure for international relations. The pursuit of this vision provides an opportunity for big power relations to move from a traditional confrontational structure to a negotiated governance structure.[7]

The BRI initiative further reflects the growing importance of China as a responsible power. China plans to lead the new global economic order through new development norms, helping form a new dimension to international state relations. The Belt and Road Initiative is thus a Chinese program which aims to promote global peace, cooperation and

---

[7] Su Changhe, "Governance and Order in a Connectivity World," *World Economics and Politics*, no. 438 (February 2017): 32.

common development. China advocates that all countries participate equally, openly and transparently, regardless of size, and financial capability to pursue mutual benefits.

The goal here is to build a new system of global economic governance in order to promote the efficient flow of people, capital, goods and services; to broaden the market; realize diversity, autonomy, and balance with sustainable development; and to further expand dialogue and mutual understanding.[8] These are the inherited and the logical extensions of the very same international norms that have been in place since the end of World War II; the overall aim of which was to help foster global development, stability and prosperity.

BRI as Part of China's Development Policy Framework

Since the Belt and Road Initiative was proposed, all departments of the Central Committee have recognized its far-reaching importance and have responded positively, taking concrete actions for its implementation. The China National Development and Reform Commission, the Ministry of Foreign Affairs, the Ministry of Commerce and various other departments at both local and national levels have all played a key role in the planning and implementation of this massive initiative across multiple tiers of policy-making.

China National Development and Reform Commission (NDRC)

In 2013 the organizational body responsible for the Belt and Road Initiative was set up. The office of this leading body is located in the National Development and Reform Commission. For the Belt and Road Initiative, the China National Development & Reform Commission is responsible for policy coordination and infrastructure connectivity across the project. The NDRC actively promotes research and development of the Belt and Road Initiative's planning, with all-round support for its interconnection. On January 6, 2017, the National Development and Reform Commission, the Ministry of Foreign Affairs, the Ministry of Environmental Protection and 10 other departments and

---

[8] "Building the Belt and Road: Concept, Practice and China's Contribution," *Belt and Road Portal*, May 5, 2017, https://eng.yidaiyilu.gov.cn/zchj/qwfb/12731.htm (accessed May 10, 2017).

units combined together to form the Belt and Road PPP work mechanism with other countries to strengthen cooperation and ensure the timely completion of various infrastructure projects.[9]

Ministry of Commerce
The Ministry of Commerce promotes communication and the pragmatic cooperation of trade, investment and foreign aid.[10] With respect to the Belt and Road Initiative it is responsible for ensuring the smooth flow of trade between China and participating countries. Since the introduction of the Belt and Road Initiative, the Ministry of Commerce has embarked on a number of partnerships, highlighting the vast and all-encompassing vision of the BRI. This includes setting up a Eurasian Division to promote the construction of the Silk Road Economic Zones, recently signed memorandums with Moldova, Sri Lanka, Maldives and Nepal, and finalized negotiations with ASEAN's free trade zone. Furthermore, it has also engaged with Georgia's free trade setup, advanced negotiations with the Maldives Free Trade Area and has recently started negotiations with the GCC, Israel and other free trade areas as well.

Ministry of Foreign Affairs
The Ministry of Foreign Affairs cooperates with various administrations to actively publicize the background narrative, planning and construction behind the BRI. By coordinating with countries along the Belt and Road it plays a key role in drumming up support for important projects across diverse regions and areas. From the end of 2013 to April 2017, the Ministry of Foreign Affairs has helped liaise with almost 80 countries fostering successful partnerships with regard to trade, infrastructure development, people to people connectivity and greater financial access. It has played a crucial role in sharing and presenting a

---

[9] "National Development and Reform Commission with 13 Departments and Units to Establish the Belt and Road' PPP Work Mechanism," *National Development and Reform Commission of PRC*, January, 2017, http://tzs.ndrc.gov.cn/zttp/PPPxmk/gzdt/201701/t20170106_834560.html (accessed January 6, 2017).
[10] "The Belt and Road Initiative's Economic and Trade Cooperation to Achieve Positive Progress," *Government of China, Ministry of Commerce*, December 27, 2016, http://www.mofcom.gov.cn/article/difang/201612/20161202388848.shtml (accessed December 27, 2016).

common ground for Chinese interests abroad with particular regard to the BRI.

Within China, the Ministry of Foreign Affairs has also used the existing institutional platform to assist local provinces and municipalities in formulating local plans for convergence with the Silk Road economic zone, and has also supported numerous local special events.[11]

International Department, Central Committee of CPC

This department is mainly responsible for promoting people-to-people contacts creating opportunities for greater interaction amongst parties, governments, non-governmental organizations, think tanks, enterprises, the media and even ordinary citizens along the Belt and Road. By strengthening these relationships, the International Department of the Central Committee of the CPC aims to foster greater cooperation through consensus, improve people to people ties, and enhance mutual understanding and trust between a diverse range of societies and cultures. For instance, on May 17, 2016, the International Department, Central Committee of CPC hosted the Fifth China-EU Political Party High-level Forum. During this event, the Chinese Communist Party and 30 European political parties discussed the potential for strategic partnerships under the Belt and Road Initiative.[12]

Ministry of Industry and Information Technology

The Ministry of Industry and Information Technology has been involved in the development of the 'Digital Silk Road' as part of its 'Peripheral Connectivity Infrastructure Plan'. The ministry is tasked with achieving connectivity across data and information services by planning the construction of an information superhighway between China and its neighboring countries.[13] It plays a key role in sharing and implementing

---

[11] Yan Shanmin, *Global Action Report of the Belt and Road Initiative* (Beijing: Social Sciences Academic Press, 2015), 92.

[12] "The CCP Talks with More than 30 European Political Parties and Explores the Strategic 'Docking' Strategy," *The International Liaison Department of the CPC Central Committee,* May 23, 2016, http://www.idcpc.gov.cn/ztzl/jd95/ttxx/xw/201606/t20160616_83948.html (accessed May 23, 2016).

[13] "Create an Online Silk Road, Promote Connectivity Efficiency," *Guangming Online*, April 13, 2017, http://theory.gmw.cn/2017-04/13/content_24198662.htm (accessed April 13, 2017).

China's cutting edge research and development of the latest technologies as part of its overall development policy framework. Thus, it helps further leverage China's growing role as a global innovator and leader in the realms of technological advancement.

Ministry of Transport

The Ministry of Transport serves a crucial role in the area of infrastructure connectivity and is focused on improving the Belt and Road's integrated transport system. It is aimed at planning the "Silk Road's" traffic construction and to help form a new pattern of interconnection between China and its neighboring countries across the wider region. The Ministry of Transport has focused on promoting the layout of land and water transport corridors, regional traffic cooperation, international transport; international logistics and all related support systems.[14]

Ministry of Culture

Enhancing "People-to-people bonds" is an important part of the construction of the Silk Road economic belt. The Ministry of Culture has proposed a culture-oriented way to build a cultural belt along the Silk Road, by promoting increased dialogue and cooperation between China and partner countries. Cultural holidays, arts festivals, book exhibitions, film festivals, tourism festivals and other exchange activities will be held by China and partner countries along the Belt and Road. For these purposes, numerous Chinese cultural centers have been established in Sri Lanka, Laos, Pakistan, Nepal and other countries. Government grants are provided to these countries to carry out such culture based activities with the aim of bridging societal and cultural divides between these countries and China. In January 2017, "the Belt and Road Cultural Development Action Plan (2016-2020)" was published by the Ministry of Culture, drawing a road map for cultural development. The plan of action includes plans for the international exchange mechanism, the domestic cooperation mechanism, the Chinese Cultural Centers, the cultural exchange and cooperation platforms, the Silk Road Cultural Tour

---

[14] "Ministry of Transport Will Promote the 'Silk Road' Traffic Construction from Six Aspects," *Xinhua News*, March 27, 2014, http://news.xinhuanet.com/politics/2014-03/27/c_119981612.htm (accessed March 27, 2014).

program, the Silk Road cultural industry belt construction plan and numerous other programs.[15]

Local Governments

Since the autumn of 2013, when President Xi Jinping put forth his plans for the Belt and Road Initiative, local governments at the provincial level have actively participated in its construction playing an important role in organizing various activities. They have held forums, seminars and numerous press conferences emphasizing their advantages. These include potential advantages such as serving as a "bridgehead", "core area" or "hub" hoping to promote their own economic and social development as part of the overall initiative. Owing to their unique position, local governments also have the potential of playing a key role in the final landing process of major projects under the BRI.

Enterprises

Central enterprises belonging to China's state-owned assets' management committee regard the Belt and Road Initiative as a chance to build on their successes outside of China. With immense technical advantages and vast development experience in the fields of high-speed rail, nuclear power, oil and gas, infrastructure, machinery, communication and port transportation; State owned corporations such as the likes of China Communications Construction Company Limited, China State Construction, Power China, China Railway Construction Corporation Limited, China Railway Group Limited, "China North Railway", China National Nuclear Power Corporation Limited, State Grid, China Three Gorges Projects Development Co., Ltd, China National Petroleum Corporation, Sinopec, China National Offshore Oil Corporation, China Mobile and China Unicom have all collectively become a major force pulsating through the entire Belt and Road Initiative. For example, China Communications Construction Company

---

[15] "The Belt and Road Cultural Development Action Plan (2016-2020)," *Government of China, Ministry of Culture*, December 28, 2016, http://zwgk.mcprc.gov.cn/auto255/201701/t20170113_477591.html (accessed December 28, 2016).

Limited has built 10320 kilometers of roads, 152 bridges, 95 deep-water berths and 10 airports along the Belt and Road.[16]

A large number of private enterprises have also been active in the construction of key projects. These include projects led by Shenzhen Huawei Technologies Co., Ltd., Lenovo Group Co., Ltd., Dalian Wanda Group Co., Ltd., Shanghai Greenland Construction Group Co., Ltd. and Sany Heavy Industry Co., Ltd. and other private enterprises, all of whom have effectively promoted the overall drive towards greater regional integration.

Financial Institutions

In terms of the overall monetary requirements, the Belt and Road Initiative however, is still faced by long-term investment and financing gaps. As a result, many areas of infrastructure construction are underdeveloped. Whereas financial strength is relatively weak, infrastructure needs are huge. At present, the financial network to support the construction of "the Belt and Road" is still taking shape.

Still numerous banks and financial institutions have been actively engaged in the initiative's financing requirements. At the end of 2017 for instance, the China Developmental Bank had accumulated more than 600 projects in countries along the Belt and Road,[17] with a loan balance of more than 110 billion US dollars.[18] The projects covered infrastructure, production cooperation, financial cooperation and numerous other areas. In 2016, the Import and Export Bank supported 603 international production capacity and equipment manufacturing cooperation projects.

The Silk Road Fund too plays an important role in the Belt and Road Initiative's financial cooperation network. Since being established in December 2014, the Silk Road Fund's purpose has been to fully serve the

---

[16] "China Communications Construction has Built 10320 Km Highway in the Belt and Road," *China Communications Construction*, May 12, 2017,
http://www.cccltd.cn/news/mtjj/201705/t20170512_88580.html (accessed May 12, 2017).
[17] Chen Weihua, "BRI 'fruitful', but Debt Risk an Issue," *China Daily*, April 19, 2018,
http://www.chinadaily.com.cn/a/201804/19/WS5ad8293da3105cdcf6519467.html (accessed September 19, 2018).
[18] Nikki Sun, "China Development Bank Commits $250 billion to Belt and Road," *Asian Review*, January 15, 2018, https://asia.nikkei.com/Economy/China-Development-Bank-commits-250bn-to-Belt-and-Road (accessed September 19, 2018).

initiative with a view to promoting greater regional integration. The three 'big things' that stand out with respect to the Silk Road Fund include (a) supporting the Three Gorges Group in Pakistan and other South Asian countries to invest in the construction of hydropower stations and other clean energy projects, (b) supporting China Chemical Group's acquisition of Italian Pirelli Tire Company, and (c) taking part in Russia's Liquefied Natural Gas investment and financing activities. Data shows that by the end of 2016, the Silk Road Fund's actual investments reached about 40 billion US dollars.[19] Under its founding Chairman, Yang Zejun, the Silk Road Fund has focused on tracking more than 100 projects across Russia, Central Asia, Bangladesh, India, Southeast Asia and other regions since its inception.

Furthermore, a large number of Chinese commercial banks have also played a significant role within the overall BRI framework. These banks have established more than 56 first-tier branches across nearly 30 countries in key regions. These straddle across numerous industries, such as energy, transportation, oil and gas, minerals, telecommunications, heavy machinery, construction, agriculture and shipping.

Regional Connectivity with 'Chinese Characteristics'

Building on the all-encompassing policy framework of the Belt & Road Initiative, its construction and implementation can be thus viewed as being imbibed with distinctly 'Chinese Characteristics'. This involves emulating the kind of development that is borne out of China's own experience of unprecedented economic growth over the last few decades. The construction of the Belt and Road Initiative, as part of China's overall plan for regional connectivity is thus laid out through a distinctly Chinese approach to growth and development at the policy level. This approach is underlined by the following characteristics:

---

[19] Betty Huang and Le Xia, "China ODI from the Middle Kingdom: What's Next after the Big Turnaround?," *BBVA Research*, February 2018, https://www.bbvaresearch.com/wp-content/uploads/2018/02/201802_ChinaWatch_China-Outward-Investment_EDI.pdf (accessed September 24, 2018).

Centrally Planned State Implementation

The entire Belt & Road Initiative is being coordinated and promoted by the Chinese State across multiple levels of government. At the national level, these strategic partnerships require a level of authority and accountability derived from the standpoint of an overarching national interest. The argument being that the benefits to be derived from this initiative are the same as those derived from any form of public good.

Based on these factors and the immense scale of this initiative, the government is best placed in terms of its ability and policy tools to be able to lead its implementation. Hence, the Chinese government has made great efforts to promote the "the Belt and Road Initiative", not only in the numerous meetings and work arrangements at domestic levels, but also at the international level during a number of key occasions and external visits.

From a domestic point of view, the Chinese government while promoting the Belt and Road Initiative has fostered an all-encompassing approach ensuring that all ministries and departments are working towards a common direction. For instance, at the central government level, the Politburo Economic Work Conference made it clear in December 2014 that the Belt and Road Initiative would be implemented as a key task as part of the national politico-economic framework.[20] A month prior to this announcement, President Xi Jinping had already presided over the eighth meeting of the Central Financial Leading Group, which involved a careful study of the plans for the Silk Road economic zones and the 21st century Maritime Silk Road.[21] The State Council executive meeting had also discussed how to develop specific industries within the context of greater international cooperation though comparative advantages. All ministries and commissions have since been actively working to realize these plans from their respective domains and areas of expertise. This is evident in the tremendous work being

---

[20] "Highlights of China's Central Economic Work Conference 2014," *China Daily*, December 15, 2014, http://www.chinadaily.com.cn/bizchina/2014-12/15/content_19086822.htm (accessed May 12, 2017).
[21] "Xi Jinping Presided over the Eighth Meeting of the Central Finance Leading Group," *Xinhua News*, November 6, 2014, http://news.xinhuanet.com/video/2014-11/06/c_127186401.htm (accessed November 15, 2014).

carried out by the Ministry of Foreign Affairs, Ministry of Commerce, Development and Reform Commission, Ministry of Transport, the central bank and other central ministries as discussed previously.

At the local level, provinces along the route have also taken up responsibility, contributing extensively from within their domains. Under the Chinese politico-economic framework, the joint support of all levels of government is one of the key elements of the success of its overall economic policy initiatives.

At the international level, Chinese heads of state ranging from President Xi Jinping to Premier Li Keqiang and Deputy Prime Minister Zhang Gaoli have led numerous international delegations, in their efforts to promote the regional and global benefits of the BRI initiative. This has been carried out across a number of international forums while also forming a key component of expanding bilateral ties with BRI partner countries. Based on the development status of Asian countries (large investment, long construction period, and extremely high risk), the required level of policy coordination can only take place through close coordination at the state level.

Mutually Beneficial Partnerships
Throughout the process of implementing the BRI, China is focused on creating strategic, mutually beneficial partnerships with all related countries and international organizations. The Chinese government has gone to great lengths in ensuring that the national development strategies of all countries along the BRI route are in line with its overall vision. These include indigenous plans such as Kazakhstan's 'Bright Road', Saudi Arabia's 'Western Plan', Mongolia's 'Grassland Road', the EU's 'European Investment Plan', the ASEAN interconnection plan 2025, Poland's 'Responsible Development Strategy', Indonesia's 'Global Ocean', the 'Re-industrialization Strategy' of Serbia, the Asia-Pacific OECD Interconnection Blueprint, the Asia-Europe Interconnection and Cooperation, and the United Nations' 2030 Sustainability Agenda. It can be argued that all of these plans and initiatives are in their very essence, closely aligned with China's 'Belt and Road Initiative'.

Therefore, on the basis of mutual respect and mutual trust, China has established a relatively robust cooperation mechanism with all countries along the BRI. Bilateral dialogue has remained the main channel of policy communication as China and these countries continue to strengthen, their integration of infrastructure, trade and investment, production cooperation and cultural exchanges, etc.

Market driven Enterprise

While the planning and vision of the BRI has been derived at the State level, the actual implementation and construction of projects under the BRI initiative is driven wholly by market forces. The underlying idea being that all these projects despite being centrally planned as such are wholly demand driven from the point of view of end-consumers, while also potentially being profitable for its owners and operators. Out of the main stakeholders, centrally owned enterprises, local state-owned enterprises, private enterprises and foreign enterprises are all contributing to the BRI across various levels of its implementation and development.

Chinese-funded enterprises have taken the lead on projects such as the China-Laos railway, Yavan high-speed railway, numerous oil and gas pipelines in Central Asia, as well as the Gwadar port and its complementary Karakoram Highway project (currently taking place within the China-Pakistan Economic Corridor framework). At this stage, the central enterprises are given greater importance as they have a more prominent position and experience as transport, energy, construction and heavy industry related contractors. They have in essence, significant economic, organizational and institutional advantages that can help implement the national initiative to its fullest.

Among the type of state-owned enterprises, the central enterprises managed by the State-owned Assets Supervision and Administration Commission (SASAC) are arguably the most important carriers for the construction of major projects within the BRI. These enterprises serve as the largest providers of direct investment in neighboring countries, and also the main force in undertaking such contracts. The presence of Sinopec and Petro China in the Central and Southeast Asian oil and gas ventures, Shenhua's investments in Mongolia, China Power Construction, China Energy Construction and China Water Construction's water and electricity investments in neighboring countries can all be regarded as typical cases within this framework.

China-financed financial enterprises have in conjunction directly expanded financial cooperation with neighboring countries. The Shanghai Cooperation Organization (SCO) Development Bank proposed and promoted by the China Development Bank, the China - ASEAN Investment Cooperation Fund initiated by China Export - Import Bank, and the newly established Asian Infrastructure Investment Bank and Silk Road Fund, have all effectively promoted the financial influence of China as part of the BRI framework.

Local state-owned enterprises are also actively involved in the construction process, particularly in states with strong state-owned enterprises, such as Shanghai, Shandong, and Jiangsu. Furthermore, state-owned enterprises along the BRI route, such as in Xinjiang, Heilongjiang, Guangdong and Chongqing provinces are also fast emerging as key players within the BRI framework. Examples include Shanghai Electric's State Power Station project in India, Shanghai Construction's stake in the Cambodia Bridge and other infrastructure projects that have played an important role in promoting economic development at various levels across partner countries.

Private enterprises have also seized the opportunity to trade and invest in terms of their comparative areas of expertise. These include new business opportunities for foreign companies already invested in China, providing them with a wider platform to further engage in enhanced trade and investment.

In the long run, as the BRI initiative is further developed, all kinds of enterprises can find the right place within it. The seamless integration of operating companies and government and regulatory bodies overseeing these projects, paves the way for the realization of the grand blueprint of the Belt and Road Initiative. Enterprises in the specific operation process can identify problems and be given timely feedback by the government through an ongoing dialectic process. For common problems, the

Government can even supplement and improve the planning accordingly.[22] In this way market incentives driven by demand, competitiveness and profitability are coupled with strong oversight from the State as part of a two-way process.

The role of state-owned enterprises however needs to be further strengthened keeping in mind the long-term economic dynamics of the region. While ensuring that the state-owned enterprises operate in accordance with the market logic, the government should pay more attention to encouraging the participation of private enterprise within the BRI framework over the long -run.

Emerging Opportunities and Challenges

China's regional integration prospects carry with them a whole host of opportunities and challenges; opportunities that should be seized and challenges that need to be overcome if the BRI's vision of wide scale regional integration is to be fully realized.

Opportunities:

Prevailing Peace and Stability across the Wider Region
The present multi-polar world order is being increasingly characterized by greater economic interdependence as part of current globalization trends. As the intertwined interests of major powers become increasingly complex, there is much greater scope for fostering increased cooperation within numerous political, economic and cultural frameworks. This multi-dimensional pattern of varied interests offers the chance for the international community to find a common ground as the basis for resolving outstanding issues, while promoting mutual restraint among the great powers to avoid any potential large scale conflicts. Thus, in the absence of such large-scale conflicts, the prevailing situation of relative peace and stability within the broader Asian region should be capitalized on as an opportunity to further promote greater regional cooperation.

---

[22] Song Guoyou, "The Strategic Conception of 'the Belt and Road' and the New Development of China's Economic Diplomacy," *International Review* 46 (2015): 29-30.

BRI as a Case for Internationalizing the Chinese Development Model
After the 2008 global financial crisis, the more developed economies of the West have experienced sharp downturns, while the Chinese economy has more or less maintained its levels of growth.[23] China has become a veritable world economic developmental engine. In the context of deepening internal and external economic linkages, China has become a major Asian economic hub by virtue of its strong comprehensive national strength as well as its growing integration with the economies of neighboring countries within the region.[24]

Historically, China's economic reforms and opening up have allowed it to reap solid financial advantages, with the technical means and experience of a working development model. The tremendous economic growth experienced by China over the last decade, stands as a testament to exporting the Chinese Development model in other developing countries as well. For example, China's vast experience in indigenously developing and expanding its vast state infrastructure through key energy and transport projects based around important Special Economic Zones (SEZs) has allowed it to directly assist Pakistan in helping develop and implement the $62 billion China-Pakistan Economic Corridor (CPEC).

Regional Integration as Part of Globalization
With rapid socio-economic development, the bonds based on mutual interests between countries have continued to strengthen. However, at the same time challenges are growing as well. In the 21st century, the world political and economic situation has undergone a series of changes, especially since the international financial crisis in 2008. Global economic growth has been weak and the traditional growth engine used to stimulate the economy has weakened. This has led many countries to face widespread economic downturns. At the same time, globalization itself is faced with new difficulties and obstacles including; trade

---

[23] "China 2008: The Global Financial Crisis," *China Digital Times*, December 8, 2008, https://chinadigitaltimes.net/2008/12/2008-financial-crisis-and-china/ (accessed September 20, 2018).
[24] Hu Bin and Zheng Liansheng, "Asia Connectivity: China's Strategy, Policy and Action," *Frontiers*, no. 23 (2015): 76.

protectionism, isolationism, populism and numerous other destabilizing trends. The global economic governance system has failed to reflect these changes.

Institutional mechanism innovation has also been slow and the global trade and investment system needs to be improved accordingly. The mutual benefits of having a broad and diverse global value chain have yet to be fully realized. This is because the required state infrastructure is inadequate across a large number of States. As a result, regions and sub-regions have been facing bottlenecks which need to be dealt with by greater regional integration.

Facing the opportunities and challenges brought by economic globalization, it is the correct choice to solve these problems by strengthening policy communication and partnerships between countries. The BRI is an attempt to directly address these gaps and within the current global context is extremely well-placed to take on its role as a key driving force behind Globalization for many decades to come.

There is a Genuine Need for Infrastructure Development within the Region
As mentioned in the previous point, there is a significant lack of infrastructure development within the region which has greatly limited its economic potential. The Asian Development Bank in a recently released report pointed out that to maintain its current levels of growth, the Asia-Pacific region's infrastructure requirements would exceed $22.6 million ($ 1.5 trillion per year) by 2030.[25]

Most Asian countries are facing an uneven development situation. The lagging infrastructures of some low and middle-income developing countries in particular have come to serve as a major bottleneck in the overall region's economic development. In view of this, the vast majority of these countries have welcomed China's initiative. The infrastructure requirements of these countries have presented a highly relevant context within which to promote China's vision of greater regional integration through the Belt and Road Initiative.

---

[25] "Meeting Asia's Infrastructure Needs," *Asian Development Bank*, n.d., https://www.adb.org/publications/asia-infrastructure-needs (accessed February 2017).

Challenges

Competing Interests and Power Relations within the Region

To some extent however, the implementation of the Belt and Road Initiative is restricted by international geo-political power relations currently being played out in the region. The BRI initiative straddles across countries in Europe, Asia and Africa. Relative to the majority of small and medium-sized countries' expectations, the competing interests of major powers remain within a complex web of power dynamics. First of all, before China put forward the initiative, the major powers had put forward their own "Silk Road plans" based on their interests. These include the United States' 'New Silk Road Plan', the EU's 'Silk Road Plan' and so on. The focus of these different programs however had led to a certain degree of exclusion. The conflict of interests and competition of these powers have long hindered the implementation of China's initiative, especially as a result of the United States', Japan's, and India's resistance to the initiative. At the same time, the major powers maintain greater influence on the small and medium-sized countries along the BRI route. This is exemplified by current US interests within Southeast Asia and the Middle East, Russian interests in Central Asia, Indian interests in South Asia and so on. The influence of these powers thus greatly limits the willingness and flexibility of countries wishing to take part in the BRI at the policy level.

Conflicting Interests and Development Priorities

Within the region, there is a certain lack of political security and mutual trust between partner countries. The contradictory attitude of the relevant countries to the BRI initiative limits the scope for steady cooperation on certain projects. This contradictory attitude is manifested in the sense that on the one hand, partner countries are eager to take China's car to drive their own economic and social development. On the other hand, however they are worried about losing financial and political autonomy as a result of increased politico-economic interdependence with China.

Secondly, varying economic structures, levels of development and differing priorities of these partner countries greatly limit these partnerships from realizing their full potential. In some cases an unstable political situation has also greatly delayed and limited the scope of development that could have otherwise proved more conducive to regional prosperity.

Finally and more importantly within the present context, there is a glaring lack of a joint politico-economic organizational platform that provides a formal mechanism to address these and other issues affecting the region as a whole.

Funding Gaps for even Riskier Investments
This entire initiative currently lacks a relatively multilateral financing system backed by institutional arrangements. There still exists a large funding gap with plenty of scope to expand and build on the current financial mechanism. According to the Asian Development Bank's estimates; between 2010 and 2020 the Asian region would require nearly $8 trillion in energy, transportation, telecommunications, water supply and healthcare infrastructure. China's Silk Road alone cannot guarantee to fill this huge gap in funding.

Furthermore, the financial burden of this large scale regional integration project is led mainly by states with the glaring absence of large financial institutions and little involvement from the private sector. What's more, the level of investment required is immense, with limited scope for returns in the short-run. At the same time, there are a number of variables at play such as politico-economic stability, exchange rate fluctuations and emerging security threats all of which compound the financial risks of the entire initiative. For example, when Central Asian countries devalued their currencies in early 2016, it brought about even greater uncertainty to investment enterprises in the Central Asian region.[26] Despite the immense potential of the entire project, there is still a modicum of financial risk involved that has caused institutional and private investors to shy away.

---

[26] Guo Huijun, "Investment Cooperation between China and Central Asia in the Context of 'the Belt and Road' - Based on the Perspective of Transportation Infrastructure Investment," *International Economic Cooperation*, no. 2 (2017): 74.

Security and Political Risks

For different investment projects and different investment areas, there is a considerable level of political risk involved that can manifest itself in a whole host of different forms. These can occur in the form of regime change, ethnic/sectarian conflicts, military conflict, public outrage amounting to large-scale protests, a lack of governance capacity, and ultimately the risk of governance failure. In addition, there are risks arising from third-party factors, such as potentially damaging actions taken by rival multinational companies, the media, and non-governmental organizations all of which pose certain risks and limitations to China's credibility and investments in these countries. These political risks often do not exist alone, but can prove detrimental when acting together.

To better protect China's interests in the countries along the route; it is necessary for China to strengthen the political, diplomatic and military capabilities of partner countries. China's total investment is likely to reach hundreds of billion dollars throughout these countries. For the banks and companies investing into this venture, such political risks are tantamount to economic loss. This means that tens of millions or even more of their investment is at the risk of being completely wiped out. In extreme cases, the cumulative loss may even be higher than what they initially invested. Even for the well-funded central enterprises, such losses are unacceptable in the short term, not to mention those private enterprises with still relatively limited liquidity.

These losses in turn, have the potential of spilling over to the diplomatic level causing even further damage with respect to bilateral relations. In many cases in the past, certain domestic and international political forces in such countries have tended to use and enlarge some of the problems in Chinese investment projects, to attack China's foreign policy, belittle its supporters within these countries, and weaken public opinion towards China. In other words, China's foreign investments have not only become a catalyst for promoting bilateral relations between China and the investment countries, but have come to serve as a highly sensitive and key factor in bi-lateral relations as well. The two sides are bound to invest considerable diplomatic resources to solve such potential issues that can arise from any such scenarios. If handled improperly, such negativity can easily undermine the trust relationship between China and partner governments. Hence, the prerequisite for avoiding such risks are to properly evaluate such political risks beforehand.[27]

Environmental Protection and Sustainability as Part of Regional Integration

To create a green Belt and Road, not only should it be adapted to international environmental protection standards taking into the account the inherent requirements of promoting an ecological civilization, but it should also be in line with the particular requirements of developing countries to promote green and sustainable development. The initiative covers developing countries and emerging economies, where the ecological environment is already fragile, with economic development highly dependent on the extraction of resources. This often involves the large-scale implementation of numerous energy related, infrastructure construction projects which carry with them the inherent potential risk of ecological damage. In recent years, environmental disputes cases caused by China's foreign investment projects have been common, causing a number of such overseas projects to be shelved due to such environmental problems.[28] These need to be considered and addressed accordingly, in line with the BRI's vision of promoting sustainable development.

Conclusion – Connecting Hearts and Minds

This chapter has presented an overview of the goals, assumptions and overall vision of the Belt & Road Initiative as part of China's Development Policy framework. It has argued for its need and credibility within the current international scenario and attempted to dispel certain notions and misconceptions that have arisen in its opposition.

---

[27] Song Guoyou, "The Strategic Conception of 'the Belt and Road' and the New Development of China's Economic Diplomacy," *International Review* 46 (2015): 33.
[28] Xie Ran and Zhou Jun, "Environmental Protection is the Best Background Color of the Belt and Road," *Environmental Economy*, no.198 (2017): 55.

It should be noted however, that this discussion has been limited more to the technical aspects of this vision focusing more on the BRI's impact from the perspective of the Global Political Economy. What it has lacked is perhaps an appreciation of the way the BRI envisions greater peace and stability through greater people to people contacts by celebrating societal integration and cultural diversity.

As it stands, people-to-people contacts form the cornerstone of the stable development of bilateral relations between countries. The recognition of the people is the ultimate criterion for measuring the success of such large-scale integration. Policy coordination, infrastructure connectivity, unimpeded trade and financial integration are hard power areas, whereas people-to-people contacts can be categorized under soft power. Without the understanding, recognition and support of the people of the countries along the way, the implementation of the Belt & Road initiative, its planning and the construction of its related infrastructure projects would be severely constrained and prone to changing domestic political trends.

It can be seen that the Chinese government has invested a lot of manpower, material and financial resources for regional interconnection. However, the end goal of this massive initiative is to foster a joining of hearts and minds of a diverse range of people beyond societal, cultural, national and economic barriers. Only through this can we truly achieve the shared dreams of wide-ranging peace and prosperity that is the true aim and vision of the Belt & Road Initiative.

Chapter 6: CPEC as part of the 'New World Economic Order'

Dr. Liu Jun[*]

Introduction

On September 15, 2008, the Lehman Brothers, a U.S. investment bank with more than 150 years of history, filed for bankruptcy. This milestone event immediately triggered the U.S. Sub-prime crisis, which subsequently led to the international financial crisis. Overnight, the world's confidence in Wall Street collapsed. Financial assets depreciated dramatically amidst mass selling. Several major U.S. investment banks closed down, or got taken over. Credit squeezed, the stock market crashed, and corporate investment shrank. All these factors converged and resulted in the significant decline of the U.S. economy. As the world's largest economy since 1894, the negative impacts of this rapid economic decline spread worldwide swiftly, and triggered the European sovereign debt crisis. The resonance of both the American and European economic crises led to a global economic downturn, with no country left aside. As a result, the international financial crisis evolved into a global economic recession, and the original world economic order was in peril.

The world economic crisis that has followed these events has lasted for nearly ten years now. As a result, there have emerged a number of new trends within the world economy with wide-ranging affects that are likely to play a major role in shaping the trajectory of global growth and development. This chapter identifies these trends and presents them as a point of departure towards a 'New World Economic Order.' A World

[*] Dr. Liu Jun is Associate Professor and Director South Asia Institute at the Yunnan University, China.

Order that has become largely characterized by the immense rise of China as a major economic power. The ensuing discussion thus while building on this premise, examines the kind of role being taken on by China within this new emerging paradigm. It aims to contextualize China's Belt & Road Initiative within this context and highlights the importance of the China Pakistan Economic Corridor within this 'New World Economic Order.'

Defining the New World Economic Order

Emerging in the wake of the 2008 Global Financial Crisis, the following trends have been identified as some of the most salient factors to have emerged as part a New World Economic Order. These in turn directly affect the stability and sustainability of its recovery and thus merit closer examination:

Shifting Contributions to Global Economic Growth
Data from the World Bank has shown that in 2008, the top four countries ranked by GDP were the United States (US $14.719 trillion), Japan (US $5.03 trillion), China (US $4.59 trillion) and Germany (US $3.75 trillion). During this period China's GDP was equivalent to 24.10% of that of the United States, 63.70% of Japan, and 276.23% of India (US $1.22 trillion).[1]

By 2016 China had overtaken Japan in terms of total GDP. During this year, the United States (US $18.3 trillion), China (US $11 trillion), Japan ($4.94 trillion) and Germany (US $3.47 trillion) comprised the top four countries ranked by GDP. At this point, China's GDP was equivalent to 61.01% of that of the United States, 251.14% of Japan's, and 562.32% of India's GDP (US $2.9 trillion)[2].

---

[1]"GDP (current US$) China, United States, Germany, Japan and India," *World Bank,* n.d., https://data.worldbank.org/indicator/NY.GDP.MKTP.CD?locations=CN-US-DE-JP (accessed November 15, 2017).
[2] Ibid.

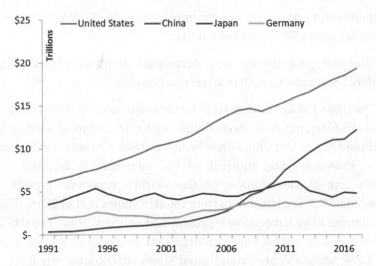

Graph 6.1- A comparison of the GDPs (current US$) China, the United States, Germany and Japan (1990-2017). "(current US$) GDPs of China, the United States, Germany and Japan (1990-2017)," *The World Bank, n.d.*, https://data.worldbank.org/indicator/NY.GDP.MKTP.CD?locations=CN-US-DE-JP (accessed November 15, 2017).

A simple analysis of this data reveals that even though the United States is still the largest economy in the world, its economic aggregate is less than twice than that of China. Within the last decade China has also exceeded Japan and become the world's second largest economy, with the gap between the two still expanding. Furthermore, during the past eight years, China has maintained a relatively higher and steadier economic growth rate while the United States, Japan and Germany have consistently faced low economic growth rates. As a result China's overall share in the world economy has kept increasing consistently. China's economic growth rate in 2016 was 6.7%, which means that, in this aspect, China still maintained the highest economic growth rate out of all the major economies in the world.

It is clear that, during the past eight years, key changes have taken place among the world's major countries. The share that developed countries occupy in the world economy has decreased, in contrast to the rising share of emerging markets which are making ever-increasing contributions to global economic growth. Commenting on this development, President Xi Jinping in his speech at the World Economic Forum in January 2017 pointed out that:

"The emerging markets' and developing countries' contribution to the global economic growth rate has reached 80%."[3]

The United States once used to be the major driving force behind the global economy, but, nowadays, a dual-engine driven model – led by both the United States and China - has brought about a new World Economic Order. Ever since the outbreak of the international financial crisis, China's annual contribution to the world's economic growth has exceeded 30%.[4] The latest data from the IMF shows that in 2016, China's contribution to global economic growth had reached 39%.[5] The IMF also believes that in 2016 China's contribution to global economic growth was 1.2%, while a debt-ridden United States contributed only 0.3% and Europe just 0.2%. This means that China's contribution to global economic growth was far more than the combined contributions of the developed countries during this time period.[6]

With the relative decline of developed economies and the relative rise of emerging countries, the rising international status and influence of emerging countries has had a significant impact on the global economic governance structure. Developed countries have been unable to cope with the global financial crisis independently. This is evident by how the Group of 20 (G20), including 10 emerging countries, has more or less replaced the economic relevance of the Group of 7 (G7) and become the primary platform for global economic governance. Among all the current members of the G20, China has the largest economic aggregate, and has maintained the fastest growth rate among members for many years.

---

[3] "Keynote Address by President Xi Jinping at the Opening Ceremony of the World Economic Forum's," *Xinhua News*, January 18, 2017, http://cpc.people.com.cn/n1/2017/0118/c64094-29031339.html (accessed January 12, 2018).

[4] Ibid.

[5] "China's Contribution to Global Economic Growth 39% The World is Still Doubting China," *CCTV*, January 20, 2017, http://money.163.com/17/0120/02/CB6K1CIH002581PP.html (accessed November 15, 2017).

[6] Hao Yin Wei, "German Media: China Contributes Far More to the World Economic Growth than Europe and the United States," *China News*, December 30, 2016, http://www.chinanews.com/cj/2016/12-30/8109467.shtml (accessed November 12, 2017).

In September 2013, as President Xi Jinping attended the G20 summit for the first time he called for a more balanced and sustainable approach to global economic growth and proposed a series of new ideas on innovative development, interconnected growth, and integrated interests. Many of his views and suggestions were incorporated into the summit declaration, a clear indication of China's increasingly prominent position and role in global economic governance.

Furthermore, at the opening of the G20 Hangzhou Summit three years later, President Xi Jinping stated:

> "In face of the current challenges, we should improve global economic governance and strengthen its guarantee mechanisms. The Group of 20 should constantly improve the international monetary and financial system, optimize the governance structure of international financial institutions, and give full play to the role of the IMF Special Drawing Rights (SDR). We should improve global financial safety nets, strengthen cooperation in financial regulation, international taxation and anti-corruption, and improve the ability of the world economy to resist risks."[7]

In the face of the current challenges, he also stressed that we should build an open world economy, continue to promote the liberalization and facilitation of trade and investment, implement the 2030 Agenda for Sustainable Development, and promote more inclusive development.

It is however entirely conceivable that currently the world's developed countries are unwilling to see a new world economic order that is not led by them. It is thus doubtful that the road to a new world economic order will be a smooth one.

The Rise of Protectionism and Anti-globalization in the West

---

[7] Professor Zhang Zhanbin, "Six Characteristics and Ideas of New Normal of China's Economy," *Guangming Daily News*, January 11, 2016, http://economy.gmw.cn/2016-01/11/content_18447411.htm (accessed December 12, 2017).

Continued globalization, despite having actively promoted the transfer of industry in the past several decades, has given way to certain anti-globalization trends and movements that have emerged more recently. Developed countries have more recently, actively supported real economy and re-industrialization policies, both of which are aimed at attracting overseas industries back into their economies. The United States for instance has especially proposed to rebuild its manufacturing industry and bring manufacturing jobs back to the US. Similarly, Germany, Japan and South Korea have also re-planned their industrial strategies with the purpose of retaining high-end core manufacturing industries at home.

During his presidential campaign, Donald Trump declared that he would never sign a trade agreement that would harm American workers or undermine American freedom and independence. On January 23, 2017, only two days after he was sworn in as the President of the United States, President Trump signed an executive order which officially announced the withdrawal of the United States from the Trans-Pacific Partnership Agreement (TPP). The TPP, formerly known as the Asia-Pacific Free Trade Zone, was originally initiated by four APEC members (New Zealand, Singapore, Chile and Brunei), and was launched at the beginning of 2002 as a bilateral free trade agreement with the aim of promoting free trade in the Asia-Pacific region. As the new edition of the free trade agreement, TPP's biggest feature was to break restrictions on free trade, enforce environmental protection, an address a number of issues related to government procurement, intellectual property, investment and other trade items.

On April 18, 2017, President Trump signed the executive order titled, "Buy American Goods, Hire American People", changing the employment procedures of foreign specialists in Facebook, Apple, Google and other American technology companies.[8] The order was enacted to promote domestic production and the purchase of domestic goods, as well as to

---

[8] "Presidential Executive Order on Buy American and Hire American," *White House*, April 18, 2017, https://www.whitehouse.gov/presidential-actions/presidential-executive-order-buy-american-hire-american/ (accessed October 5, 2018).

tighten the process of acquiring employment by foreigners under the H-1B work visa, to protect the U.S. labor market.

Developed countries have held the banner of free trade high in the past. At the present however they have turned more towards trade protectionism. In his presidential campaign, Donald Trump chose "Make America Great Again" as his slogan which served as a poignant rallying cry for his supporters. In order 'To make America great again' however, the core of Donald Trump's economic policies are premised on anti-free trade and anti-globalization policies. In his campaign speeches and debates, Mr. Trump repeatedly proposed to encourage enterprises and capital to return to the United States by means of implementing a new tax policy, labeling China as a currency manipulator, revising the North American Free Trade Agreement, and withdrawing from the Trans-Pacific Partnership Agreement (TPP). These anti-globalization economic policies were not simply election campaign rhetoric either. On January 3, 2017, President Donald Trump threatened General Motors (GM) via his Twitter account, to either move the manufacturing of the Chevrolet Cruze back to the United States from Mexico, or wait for a high border transaction tax.[9]

Data from the U.S. Department of Labor has shown that the share of its labor force employed in the manufacturing sector stood at 17-18 million before 2000. However, since then more than 5 million jobs have disappeared from the sector. The latest Rasmussen Reports also shows that 72% of Americans supported President Trump's move to sign the new protectionist executive order discussed above.[10]

Capital Flight from Emerging Markets
In response to the international financial crisis in the beginning of the last decade; rescue measures aimed at expanding the money supply,

---

[9] Ben Chapman, "Donald Trump Blasts General Motors for Making Cars in Mexico Temporarily Damaging the Company's Stock," *The Independent,* January 3, 2017, https://www.independent.co.uk/news/business/news/donald-trump-general-motors-gm-twitter-blast-making-cars-mexico-stock-value-president-elect-a7507356.html (accessed December 12, 2017).

[10] "Opinion Polls: More than 70% of Americans Support Trump "Executive Order to buy U.S. Goods and Hire Americans," *Sputnik News*, April 24, 2017, http://sputniknews.cn/politics/201704241022443387/ (accessed November 11, 2017).

such as printing more bank notes and decreasing interest rates, were taken by developed economies across the world. This in turn led to an excess in global liquidity giving rise to a flood of speculative capital flowing into emerging market countries. This subsequently brought about larger trade surpluses, but at the cost of greater inflationary pressures and rapid appreciation of domestic currencies leading to dramatic reductions in the foreign exchange reserves of these developed countries.

In early 2014 however, the Federal Reserve enlarged its scale of debt reduction, resulting in a massive withdrawal of foreign capital. This led to sharp falls in exchange rates in Brazil, India, South Africa and other emerging markets, followed by heavy losses in global stock and bond markets. The Argentinean Peso for instance, devalued 15% in just a week. More recently, the U.S's. withdrawal from its quantitative easing policy has exacerbated this development bringing in further risks with their own set of impacts.

On December 17, 2015, the United States announced the lifting of the federal benchmark interest rate, which also marked the end of its quantitative easing monetary policy and the start of an interest-hike cycle. The Federal Reserve further clarified that its monetary policy of raising interest rates was based on reducing the size of its balance sheet. Major central banks in other countries also began to signal the normalization of their monetary policies. This large scale pull back from the quantitative easing policy has a high chance of bringing about a new global economic cycle that may in turn have a sizeable knock-on effect on emerging markets.

Such financial turmoil in emerging markets shows that the road to recovery of the world economy is still tortuous, with uncertainty still looming ahead. Emerging and developed markets represent the two poles of global capital flows and financial cycles. Over the long term, excess savings and trade surpluses in emerging markets have historically flowed to the United States and compensated for the US's current account imbalances. The United States' steady recovery and withdrawal from its quantitative easing policy has already triggered major capital outflows from emerging markets, and attracted a large amount of global capital into US Dollar assets. Thus, as the US dollar strengthens, it reduces the value of other foreign exchange assets held by central banks across the world. Even though the international community's confidence in the US dollar may have fallen, its dominance within the global economy is still currently irreplaceable.

The Rise of the Chinese Renminbi as a Major Currency
The reform of the international monetary system is a long drawn process, with many uncertainties. Yet, emerging economies such as China have played an important role in reshaping the prevailing status quo. The gradual internationalization of the RMB and its steady adoption as a major currency has played a significant part in bringing about such change. For instance, in the wake of the international financial crisis nearly a decade back, when Iceland's major banks collapsed, China offered a helping hand and signed a currency swap agreement with the Central Bank of Iceland. Later in 2014, China became a net foreign investment country for the first time in history, with its actual foreign investment standing at US $20 billion more than the amount of foreign investments it had attracted.

In July of the same year, China, Brazil, Russia and other countries signed an agreement to establish the BRICs Development Bank and made arrangements for establishing a contingency reserve. The Silk Road Fund Co. Ltd. was also established in Beijing later that year laying the financial ground work for the Belt & Road Initiative in its early stages. The following November in 2015, the Executive Board of the IMF decided to include the RMB as part of its Special Drawing Rights (SDR) currency basket. This served as a key milestone for the currency as part of the Chinese government's efforts to further internationalize it. A few months later that the Asian Infrastructure Investment Bank (AIIB) was formally established, allowing for the RMB to play an even greater role in the future economic trajectory of Asia.

Since September 2016, the People's Bank of China has successively signed currency swap agreements with 37 countries. These include emerging economies as well as BRI partner countries that have shown interest in adopting China's model for economic development. With many more agreements to be signed soon, the RMB is well-poised to play a significant role amidst the structural shifts occurring within the global economy.

Based on the above discussed factors, the outbreak of the international financial crisis marks the end of the world economic growth model based on the singularly driven excessive consumption of the world's largest economy (i.e. the US economy). As a result the world's more developed economies have entered a difficult period of restructuring based on boosting self-sufficiency and growing their real economy, all in an attempt to insulate themselves from the global shocks that emanate from the US economy. These attempts at wide scale restructuring however are fraught with difficulties mainly because of the slow progress of these structural reforms. For example, lagging social reform and increasing income inequality in the US, political, economic and social resistance to labor market reforms in Europe, and the impact of Brexit are just some of the factors which are likely to limit global economic recovery within the coming years.

Shifting Trends in the Chinese Economy

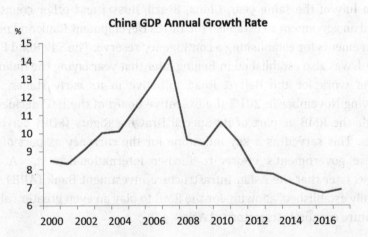

Graph 6.2- China's Annual GDP Growth (2000-2017). "GDP growth (annual %) 2008-2016," *World Bank*, n.d., https://data.worldbank.org/indicator/NY.GDP.MKTP.KD.ZG (accessed July 20, 2018).

Over the last few years, China's rapid economic growth has experienced a relative drawdown owing to a number of local and external factors. Its annual average growth rate of around 10% from the past 30 years has been replaced by a steady to medium growth rate of about 6.5%.[11]

This can be attributed to the fact that nine years after the international financial crisis, China has experienced a significant transition with respect to its model of economic growth and development. This has been characterized by a rebalancing of its economic structure as a well as significant shift in its overall impetus for growth, pointing towards a brand new stage in China's economic development.

Mitigating Drawdowns in Growth
Owing to the cyclical nature of economic growth, no economy can constantly maintain high- levels of growth for long. In fact numerous studies have shown that extremely high levels of growth have been often followed by economic drawdowns that have had little impact on the overall growth trajectory in the long-run.

For instance, from 1950 to 1972, Japan achieved an annual growth rate of 9.7% in GDP, which declined to 4.26% between 1973 and 1990, let alone the more stagnant growth rates of 0.86% between 1991 and 2012.[12]

It is worth noting however that in 2016, China's 6.7% GDP growth rate was still relatively higher than the US's growth rate of 1.6% (a record low since 2011), Germany's growth rate of 1.9% (a record high since 2011), Japan's rate of 1.0% and the UK's 1.8%.[13]

---

[11] "GDP Growth (Annual %) 2008-2016," *World Bank,* n.d., https://data.worldbank.org/indicator/NY.GDP.MKTP.KD.ZG (accessed July 20, 2018).
[12] "Xi Jinping at the G-20 Summit in Hangzhou, The Opening Address (full text)," *Xinhua News Agency*, September 5, 2016, http://www.xinhuanet.com/world/2016-09/04/c_129268987.htm (accessed November 12, 2017).
[13] "GDP Growth (annual %) China, United States, Germany, Japan and UK," *World Bank*, n.d., https://data.worldbank.org/indicator/NY.GDP.MKTP.KD.ZG?locations=CN-US-DE-JP-GB (accessed July 20, 2018).

On the other hand, both the domestic and external economic situations still pose a number of challenges, with the current uncertainty prevailing in the global economy posing additional risk. In order to cope with the international financial crisis, China has implemented an unprecedented economic stimulus policy to maintain its high growth and low unemployment rates. However, this has had its drawbacks as well in the form of high housing prices, rampant inflation and huge local debts, which will definitely hamper its economic growth in the medium to short term.

Transitioning Towards a More Optimized Economic Structure
In order to adapt to the slowdown in its growth rate, China's economic transition has been placed on a number of structural changes. In the recent past, China's economic structure has been perceived as being led by an investment, industry and export-oriented structure. But due to the slowdown in its growth rate, the long-standing effects of the international financial crisis and an overall shift in the policies of major economic powers, China has had to slightly alter its development model, reprioritizing certain sectors within its economy.

For instance, China's production structure has seen a significant shift with the share of its agricultural and manufacturing industries declining markedly, while its service industry has risen dramatically. In recent years, the service sector has replaced industry as the main driving force of China's economic growth. In 2013, the added value of China's tertiary industry, in the form of the service sector, accounted for 46.1% of GDP, exceeding the secondary industry for the first time. This indicates that China's economy has officially entered the era of "service".

Also, investment in China's economic demand structure has also declined, while domestic consumption has risen. Thus it is consumption as opposed to investment that has now become the mainspring of economic demand. In 2014, the share of consumption in China's GDP exceeded that of investment, reaching 51.2%. At present, household consumption in China has entered a new stage of steady growth, which has become the main driving force for China's economic growth. In 2014, China's total retail sales of consumer goods exceeded 27 trillion RMB, rising 10 times since 1995; making China the world's second largest retail market second only to the United States.[14]

Furthermore, the proportion of enterprise income in China's income structure has also declined, while the proportion of household income has risen significantly. In recent years, the income of rural residents in China has risen faster than that of urban residents. This indicates that the urban-rural dualistic structure is transforming into a unitary one as economic growth in regions of Central, Western and Northeastern China are growing faster than Eastern China.

Transitioning from an Element-Driven Model to an Innovation-Driven One
With a total population of around 1.3 billion, if China were to continue its previous growth model built on high investment, high input, high energy consumption and high pollution, then China alone would consume global resources.[15] For a more sustainable alternative to be implemented, a new pattern of economic growth is required that is based on innovation, as opposed to the previous element and investment-driven models. In recent years, China has made a series of major technological breakthroughs in communications, large scale computing, digital television and various other fields. At the same time, the cyber-economy as well as other emerging business models have also flourished and penetrated into the production, consumption and investment cycles, providing a new driving force within China's economic development. China's recent emphasis on promoting cutting edge research and development has thus directly contributed by adding immense value to its produced goods and services. Thus the emphasis has shifted more on quality over quantity with regard to overall production.

Mitigating Associated Risks
On the whole, all of the above factors carry with them significant risks bringing about greater uncertainty within the Chinese Economy. If not managed properly, China's economy remains prone to excessive

---

[14] "China Enters the New Normal of Consumption, Internet" to Lead the Transformation of the Retail Industry," *Xinhua News*, July 10, 2015, http://news.xinhuanet.com/fortune/2015-07/10/c_1115886099.htm (accessed December 10, 2015).
[15] "China, Population Total," *World Bank Data*, n.d., https://data.worldbank.org/country/china (accessed July 20, 2015).

fluctuations that would greatly limit any efforts at creating a sustainable and stable growth environment. At the present, the most prominent risks to China's economy comprise of liquidity risks, real estate bubbles, rising local debt and excess production capacity among others. These risks are intertwined together and must be resolved in a coordinated manner. Therefore, China must coordinate its reforms regarding public finance, taxation, land zoning, real estate and public administration to be able to successfully overcome these risks, and allow its economy to smoothly transition towards the above mentioned objectives.

China's Role in the New World Economic Order

Over the last few decades, China's rise as a major economic power has led to widespread speculation over its impact on the international system. Even as the Chinese economy is undergoing a major transition as discussed in the previous section, the effects of China's rise still form a key part of academic and policy discourse throughout the world. The following section discusses these impacts from the varying perspectives of leading academic authorities, as well as China's top leadership, in order to evaluate its impact on some of the world's most under-developed economies.

Perspectives from within Academic and Policy Discourse
Critics often claim that China's development is like a house of cards that is about to collapse. Some even believe that the continued rise of China will pose a huge threat to the world. Professor John Mearsheimer from the University of Chicago for example believes that the rise of China's economy will inevitably lead to China's expansion, posing unavoidable conflicts of interest between China and the United States. In the concluding chapter of his book *The Tragedy of Great Power Politics*,[16] he writes: "The rise of China appears to be changing this situation, because this development has the potential of fundamentally altering the architecture of the international system. If the Chinese economy continues growing at a brisk clip in the next few decades, the United

---

[16] John J. Mearsheimer, *The Tragedy of Great Power Politics* (USA: W. W. Norton & Company, 2014), 316-351.

States will once again face a potential peer competitor, and great-power politics will return in full force."[17]

Professor Susan Shirk of the University in San Diego on the other hand believes that despite its rise, China is unlikely to pose a threat to the United States. She argues that China has always prioritized the maintenance of domestic order, as a "Fragile Superpower". That although the economic development of China has greatly enhanced its international status, China may sink into total chaos at any time due to certain systemic and historical reasons, as well as the ineffective settlement of certain long-term accumulated problems that threaten the stability of its internal politics.[18]

Thus, while a large number of western scholars believe that China will soon be able to challenge and reshape the prevailing international order, not all of them agree to the merits of such a development. For instance, Gilford John Ikenberry believes that the rise of China is one of the greatest events of the Twenty-First Century, and thus, would have a profound impact on the future of East Asia and wider region.[19] Former U.S. Secretary of State Condoleezza Rice also believes that the China Model and the Democratic Development Model upheld by the United States and other western countries run in opposite directions and that the rise of China will undoubtedly counteract the western liberal democratic values' appeal to the world.[20]

In contrast, Martin Jacques, a left-wing British thinker and the author of *When China Rules the World: The End of the Western World and the Birth of a New Global Order,* presents a different viewpoint.[21] While critics argue that wealth, globalization and political integration will turn

---

[17] John J. Mearsheimer, "Can China Rise Peacefully?," *National Interest*, October 25, 2014, http://nationalinterest.org/commentary/can-china-rise-peacefully-10204?page=show (accessed November 23, 2014).

[18] Susan L. Shirk, *China: Fragile Superpower: How China's Internal Politics Could Derail its Peaceful Rise* (Oxford: Oxford University Press, 2007), 12.

[19] G. John Ikenberry, "The Rise of China and the Future of the West," *Foreign Affairs* 87, no. 1 (January/February 2008): 23-37.

[20] Condoleeza Rice, "Campaign 2000: Promoting the National Interest," *Foreign Affairs* 79, no. 1 (2000): 1-8.

[21] Martin Jacques, *When China Rules the World: The End of the Western World and the Birth of a New Global Order*, Second Edition (UK: Penguin Books, 2012), 23.

China into a gentle giant, Martin Jacques believes that China and Asia, with the particularities of its civilization, will develop on a different road of modernization from western countries. By presenting an economic, political and cultural analysis of waning Western dominance, Martin Jacques believes that the rise of China would change global rules and dominate the world offering a much better alternative to the prevailing status quo.

On the other hand, ever since the 2008 global financial crisis, the world economic and political environment has become rather complex and turbulent. Subsequently, the implementation of America's Asia-Pacific Re-balancing Strategy has further added to this complexity, specifically within the context of the Asia-Pacific region. Various narratives espousing a 'New Cold War' or a 'Cool War' between China and America, or even 'Hot War' between China and Japan, are becoming popular. In China, some hawkish scholars, especially those from the military, believe that China should make a fresh start and rebuild the world order.[22]

In any case, considering China's impact on the global economy, whether it collapses or rises, China's current trajectory would inevitably lead it to having a significant and profound impact on a New World Order. As discussed earlier in this chapter, China has long surpassed Japan as the world's second largest economy, next only to the United States. Since then, the perceived impacts of China's rise on the world economic and political situations have increasingly become hot topics within global academic discourse. All of these differing voices and opinions however still imply a core contradiction that merits further examination. Thus, the question that all these arguments give rise to is:

Will the world order change fundamentally? Or in other words, should China continue to participate in the existing international system or set up a new one?

---

[22] "The Cold War is history, Now it's the Cool War," *The Guardian*, February 24, 2013, https://www.theguardian.com/commentisfree/2013/feb/24/cool-war-cyber-conflict (accessed October 12, 2018).

This very question implies that there already lies a schism between established universal values and the up and coming China Model. On the one hand, some believe that it is impossible for China to break away from these universal values, and that China must comply with the existing international order and its values. On the other hand, some insist that China has its own unique development model, and that 'another world' led by China is possible.

Perspectives from China's Top Leadership
With regard to the above dichotomy, President Xi Jinping has himself responded to this particular issue on several occasions. Acknowledging the basic underlying trends of world peace and development, he put forward the "Five Unchangeable Situations" outlining the following constants as the basis of his vision: (i) The multi-polarization of the world situation will not change; (ii) economic globalization will keep moving forward; (iii) peace and development will remain the themes of the era; (iv) the trends of international systematic reform will not change; (v) and the overall state of a prosperous and stable Asia-Pacific region will not change".[23]

At the same time, he has also emphasized the unique characteristics of the China Model saying, "As no two leaves are exactly the same, there is no universal experience which is fully suited to all countries around the world, nor is there an immutable development model. Socialism with Chinese characteristics must continue to develop and improve. The world is changing, China is changing, and socialism with Chinese characteristics must develop with the change of situations and conditions. Only by keeping pace with the times can China be full of vitality."[24]

Within this statement, it is evident how China's leadership has adopted a balanced attitude and position with respect to China's

---

[23] "Xi Jinping to Attend the Central Foreign Affairs Working Conference and Deliver an Important Speech," *Xinhua Net*, November 11, 2014, http://news.xinhuanet.com/politics/2014-11/29/c_1113457723.htm (accessed July 23, 2017).
[24] "Xi Jinping Presided over Non-Party Forums and Democratic," *Xinhua News Agency*, March 3, 2013, http://news.xinhuanet.com/politics/2013-03/20/c_124478704_7.htm (accessed November 13, 2016).

participation within the prevailing international system. On the one hand, they have stressed the unity of China and the world, emphasizing that the international community has become a 'Community of Common Destiny' sharing weal and woe.[25] China's emphasis on the 'win-win cooperation' resulting from its rise is derived from this principle.

On the other hand however, China' also claims adherence to its self-professed "Four Principles of Self-confidence" or the Confidence Doctrine, as outlined by its leaders. This entails (i) Confidence in their chosen path, (ii) Confidence in their guiding theories, (iii) Confidence in their institutions, and (iv) Confidence in their culture.[26] This is based on the fact that on certain issues, "China is willing to learn from all the achievements of human civilization, but never copy any country's development model".[27]

It thus follows that China is hedging its bets on the existing world order while perfecting its own domestic order. President Xi Jinping pointed this out when he said that, "When we observe and plan for reform and development, we must have the comprehensive consideration and utilization of both international and domestic markets, resources, and rules".[28] This statement clearly shows that China's leadership while acknowledging the long-embedded realities of the international system is balancing such constraints with regard to its own domestic interests, and its own perceived role as an emerging global power.

---

[25] Jacob Mardell, "The 'Community of Common Destiny' in Xi Jinping's New Era," *The Diplomat*, October 25, 2017, https://thediplomat.com/2017/10/the-community-of-common-destiny-in-xi-jinpings-new-era/ (accessed 6 October, 2018).

[26] Zheping Huang, "All the Buzzwords Xi Jinping Added to the Chinese Communist Party's constitution," *Quartz*, October 25, 2017, https://qz.com/1111474/chinas-19th-party-congress-all-the-buzzwords-xi-jinping-added-to-the-chinese-communist-partys-constitution/ (accessed 6 October, 2018).

[27] "Xin Jinping: China Wishes to Draw on all Civilized Achievements but will not Copy it," *China News*, March 19, 2013, http://www.chinanews.com/gn/2013/03-19/4657500.shtml (accessed January 12, 2017).

[28] "Xi's Two Overall Situation of Economic Development in China," *People's Daily*, March 28, 2016, http://politics.people.com.cn/n1/2016/0328/c1001-28231742-4.html (accessed March 29, 2017).

Hence, instead of a relationship borne out of conflict or antagonism to the existing status quo, China considers its impact on this New World Order as part of a dialectic process between the Chinese development model and the prevailing status quo. Instead of one dominating the other, the relationship between these two systems can be thus seen as one of synthesis as opposed to an anti-thesis.

Impact on the Developing World
With regard to the case for the vast majority of developing countries however, it is evident that for the past several decades, leaders of international financial institutions like the International Monetary Fund (IMF), the World Bank (WB) and the Asian Development Bank (ADB), have largely represented the interests of Europe, the United States and other developed countries and regions. To some extent, these international financial institutions are essentially reduced to promoting the hegemonic economic policies of Western Countries led by the United States. However, as the world's Developing Countries continue to gain economic strength and international influence, Western Countries have become increasingly reluctant to re-examine issues of equality and justice within the international economic and financial system. At the same time, Developing Countries require a considerable amount of construction funds, which cannot be met by these international financial institutions by themselves.

In order to fill these gaps, the AIIB and the BRICs Banks were set up to provide an important opportunity for financial cooperation among such developing countries. Beyond helping facilitate the international expansion of Chinese enterprises, the internationalization of the RMB, and as countermeasures against the challenges posed by the TPP and TTIP; cooperation mechanisms like the AIIB and the BRICs Bank have been advocated by China to lead and help emerging markets and Third World countries to participate in the construction of the New World Economic Order.

Viewed from either the specific outcomes, or the stated objectives of China's national strategy, the underlying premise of the AIIB, the BRICs Banks and even the Belt and Road Initiative is thus evident when taking into account the following objectives: i.e. upholding the sovereignty, security and development interests of developing countries, strengthening cooperation with developing countries, safeguarding the legitimate rights and interests of developing countries, and promoting the common revitalization of China together with a vast number of developing countries.

In January 2017, President Xi Jinping pointed out in his speech at the World Economic Forum that the most urgent task for China was to lead the world out of economic difficulties. He was clear that according to China, the long-term downturn in the world economy, the gap between the rich and the poor and the gap between the North and the South are all indicative of major problems in the world economy's growth, governance, and development models.

He stated: "...the contribution of emerging markets and developing countries to global economic growth has reached 80%. Over the past few decades, the contrast among international economic powers has undergone profound changes, but the representativeness and inclusiveness of the global economic governance system is far from enough to reflect these new economic trends. While the global industrial layout is constantly under adjustments, new industrial chains, value chains and supply chains are gradually formed. But, international trade and investment rules, handicapped by enclosed mechanisms and fragmented regulations have failed to keep up with these new conditions. The global financial markets need to enhance their ability to resist risks. But, the global financial governance mechanism cannot adapt itself to these new requirements, which makes it unable to resolve the frequent turmoil in the international financial market or the accumulation of asset bubbles, and so on."[29]

Thus although the AIIB and the BRICs Banks are different in many aspects, both constitute a solid foundation for China's foreign policy strategy. The AIIB, the BRICs mechanism, and the Belt and Road

---

[29] "Keynote Address by President Xi at the Opening Ceremony of the Annual Meeting of the World Economic Forum, 2017," *People's Daily*, January 18, 2017, http://cpc.people.com.cn/n1/2017/0118/c64094-29031339.html (accessed July 5, 2017).

Initiative are not only China's response as effective countermeasures against the blockade set by Western Countries, but are also ways to realize the rejuvenation of the Chinese Nation and the Chinese Dream.[30]

Based on these arguments it can be seen that China has thus no intention of subverting the existing international order. On the contrary, China seeks to participate in and maintain the current international order. In other words, China views the world economic order led by the West as a kind of international public good in its essence. Upsetting this international public good would neither conform with Chinese interests nor with those of any other country in the world. By adding to this international public good, China is exploring a new path to reforming the current international order that is more complementary in nature as opposed to an incompatible one.

It is thus, in this sense that China is positioning itself within this new World Economic Order. In the past, China had emphasized '*participation*', focusing on "cooperation between countries". Now, China holds the view of '*sharing*', emphasizing the importance of fostering a 'Community of Shared Destiny'. While pursuing its national interests, China takes into account the legitimate concerns of other countries. In this way, as an extension of its own domestic development, China promotes the shared development of other countries as well. This has become an important part of China's concept of the New World Economic Order, of which the Belt & Road Initiative is a telling example of.

The China–Pakistan Economic Corridor and the New World Order

Building on this framework, the China Pakistan Economic Corridor (CPEC) which is a key component of the Belt & Road Initiative is by extension a key facilitator of this New World Order. Stemming from China's tremendous rise as an economic power, both the BRI and CPEC represent the above discussed notions of shared development and a common destiny for Nation States. This is embodied in CPEC's objectives

---

[30] David Dollar, "The AIIB and the 'One Belt, One Road," *Brookings Institute*, 2015, https://www.brookings.edu/opinions/the-aiib-and-the-one-belt-one-road/ (accessed July 5, 2017).

of fostering greater regional integration and enhanced people to people relations built on the thriving Pak-China Bilateral framework.

Over the last five years, CPEC has resulted in large-scale cooperation between Pakistan and China across a broad range of sectors straddling transportation, energy, trade, finance, administration, education and cultural exchange. Already as part of the 'Early Harvest Phase' key projects such as major highways, energy plants and fiber optic cables have been completed with the construction of key rail lines, oil and gas pipelines, and major industrial zones currently underway.

As the flagship project of the Belt and Road Initiative, CPEC is thus playing a key role in realizing President Xi Jinping's vision of a broader 'Community of Common Destiny'. As Chinese Foreign Minister Wang Yi has stated "if the Belt and Road Initiative is a symphony in favor of many countries, then the CPEC is its sweet opening melody."[31]

CPEC as a Major Globalizing Force

Considering that economic globalization is a major trend in the world's development, China and Pakistan need to expand on their potential and actively participate in the process of economic globalization and marketization. The construction of the CPEC will promote China's industrial transfer, attract a large number of Chinese enterprises and personnel to Pakistan, promote the formation of a regional supply chain, and enhance Pakistan's influence across the wider region. As a growth boosting trade corridor, CPEC would not only make it easier to ship raw materials from the Middle East and Africa from Pakistan, Central Asia and China, but would also make it easier to ship the manufactured goods of both countries to the Middle East, Africa and other markets. This will further expand and strengthen multi-lateral trade greatly contributing to the globalization and marketization of all countries across the wider African, South Asian, Central Asian, Middle Eastern and Gulf Regions.

---

[31] "China's "Belt and Road Initiative" to Build a Sweet Opening Speech: China-Pakistan Economic Corridor," *World Huanqiu*, April 18, 2015, http://world.huanqiu.com/exclusive/2015-04/6220458.html (accessed October 1, 2017).

CPEC as a Key Bridgehead for China in the Indian Ocean

As a key ally of China, Pakistan is strategically located between the Middle East, South Asia and Central Asia with the potential of serving as a key conduit for supplying energy to China. Pakistan provides convenient access to the sea for the Central Asian countries and Western China, and is to be developed into a key bridgehead for the region. As the flagship project of CPEC, Gwadar Port has the potential of becoming the largest deep-water port in the region. Its annual cargo throughput is likely to reach 300 to 400 million tons, which is ten times more than the capacity of the Karachi Ports Complex.

Considering its close proximity to the maritime supply routes emanating from the Middle East and Persian Gulf regions, the Gwadar port, as a key component of CPEC allows for the much needed diversification of existing maritime trade routes. These include particularly those sea routes linking China with the Middle East & Africa via the South China Sea. Since the rise of China as part of the New World Economic Order has coincided with escalating tensions in the South China Sea, the Gwadar led CPEC route presents a viable alternative to help fuel China's growing economy, as well as the economies of its neighboring countries. Thus CPEC holds immense potential in redrawing existing supply lines that are to fuel the growing energy needs of some of the world's most promising developing economies. As a result, it is likely to play a crucial role in China's participation within the New World Economic Order.

CPEC as a Link between China and the Islamic World

As an Islamic Republic with a majority Muslim population, Pakistan enjoys a central position in the Muslim world. To its West lies the core, historic area of the Islamic world, comprising of the Arabian Peninsula and the Persian Gulf. To its north are Afghanistan, China and Central Asia while to its east lie India and Bangladesh with the Muslim dominated Nations of Malaysia and Indonesia also lying further South East. Considering its storied history as well as its standing as a major military and nuclear power in its own right, Pakistan holds immense influence within the Islamic world. This is evident in the privileged status it holds in the Organization of Islamic Cooperation (OIC), as well as its close ties to key OPEC member states such as Iran and Saudi Arabia. Coupling Pakistan's geo-strategic importance with its ideological affinity to the Islamic world, CPEC allows the Pak-China bilateral framework to embark on a broader impetus for regional connectivity. This opens up a wide array of potential opportunities with regard to trade, energy, financial and even cultural integration forming a key component of the New World Economic Order.

Conclusion

At the present there are profound changes taking place in the international system. These are manifest in the historic changes in the balance of power, global governance structure, and the geo-strategic landscape across the world. Increased competition in the economic, scientific, technological, and military fields across the world has done away with the last few decades' unipolar international structure. The New World Order, built on the economic rise of developing countries beckons the start of a new era in International Relations.

Based on this context, the opening words of Henry Kissinger's *Diplomacy* come to mind with regard to how this discussion has taken shape so far in this chapter. He states that, "Almost as if according to some natural law, in every century there seems to emerge a country with the power, the will, and the intellectual and moral impetus to shape the entire international system in accordance with its own values."[32] Here, Henry Kissinger points out the two main elements of analyzing comprehensive national strength: power and will.

Power refers to a country's material strength, including economic, military and other strengths. The will refers to a country's spiritual strength, including its view of world order, the values it pursues, and so on. In more realistic terms, a country needs a mechanism to serve as an intermediary between this power and will. This mechanism can translate a country's will into concrete policy. At the same time, it can also make up for the gap between its professed goals, and its actual achievements.

---

[32] Henry Kissinger, *Diplomacy* (New York: Simon & Schuster, 1994), 17.

CPEC as part of the BRI offers this very mechanism. While serving as a roadmap for Pakistan's entry into the New World Economic Order, it allows it to build on the thriving Pak-China bilateral framework, and extend it beyond the wider region as part of the BRI. Although the Belt and Road was initiated by China, it has achieved global consensus. Over the past 3 years, more than 130 countries and international organizations have responded positively to it.

Against this background of increasing economic globalization, CPEC will not only bring about development and prosperity for both China and Pakistan, but would also help in building a vibrant emerging market across the wider region. Thanks to the implementation of the CPEC, other countries will enjoy a better investment environment and wider business space in Pakistan, so as to achieve mutual benefits amidst a win-win situation. They will thus be united and bound together as global community of shared prosperity and destiny. This in itself represents one of the hallmarks of the New World Economic Order.

Part III: Restructuring Pakistan's Economy via CPEC

Chapter 7: Preparing for the Next Wave of Developments under CPEC

*Dr. Vaqar Ahmed**

Contextual Background

As the benefits of the early harvest programme under the China Pakistan Economic Corridor (CPEC) start to materialize, there are high hopes for a new era of economic growth to be experienced in the near future. This is to result from an improved energy outlook, as well as through enhanced roads and port infrastructure, that form the majority of the projects completed so far under this massive initiative. It is also expected that both the governments of China and Pakistan will strongly follow through with the next phase of CPEC which could see the development of nine Special Economic Zones (SEZs) in Pakistan.

Already there is information to suggest that the development of two coal-fired power plants at Port Qasim Karachi, another two coal-fired power plants in Sahiwal, and Wind Farms in Thatta have started contributing power supplies to the national grid. These have increased the provision of energy available for industrial and residential purposes and in the longer run could help in bringing down rising energy prices currently plaguing Pakistani consumers.

The transport sector has also seen a boom as a result of CPEC. The road sector received particular attention with a large chunk of public investment from Pakistan and technical expertise from China. This was followed by the railway sector where a large development portfolio is still under discussion with Chinese partners. It is expected that achieving

* Dr. Vaqar Ahmed is the Joint Executive Director at the Sustainable Development Policy Institute (SDPI), Islamabad.

seamless connectivity across various provinces in Pakistan would greatly improve the business climate for trade, distribution and warehousing. This has been a key demand by investors from the private sector based in Western China, who wish to use the Karachi and Gwadar ports for both exporting to, and importing from regions such as Africa, the European Union, and the Middle East.

While the Eastern route of CPEC has gained a lot of attention in the media, parallel work has also been initiated on the Western route which starts at Gwadar and passes through Turbat, Hoshab, Panjgur, Besima, Kalat, Quetta, Qila Saifullah, Zhob, Dera Ismail Khan, Mianwali, Attock, Hasanabdal and onwards. This route is to connect some of the most impoverished districts across the Balochistan province, while bringing dividends in the shape of increased employment, and the more efficient transit of goods, people and services. This route is also expected to service the growing demand for oil and gas supplies to Pakistan and its neighboring countries.

For the purposes of this chapter, cooperation under CPEC has been classified according to the following areas: infrastructure and connectivity, trade and investment cooperation, agriculture development and tourism (and how this could result in poverty reduction), and financial sector cooperation. These areas fall broadly in line with the key priorities highlighted in the CPEC Long Term Plan.[1]

Keeping in view these classifications, this chapter extensively draws from the first-hand research carried out by the Sustainable Development Policy Institute on the many challenges currently plaguing businesses in Pakistan. This includes a particular emphasis on the export sector, which is likely to prove crucial in the country's economic growth and development in relation to the next phase of the CPEC initiative. This also relates directly to some of the most salient risks being posed to Pakistan's economy which point towards the need to expedite structural economic reforms – a failure of which could result in greater external

---

[1] "Long Term Plan for China-Pakistan Economic Corridor (2017-2030)," *Ministry of Planning Development and Reforms*, 2017, https://www.pc.gov.pk/uploads/cpec/LTP.pdf (accessed October 17, 2018).

debt commitments not only towards China, but also other multilateral or bilateral fund providers.

Impact of CPEC on Bilateral Trade

CPEC's trade potential will increasingly depend upon how fast Pakistan can foster an enabling environment for local businesses. This holds particular importance in key sectors which are currently witnessing rising demand in China. Based on these developments, an economy-wide analysis is still awaited as to which goods and services Pakistan can likely export to China in the short, medium and longer run. While it may be easier to forecast the bilateral trade potential of individual goods or services, it becomes harder to quantitatively assess the commercial advantages from longer term commitments. For instance, considering its broad ranging impact on Pakistan and the wider region, assessing the total sum of the benefits to be gained from the development of the Gwadar port would involve taking into account a number of intangible factors that are difficult to quantify. With respect to the projected impact on bilateral trade however, these figures are currently readily available.

During the 2018 fiscal year, China remained Pakistan's largest trading partner with merchandise exports (of China) worth USD 11.5 billion. This marked an increase of USD 1.4 billion compared to the previous year. Pakistan was also able to increase its exports to China which now stand at USD 1.7 billion - an increase of USD 120 million compared to the previous year 2017[2]. Some sectors of the local business community have raised concerns over this emerging trade gap with China (also owing to CPEC related imports) amounting to USD 9.7 billion, which stands as almost 30% of Pakistan's overall trade deficit.[3] Some have also blamed the China Pakistan Free Trade Agreement (FTA) for this large gap between imports and exports with China. This conclusion

---

[2] Shahid Iqbal, "Trade Gap with China Rises to $9.7bn in FY18," *Dawn*, July 29, 2018, https://www.dawn.com/news/1423551 (accessed October 17, 2018).
[3] Ibid.

however is neither agreed upon by numerous empirical studies nor by the Ministry of Commerce in Islamabad.[4]

Nevertheless, in order to address the above mentioned concerns raised by the Pakistani business community, there are currently ongoing discussions in Beijing to send prospective Chinese buyers to Pakistan in order to evaluate the possibility of importing goods from the latter. As a result, Pakistan's five major export-oriented industries comprising of textiles, leather goods, carpets, surgical instruments, and sports items could soon see major orders being placed by Chinese buyers. Other industries which could see some traction from Chinese importers in the medium to longer term also (if competitiveness is ensured) include auto parts, light engineering and key service providers such as information and communication services and other business related operations. The buying missions from China are expected to generate export receipts over and above the usual trade gains seen in the recent past.

A revised free trade agreement (FTA) with China is also a near-term possibility. It was recently proposed that 'trade in services' should also be made an important part of this new FTA.[5] Pakistan's large, skilled, and English speaking labour force has a lot to gain from the services sector in China. Sub-sectors such as information and communication technologies, business services, accounting services, education, health and other related services in China have a large demand for workers who can interact with Western clients - an area where Pakistani graduates and experienced services sector professions have ample experience. A more balanced FTA would also further lend to Pakistan's value chain integration with other Central and South Asian economies providing an added boost to its economy.[6]

---

[4] "Preliminary Study on Pakistan and China Trade Partnership Post FTA," *Pakistan Business Council*, 2013, http://www.pbc.org.pk/research/preliminary-study-on-pakistan-and-china-trade-partnership-post-fta/ (accessed October 17, 2018).
[5] Vaqar Ahmed, *Pakistan's Agenda for Economic Reforms* (Oxford: Oxford University Press, 2017), 11-15.
[6] Vaqar Ahmed, Abid Q. Suleri and Muhammad Adnan, "FDI in India: Prospects for Pakistan," in *India-Pakistan Trade* (New Delhi: Springer, 2015):193-219.

Fostering Greater Cooperation and Investments under CPEC

Based on interviews with the Federation of Pakistan Chambers of Commerce and Industries (FPCCI) carried out by the SDPI, Chinese investors have now started procuring land for production purposes in select special economic zones (SEZs). In total, both governments have agreed on a longer term plan of developing nine special economic zones. These include: the Rashakai Economic Zone near the M-1 Motorway in Nowshera; the China Special Economic Zone in Dhabeji, Thatta; the Bostan Industrial Zone in Pishin; the Allama Iqbal Industrial City (M3) near Faisalabad; the ICT Model Industrial Zone in Islamabad; the Industrial Park being developed on Pakistan Steel Mills Land at Port Qasim, Karachi; the Special Economic Zone at Mirpur, Azad Jammu & Kashmir; Mohmand Marble City; and the Moqpondass SEZ in Gilgit-Baltistan. Apart from these a Gwadar port free zone is also planned to create the ancillary industries required by Gwadar Port.

To scale up this planned process of industrialization within Pakistan, China has recently also agreed over the participation of third party countries within CPEC SEZs. A delegation from Saudi Arabia recently visited several CPEC SEZ cites as well as a number of energy projects underway to explore potential investment opportunities while carrying out a number of feasibility studies. Most SEZs have also been adjusted to offer separate land spaces for Pakistani and third country investors.[7]

With regard to these SEZs in general, a basic measure of Pakistan's success would be the extent to which Pakistan is able to attract China's private sector in significant numbers across a diverse range of industries. Already we have seen a few but growing number of examples where the private sectors from both sides have entered in to joint ventures. Further expansion of investment relations is also expected if Pakistan is able to expedite: a) structural reforms which reduce the costs of doing business, b) demonstrate a more transparent tax regime for foreign investors, and

---

[7] Ayaz Gul, "Pakistan: Saudi Arabia to Join China-Funded Development Project," *Voice of America*, September 20, 2018, https://www.voanews.com/a/pakistan-saudi-arabia-to-join-china-funded-development-project/4580299.html (accessed October 15, 2018).

c) ensure the security of assets, profits and intellectual property belonging to foreign entities.

In return, Pakistan can certainly put in place an investment policy which should ensure technology transfer, greater employment of the local labour force, and more exchange programmes where the Pakistani industrial workforce is able to receive capacity building support from their Chinese counterparts.[8] Also important is to mutually study the benefits which could further strengthen the bilateral investment regime or allow an investment cooperation clause to be built into the revised FTA with China.[9]

Pakistan's Board of Investment may also like to re-visit the key sectors which have attracted Chinese FDI in the recent past, to help formulate a more structured policy to woo Chinese investors from the Private Sector. This holds immense importance considering that net FDI inflows from China have been on the uptick since 2016 (Graph 7.1).

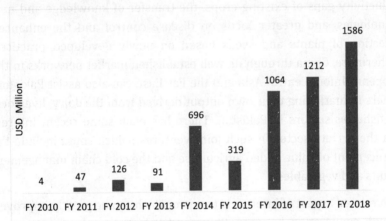

Graph 7.1- Net FDI from China. "Net FDI from China," *Board of Investment*, n.d., http://boi.gov.pk/ (accessed October 10, 2018).

---

[8] Ahmed ur Rehman and Dr. Vaqar Ahmed, "CPEC and Regional Integration," *The News International*, October 2, 2016, http://tns.thenews.com.pk/cpec-regional-integration/#.W9FfJ3szbIU (accessed October 10, 2018).

[9] For example, in the case of India see Vaqar Ahmed, Abid Q. Suleri and Muhammad Adnan, "FDI in India: Prospects for Pakistan," in *India-Pakistan Trade* (New Delhi: Springer , 2015), 193-219.

Agriculture, Tourism and Pakistan's Ocean Economy

Pakistan has a large stake in the development of its agro sector as it provides an essential livelihood to roughly 65 percent of its population.[10] The sector's contribution to the country's economy achieves even more significance considering that over 57 percent of Pakistan's exports constitute of cotton-based textiles.[11] Additionally the government aims to promote value added agriculture, in particular horticulture, which can subsequently further promote agro exports. However integrating Pakistan's agricultural sector with Chinese food value chains should be the primary goal. This will also encourage Pakistani agro-based enterprises to adopt globally certified product standards.

During a recent meeting of the Chief Agronomist of the Chinese Ministry of Agriculture and Rural Affairs and Pakistan's Minister for Planning, Development & Reforms; it was agreed that China would assist Pakistan across a diverse range of issues. These include addressing the productivity gaps of existing crops, the transfer of knowledge and new technologies, and greater focus on disease control and the enhanced protection of plants and seeds based on newly developed practices. Furthermore, China through its well established market networks in the European Union, Central Asia and the Far East, can also assist Pakistani farmers in marketing their own output derived from the dairy, livestock, and fisheries sectors in Pakistan. There has been some recent interest from the private sector in such joint ventures, which could include the enhancement of value added agriculture and the cold chain management of fruits and vegetables.

A related aspect of interest is tourism which can be greatly improved through cooperation between China and Pakistan in the forestry and ocean economy sectors. The latter sector has over the last few years assumed considerable focus against the backdrop of China's ongoing investments in Karachi and Gwadar. The ocean economy is usually defined by the economic activities that directly or indirectly take place in

---

[10] Ayesha Shaikh, "In Search of Greener Pastures," *Aurora.com*, September 25, 2018, https://aurora.dawn.com/news/1143181 (accessed October 19, 2018).

[11] "Textile Division," *Textile Industry Division Government of Pakistan*, n.d., http://www.textile.gov.pk/ (accessed October 19, 2018).

the ocean, converting a country's maritime endowments into exportable surplus. Pakistan is an important maritime state with approximately 1050 km of coastline, along which over 240,000 square kms have been designated as an exclusive economic zone (EEZ). Furthermore, Pakistan's continental shelf comprises of about 50,000 square km, with vast reserves of untapped resources. These maritime spaces offer immense prospects for Pakistan and its partner economies to benefit from a broad range of ocean-based living and non-living resources. These are likely to provide much needed economic growth and employment opportunities along a largely undeveloped coast line. The coastal highway between Karachi and Gwadar also presents an ideal opportunity to develop (coastal) tourism learning from other countries in the region, e.g. Maldives and Sri Lanka.

The Fishing industry is another major source of export earnings in Pakistan. Pakistani seafood has significant export potential in traditional and non-traditional destinations abroad. The country offers a large variety of high quality fish, shrimps and prawns. Out of the country's total exports from this sector, frozen fish accounts for 58 percent of export value. Shrimps comprise of only 23 percent despite the fact that they fetch a much higher unit value in the export market.[12] The fisheries sector is also an important source of livelihoods that provides employment to an estimated 1.5 million workers.[13] The sector is also known for employing a large number of women with a large majority working in seafood processing plants in key areas. In the rural areas of Sindh and Balochistan provinces, where there are very limited sources of alternative incomes, ocean economy-related sectors are greatly contributing to improved livelihoods and living conditions for millions. Given the rising demand for fish and fish-based products in China, Pakistan can put in place a longer term plan to remove the numerous

---

[12] Amin Ahmed, "Blue Revolution' to Enhance Fisheries Production," *Dawn,* July 02, 2018, https://www.dawn.com/news/1417342 (accessed October 23, 2018).
[13] "Fishery and Aquaculture Country Profile, the Islamic Republic of Pakistan," *Food and Agriculture Organization of the United Nations,* February 2009, http://www.fao.org/fishery/docs/DOCUMENT/fcp/en/FI_CP_PK.pdf (accessed October 23, 2018).

impediments to growth within this sector and possibly aim to supply a major share of import demand from China.

Financial Cooperation

CPEC is slated to primarily involve two channels of financial integration. The first deals with the inflow of Chinese direct and portfolio investment into Pakistan. This is illustrated by the 11% rise in the share of foreign direct investment into Pakistan during FY 2017. The second channel consists of the cross-border expansion of the numerous branches of various financial institutions.

The Private sector's joint ventures can strengthen the commercial cooperation between these financial institutions. Increased trade between the two economies is also expected to make better use of the currency swap arrangement which is already in place. Additionally China has also been supporting Pakistan with its development needs and there has been a recent rise in Chinese loans to Pakistan for both its infrastructure development as well as for maintaining its balance of payment requirements (Graph 7.2).

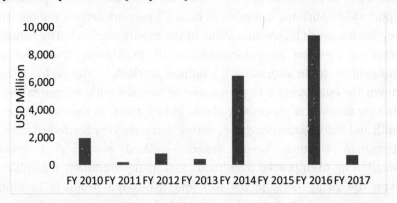

Graph 7.2- Chinese Loans and Credit Contracted. "Pakistan Economic Survey 2017-18," *Ministry of Finance,* http://www.finance.gov.pk/survey_1718.html (accessed October 18, 2018).

However, there are some challenges to financial market integration that will have to be addressed in the medium to longer term. These include: widely different legislative and regulatory systems currently governing the financial markets in both countries, a lack of coping mechanisms for systemic risks, the growing need for joint banking sector supervision systems, joint financial guarantee instruments to promote cooperation in asset and financial insurance, mechanisms for sharing capital market risks, promotion of regular portfolio investments in stock markets, supporting banks to open branches across the border, and the need to address the low uptake of the currency swap facility.

The construction sector in both countries is also willing to cooperate closely if more flexible financing options are made available to it. Some Chinese developers have exhibited interest in entering the real estate and property development markets in Pakistan's rural areas (where mainstream Pakistani developers lack interest). The low cost housing sector is also of particular interest to China, considering the rising demand for cheap housing across Pakistan. However to facilitate cooperation with China and to cater to the needs of low-income consumers, Pakistan's banking sector will need to develop better monetary and financial guarantee instruments that can protect both borrowers and lenders from the associated risks involved.

Mitigating Risks from Rising Debt and Financial Guarantees

CPEC offers an immense opportunity for Pakistan to develop its economy, if the country is able to spur the required export led growth to significantly boost its dwindling foreign exchange reserves. A failure to convert CPEC's dividends into long-term gains for commodity producing and service sectors could instead result in liabilities derived from the loans and financial guarantees provided by China to keep piling up.

It is thus important to understand that CPEC alone will not bring about export competitiveness. Certain long-pending structural reforms would need to be addressed before Pakistan will be able to experience: a) sustained export growth in traditional sectors, b) transition towards non-traditional and value added exports, and c) the entry of Pakistani merchandise into non-traditional markets abroad.[14]

---

[14] Vaqar Ahmed, Pakistan's Agenda for Economic Reforms (Oxford: Oxford University Press, 2017), 11-15.

Based on an extensive survey recently carried out by the SDPI, a key number of issues were highlighted by leading manufacturers pointing towards the long-standing impediments being faced by exporters throughout the country. This survey comprised of qualitative responses from around 254 enterprises across Islamabad, Peshawar, Karachi, and Lahore.** Out of these enterprises, around 71 percent were from the manufacturing and agro processing sectors while the remaining were from the services sector. Within the manufacturing sector, key sub-sectors represented in the survey included: textiles, steel, pharmaceuticals, cement, auto parts, chemicals, oil and gas, construction material, fast moving consumer goods, and engineering goods providers. The food processing segment was also represented in most meetings. From the services sector there was a concentration of firms from the information and communication technologies sectors, finance and insurance sectors, transport, health care and education sectors as well as numerous capacity building, and consulting services providers.

Based on the discussions held with representatives of these sectors the following challenges were highlighted as representing some of the most salient issues plaguing export led growth and development. These included challenges such as: the cost of energy still being the largest budget item faced by the manufacturing sector; tax compliance costs increasing over the past decade; the complex structure of customs duties; non-inclusivity of financial intermediation (especially timely credit availability for exporters is proving difficult); an uncertain exchange rate regime; a missing transportation, warehousing and distribution policy; a lack of fiscal support to exporters (e.g. the Prime Minister's recent Export Package not reaching new and potential exporters); difficulties in complying with foreign product standards, increasing layers of regulatory burdens at the subnational-level; the role of FTAs in enhancing competitiveness not being clear (this requires a detailed evaluation by the Ministry of Commerce); and the prevailing gaps in skilled and semi-skilled labour market.

** Purposive sampling includes current and past export enterprises.

In light of the above mentioned challenges, it can further be argued that Pakistan's youth is likely to gain considerable benefits if China liberalizes the export of services from Pakistan. However Pakistan's readiness in developing the services sector also needs significant attention.[15] The Services Sector Export Development Strategy formulated by the Ministry of Commerce should be revisited and after consultation with all services sector stakeholders, a revised strategy should be approved by the Cabinet. Given a large skilled workforce in the information technology sector, the government should prioritize IT-enabled services across the services sector (e.g. trade in IT-enabled health services and medical tourism). The Services Sector Export Development Strategy should also consider new sectors where the cost of skilled professionals within Pakistan is lower in comparison to peer economies (e.g. in the provision of medical transcription services in China).

Dedicated Special Economic Zones (SEZs) are also required for the services sectors focused on providing more targeted support. This can include the development of incubation centers for start-ups, and by promoting innovation and entrepreneurship across multiple levels. Such services-focused SEZs from China can also serve as useful models to emulate and follow.[16] Furthermore, most of these services sector start-ups or exporters are dependent upon internet penetration. Therefore overall infrastructure gaps which prevent IT-connectivity also need to be addressed in rural and peri-urban areas.

In all, there should be a more inclusive focus on promoting consultation processes and dialogue amongst multiple stakeholders. Currently there is no structured mechanism for public-private dialogue within the services sector, neither at the federal nor at the provincial government levels.

Another area of priority for the future would be to focus on making trade development more inclusive for previously marginalized groups

---

[15] Rabia Manzoor, Shehryar Khan Torub and Vaqar Ahmed, "Health Services Trade between India and Pakistan," *The Pakistan, Journal of Social Sciences* 8 (2017): 112-122.
[16] Parag Khanna, *Connectography: Mapping the future of global civilization* (New York: Random House, 2016), 40-45.

such as female and young entrepreneurs. The problem of exclusion of women from mainstream trade policy discourse in Pakistan has often been highlighted, yet without any concerted policy effort to address the gaps identified. This is also cited as a critical reason as to why gender-specific barriers to expansion of women businesses and women's participation in trade have been sidelined in the recent past. A key demand of most current women exporters is greater access to information and networking opportunities with their Chinese counterparts.

To integrate with Chinese value chains, small and medium size exporters need greater support from the government to fulfill their respective product certification requirements. Exporters have repeatedly highlighted that difficulties in getting product compliance and the relevant certification has made it increasingly challenging to remain in traditional markets. Furthermore, the ability to penetrate into non-traditional markets has also become an increasingly expensive process. It has also been suggested by business associations that a key reason why Pakistan was unable to achieve the anticipated gains from the GSP+ scheme awarded by the European Union was the lack of knowledge over certification requirements, particularly for non-textile items in which Pakistan enjoys considerable market access.

A number of startups and potential exporters have also been complaining that the regulatory burden (e.g. licenses, permits, no objection certificates etc.), faced at the provincial level is proving increasingly difficult to deal with. In order to address this issue, the Competition Commission of Pakistan should constitute a working group to study regulatory burdens on key export-oriented industries. These include the costs of delayed business transactions and the rampant corruption pervading through government institutions, all of which particularly affect SMEs. For example, automating and computerizing certain processes within the federal and provincial tax departments is cited as a viable solution that could bring down costs related to corruption.

Potential exporters to China have often highlighted that the number of days and procedural steps required to obtain connection of utilities needs to be reduced.[17] Similarly, for plant expansion and land acquisition, applications and wait times for licenses and permits also needs to be reduced significantly. Several businesses were reportedly waiting (at the time of this research exercise) to simply get electricity connections even after a wait of 12 months in the Sundar Industrial Estate – a flagship venture of the Punjab Industrial Estates Development and Management Company.

There were also variations across provinces in terms of key priority issues hindering competitiveness. In the case of Sindh for instance, the main challenges facing exporters were characterized by: a) unfair dealings with tax authorities, b) the lack of required skills in the labour market, c) the weak role of business associations in demanding reform; providing awareness regarding their dialogue with the government and demanding facilitation, d) high tariff rates on imported inputs, e) a significant lack of support for research and development in current and potential exporting sectors, f) and weak banking channels at potential export destinations.

A key concern is that Sindh is the only province which is unable to trade with a neighboring country via a land route. On the issue of utilities and related inputs, the members of this potential exporter group felt that even though formal businesses are now receiving uninterrupted energy supplies, the cost of electricity and gas is still high vis-à-vis competitor economies.

In the case of Punjab, main challenges comprised of: a) an uncertain post-18th constitutional Amendment regulatory regime faced by businesses - including the municipal, environmental and labour permits requirements, b) shortage of labour with required skills, c) complex tax regime for small exporters, d) lack of government support towards: timely coordination (within government) of export promotion measures,

---

[17] "Doing Business in Pakistan," *World Bank Group*, n.d., http://www.doingbusiness.org/data/exploreeconomies/pakistan (accessed October 11, 2018).

technological advancement support, and expansion of marketing efforts in potential export destinations.

The business associations from Punjab wanted greater interaction with their counterparts in China and India to allow exchange of ideas regarding future trade and investment cooperation. They were particularly concerned over the lack of consultation on the free trade agreement between China and Pakistan currently under revision. Current exporters felt that exports to China could be increased via land routes if the government was willing to negotiate the non-tariff barriers faced by Pakistani exports, by effectively addressing those non-tariff barriers faced by Chinese merchandise in Pakistan.

The issue of a lack of transparency in exchange rate management was also highlighted as a key concern – something which heightens expectations of a future free fall of the Pakistani rupee. There was also a desire that annual evaluation of trade missions based in Pakistani embassies abroad should be carried out against a baseline and published for the knowledge of the business community.

In the case of Khyber Pakhtunkhwa, while issues faced in compliance with taxes and refunds remained a key concern (which is also preventing formalization of businesses), the production side barriers to adoption of new technologies was also highlighted. This could be a limiting factor with respect to the future participation of enterprises from Khyber Pakhtunkhwa in the China-Pakistan Economic Corridor (CPEC). With regard to the KPK region, several other challenges were also highlighted including: a) lack of labour as per demands of the changing production requirements, b) weak coordination between the federal and provincial governments to deliver export promotion packages for Khyber Pakhtunkhwa's business community, c) weak awareness regarding government facilitation in marketing, testing services, and visa facilitation, d) an overvalued exchange rate, and e) the expensive and uncertain supply of energy. Several sector-specific associations were also concerned regarding the arbitrary imposition of regulatory duties.

Other challenges included: the lack of operationally effective dry ports in the province, changing state policies towards transit trade with

Afghanistan (a key concern of services sector exporters), damage occurring to merchandise being traded via road channels, and slow progress in the areas of mineral exploration and development – a sector which the local business community feels can bring medium to long term dividends.

In the case of Balochistan, apart from the usual constraints related to taxation, energy and the exchange rate, a key concern was the manner in which Pakistan was trying to pursue FTAs with Brazil, South Korea, Turkey, Thailand and some other trade partners. The business associations were concerned that broad based consultations had not taken place before the framework meetings of these FTAs. Similarly, the representatives of manufacturing associations showed their concern at the lack of information available to local businesses regarding opportunities in Gwadar and other SEZs under CPEC. The business community in Balochistan also wants export promotion as a key target in the recently announced 'Prime Minister's 10-year Uplift Package' for the province.

Conclusion

This chapter has highlighted several ways through which CPEC can continue to add greater value to the Pakistani economy as part of its subsequent phases of development. At the same time, it has also highlighted the growing risks associated with Pakistan's financial commitments under these CPEC projects. Based on these risks and benefits, this chapter has laid out a series of recommendations aimed at maximizing the economy's growth potential in light of the numerous challenges currently restricting it. According to the given arguments, this is only possible if Pakistan can put itself on the path towards sustained economic growth where export competitiveness is extensively and particularly promoted as part of a broad and diverse range of structural reforms. This aspect thus needs to be addressed immediately if the country's foreign exchange reserves are to improve by any standard.

Furthermore, CPEC should also be used as a basis for negotiating improved terms under the China-Pakistan FTA. The revised FTA with China should help promote key value chains between the two countries, allow for the liberalization of trade under the service sector, and promote greater investment cooperation.

All of these factors would go a long way in allowing Pakistan to maximize its growth potential in the upcoming phases of development under CPEC. Considering the broad ranging vision of CPEC as a game-changer for both Pakistan's and the wider region's economy, implementing such measures now is likely to benefit the Pakistani economy exponentially in the long-run.

Chapter 8: Special Economic Zones – Unlocking Pakistan's Economic Potential

Dr. Zafar Mehmood*

Introduction

Despite immense potential, Pakistan has been unable to develop its economy in line with global and regional development trends. While Pakistan's inability to embark on a sustainable growth trajectory can be attributed to a number of reasons, a key reason lies in the deep-rooted structural weaknesses that stem from years of economic neglect. Rather than addressing these structural weaknesses, government after government has followed ad hoc demand-side policies that have had little if any impact on more long-term prospects for sustainable growth. As a result, the country now direly needs a paradigm shift in its strategies and policies to overcome these structural weaknesses.

To make this shift a reality, Pakistan holds a number of essential natural endowments and advantages that imbibe it with immense potential for growth. It is exactly this potential that needs to be harnessed if Pakistan is to secure a bigger share in global industrial production and exports.

For instance, Pakistan's promising demographic profile, with a large proportion of educated youth, has the capability to drive the economy towards a higher growth path on the back of a vast untapped pool of

* Dr. Zafar Mehmood is a Professor of Economics and Head of Research of the School of Social Sciences and Humanities at the National University of Sciences and Technology, Islamabad.

skilled labor. Furthermore, growing urbanization and a rising middle class have created an expanding market of consumers that hold huge potential for foreign investors to tap into. Moreover, the Pakistani diaspora living abroad can play a decisive role in providing the much required expertise, knowhow and investments for a new phase of industrialization in the country.

At this juncture, as Pakistan is getting ready to take certain strategic economic decisions, the landmark China-Pakistan Economic Corridor (CPEC) has come to increasingly serve as a precursor to such fast-tracked development. Already, key infrastructure projects that have recently been completed under CPEC have laid a solid foundation for the country's industrial growth. The next step involves the proposed Special Economic Zones (SEZs) that are to further build on these foundations and help kick-start a new phase of industrialization in Pakistan. According to the most recent developments, these SEZs would provide a lifetime opportunity for Pakistani companies to work together with Chinese and other international companies for the development of export-oriented industries. The resulting cooperation between both Pakistani and Chinese companies within this framework is further expected to generate productive jobs, the transfer of technology and knowhow, develop entrepreneurship and to establish industrial and business infrastructures.

This chapter while offering a brief overview of the structure and purpose of these SEZs, presents a detailed discussion on the numerous opportunities and challenges they may arise for Pakistan as part of CPEC. Drawing on the historic impact of these SEZs across a diverse set of economies, the ensuing discussion aims to provide a set of policy directions for better managing these opportunities and challenges and to help unlock Pakistan's true economic potential.

Restructuring Pakistan's Economy through CPEC

Despite some signs of recent economic growth[1], Pakistan has been experiencing an unprecedentedly high current account deficit with its foreign exchange reserves sharply depleting. This has led to a worsening Balance of Payments (BoP) crisis, which needs to be addressed quickly[2]. Two main reasons can be put forward to explain this BoP crisis. First, domestic production levels are much lower than their potential owing to obsolete technology and an inadequate support infrastructure. Given higher domestic consumption, such low production levels have greatly limited the country's ability to generate sufficient exportable surplus that can compete both in terms of price and quality at the global level. Secondly, a high budget deficit[3] has artificially generated high demand for domestically produced goods and imported goods, which in turn has resulted in the reduction of exports and a rising import bill. This is due to the implementation of *ad hoc* expansionary fiscal policies that were carried out without any due effort to generate matching tax revenues, and were instead financed through heavy external and internal borrowing. Rising debt coupled with unsustainable levels of imports have thus further crippled growth alongside dwindling exports. The amalgam of these two reasons has thus led to a BoP crisis.[4]

This sluggish growth has not only resulted in a BoP crisis but has also contributed to rising unemployment across the country. Scores of educated youth are unable to procure any productive jobs, often despite

---

[1] It may be noted that Pakistan experienced a growth rate of 4.6% in FY16, which rose to 5.4% in FY17 and further to 5.8% in FY18 (growth rates are estimated on the basis of data obtained from the State Bank of Pakistan.) for further details see "Economic Data," *State Bank of Pakistan*, n.d., http://www.sbp.org.pk/ecodata/index2.asp (accessed September 10, 2018).
[2] The BoP crisis that is fast looming in Pakistan can be noted from the current account deficit of the past three years. It may be noted that the current account deficit as a percentage of GDP was 1.7% in FY16, which jumped to 4.08% in FY17 and further to 5.6% in FY18. See Zafar Mahmood, "Balance of Payments Crisis in Pakistan," *Hilal Magazine*, August, 2018.
[3] Fiscal deficit in FY18 was 5.8% of the GDP. For Further details see Ibid.
[4] Besides these reasons, there is undeniably a lagging brunt that Pakistan remains facing after the expiration of Multi-Fiber Arrangement (MFA) in 2008. Since then, Pakistan has not been an active participant in global production networks (GPNs) and the growth of its export markets has remained sluggish. These comprise the other main reasons for its rising current account deficit. For details See Zara Liaqat, "The End of Multi-Fibre Arrangement and Firm Performance in the Textile Industry: New Evidence," *The Pakistan Development Review* 52, no. 2 (Summer 2013): 97-126.

holding advanced degrees. As a result frustration amongst the youth class is increasing with every passing day. This situation has put Pakistan at an important crossroad which is compelling it to take the right policy decisions to adopt the most suitable growth path.

The current economic situation is essentially the result of demand-side policies used by previous governments to achieve short term growth targets. However, such policies cannot be used to achieve the required emphasis on sustainability as part of a long-term trajectory of growth. Therefore, it is high time to take a paradigm shift by switching the focus towards supply-side strategies based on leveraging productivity over the long-term. This would not only transform the whole economy but would enable the fruits of growth and development to reach all segments of Pakistani society in a more inclusive manner.

It is worth noting however that at the present, the rate of investment in the country is very low.[5] Concomitantly, the institutions responsible for the development of skills and technology have become very weak and cannot cater to the needs of a modern industrial sector. Total factor productivity has also been declining, which is a major determinant of growth.[6] These are just some of the key challenges that need to be overcome if the above paradigm shift is to be achieved.

Under this precarious economic situation, the completion of the most recent infrastructure projects under the China-Pakistan Economic Corridor (CPEC) have however, offered a ray of hope pointing towards the start of a new phase of industrialization in the country. While the launch of key energy and transport infrastructure projects have set the stage for this transition, the gradual implementation of the planned

---

[5] As compared to the Investment Rate of 19.3% in FY 06, the Investment Rate was 16.4% in FY18. See "Pakistan Economic Survey 2017-18," *Ministry of Finance Pakistan*, n.d., http://www.finance.gov.pk/survey/chapters_18/Economic_Indicators_2018.pdf (accessed August 10, 2018).

[6] Rashid Amjad and Namra Awais, "Pakistan's Productivity Performance and TFP trends 1980-2015: Cause for Real Concern," *Lahore Journal of Economics* 21(September 2016): 33-63.

Special Economic Zones (SEZs) throughout the country, is well set to further build and expand on these developments.[7]

China has vast experience in establishing successful SEZs, across a diverse range of conditions and requirements. The famous Shenzhen SEZ was established in 1979 as a testing site to implement China's open-door reform program, as part of a huge strategic shift away from a planned economy mechanism. Its success opened the door for other SEZs, not only in China, but also in other parts of the world as well. It is worth noting however that while some experienced success, others faced failure.

According to the Memorandum of Understanding signed by the governments of China and Pakistan, Pakistan has proposed nine SEZs based on their geographic strengths and existing trade and industrial setup. As discussed in the previous chapters, these include: (1) The Rashakai Economic Zone in Nowshera; (2) the China Special Economic Zone in Dhabeji; (3) the Bostan Industrial Zone near Quetta; (4) the Punjab-China Economic Zone in Sheikhupura; (5) the ICT Model Industrial Zone in Islamabad; (6) the yet unnamed Industrial Park to be developed on Pakistan Steel Mills Lands near Port Qasim; (7) the Bhimber Industrial Zone; (8) Mohmand Marble City; (9) and the Moqpondass SEZ in Gilgit-Baltistan.[8]

Most recently, three prioritized SEZs under CPEC are set to take off as both the Chinese and Pakistani governments have recently agreed to cooperate in the development of Faisalabad, Rashakai and Dhabeji industrial areas. Pakistan, inspired by the successful experience of Chinese SEZs, thus intends to adapt this revolutionary industrial growth model to its own local requirements. Both the Chinese government and private investors have so far shown keen interest and willingness to invest in these above mentioned SEZs.

---

[7] Pakistan Plans to Create Nine SEZs in Different Provinces during the Second Phase of CPEC Likely to Start in 2020. See "CPEC Enters the Next Phase," *Dawn,* November 20, 2017, https://www.dawn.com/news/1371702 (accessed August 10, 2018).
[8] Muhammad Muzammil Zia, Benaash Afzal Malik and Shuja Waqar, "Special Economic Zones (SEZs) "A Comparative Analysis for CPEC SEZs in Pakistan," *CPEC-Centre Working Paper,* no. 012 (2017): 1-18.

As to the reasons why Chinese investors are interested in investing in Pakistani SEZs, some quarters have given strategic reasons that might be true considering the scale of investment that is coming through the government sector.[9] However, it is more likely that the main reason behind these investments lies in the relative slowdown of growth in China on account of rising wages and other costs. More recently the furor created by the ongoing USA-China trade war, has further added to the slowdown of industry in China. Because of these reasons, private Chinese investors are looking for new opportunities abroad and this is where the Chinese government is giving them full support and encouragement.

While planning to invest in Pakistan, Chinese investors are keeping in mind the growing urbanization of a large middle class consumer population as well as the large educated youth population looking for productive job opportunities. Add to that the vast number of overseas Pakistanis looking to return to the country with their vast skills and financial resources, and the Pakistani market seems primed for takeoff.

On its part, Pakistan is interested in Chinese investment because other international sources of technology and foreign direct investment (FDI) are currently limited. Instead, China has shown its growing willingness to invest and better facilitate the transfer of technology and expertise. Pakistan expects that the establishment of SEZs will help in achieving the much desired structural transformation via positive technology spillovers, knowledge diffusion, skill development and greater employment, thus enabling the country to acquire new productive capabilities and by realizing a paradigm shift in industrialization levels.

While capitalizing on this lifetime opportunity, Pakistan faces a number of challenges. Unless, the country takes the right policy steps, it would be difficult to manage the numerous challenges and benefits from this opportunity which would otherwise be left only as a dream. Therefore, the top leadership should provide full support coupled with a

---

[9] Shahid Yusuf, "Can Chinese FDI Accelerate Pakistan's Growth?," *The International Growth Center Working Paper* (February 2013): 1-46.

determined political will (necessary resources) if this initiative was to successfully be the largest industrial project in the country.

Building on these arguments, the following sections discuss the potential impact of these SEZs based on their international precedents, along with the numerous opportunities and challenges that are likely to come with their establishment within Pakistan. These would then allow for the development of certain proposed policy directions for the Pakistani government which this chapter aims to conclude with.

Learning From SEZs across the World

A Special Economic Zone (SEZ) is defined as a "geographically limited area, usually physically secured (fenced-in), with a single management administration that is eligible for certain benefits based upon its physical location. It usually comprises of a separate customs area (with duty-free benefits) and streamlined procedures and regulations aimed at attracting international businesses".[10] In its essence an SEZ can thus be understood as a geographic area where business and trade laws are different from domestic zones (DZ, i.e. rest of the country). However, this difference in laws and policies can also create market and policy-related distortions in a country.

Developed countries have a long history of establishing SEZs to further their economic objectives. The first, SEZs was established in Shannon Airport in Clare, Ireland in the late 1950s.[11] Afterwards, in the 1970s, similar zones were established in Latin America and East Asia. The first Chinese SEZ was established in 1979 at Shenzhen, which paved the way for a massive influx of FDI resulting in an accelerated phase of industrialization for China.[12] China is now establishing SEZs in different

---

[10] Gokhan Akinci and James Crittle, "Special Economic Zone: Performance, Lessons Learned, and Implication for Zone Development (English)," *World Bank Foreign Investment Advisory Service (FIAS) Occasional Paper* (April 2008): 9–11.

[11] "Economic Zones in the ASEAN," *United Nations Industrial Development Organization UNIDO*, August 2015, https://www.unido.org/sites/default/files/2015-08/UCO_Viet_Nam_Study_FINAL_0.pdf (accessed August 11, 2018).

[12] Thomas Farole and Gokhan Akinci, "Special Economic Zones: Progress, Emerging Challenges, and Future Directions," *The World Bank*, August 1, 2011, http://documents.worldbank.org/curated/en/752011468203980987/Special-economic-zones-progress-emerging-challenges-and-future-directions (accessed August 11, 2018).

East Asian and African countries as part of its overarching vision for the Belt and Road Initiative.[13]

With the success of the Chinese experience, the world has seen a sharp growth in SEZs since the mid-1990s. Some of these SEZs were successful while others were not. Successful SEZs have since made significant contributions to the economic growth of host countries. Their contributions can be summarized into three gains: (1) static economic gains resulting from higher investment, job creation, and the development and expansion of exports; (2) dynamic economic gains, including technology transfers, integration with the DZ, and ultimately broad structural changes (including diversification, upgrading, and increased openness); and (3) socio-economic gains comprising of increased employment and the increased availability of goods and services all culminating to significant improvements in the standard of living. One of the main advantages that accrue to firms operating within these SEZ arises from the ability to produce goods at a much lower cost making them internationally competitive.[14] Thus, SEZs have enabled countries to make quick structural transformations and have become an important source of regional integration through trade and investment.

However, there are certain pre-requisites that are required in order for these SEZs to operate effectively. Drawing on the experience of African Nations, Thomas Farole has identified the following pre-requisites that go a long way in determining the potential success of SEZs.[15] He argues that firstly, considering the potential for boosting national competitiveness and bettering the overall investment environment, SEZs require good governance and sufficient state capacity in order for them to operate effectively. Secondly, the right domestic and

---

[13] Sean Woolfrey, "Special Economic Zones and Regional Integration in Africa," *Journal of Trade and Law Center* (July 2013): 108.

[14] Thomas Farole and Gokhan Akinci, "Special Economic Zones: Progress, Emerging Challenges, and Future Directions," *The World Bank*, August 1, 2011, http://documents.worldbank.org/curated/en/752011468203980987/Special-economic-zones-progress-emerging-challenges-and-future-directions (accessed August 11, 2018).

[15] Thomas Farole, "Special Economic Zones: Performance, Policy and Practice—with a Focus on Sub-Saharan Africa," *International Trade Department, World Bank, September, 2010*, http://siteresources.worldbank.org/INTRANETTRADE/Resources/Pubs/SpecialEconomicZones_Sep2010.pdf (accessed August 11, 2018).

regional locations and a big domestic market size are key to attracting foreign investors to these SEZs. This is because the location of an SEZ serves as the key to accessing large consumer markets, specialized supplier and ancillary firms, and a skilled workforce. Thirdly the overall investment and business environment requires quality infrastructure and trade facilitation at ports of entry and exit to help improve the overall ease of doing business in the country.[16]

He further argues that low wages, trade preferences, and fiscal incentives (including tax concessions and/or tax holidays and favorable import tariffs etc) do not significantly affect the potential success of SEZs. Rather, it's the alternative policy choices promoting productivity and a stable investment environment that are more important determinants of the success of such SEZs.

Some critics of the entire concept however, view SEZs as the "second best" policy option to wide scale economic liberalization. They argue that SEZs distort allocative efficiency and create unfair practices of competition between SEZ and DZ firms, which deprive the country of crucial national resources.[17] Furthermore, SEZs are also criticized for offering lesser social protections for their employees, for promoting the misuse of resources, tax evasion and for indulging in "rent-seeking" activities that often result in economic inefficiencies, all of which represent the opportunity costs of establishing SEZs.

Opportunities for Pakistan from SEZs

Considering the large-scale structural readjustments required within the Pakistani economy, the success of SEZs around the world, poses a number of opportunities particularly within the context of the CPEC and the BRI. For instance, the establishment of these SEZs would provide a more suitable business environment and help inspire greater confidence in Pakistan's growth prospects. This would in turn provide an

---

[16] Interestingly, Farole has shown that Trade Facilitation shows a similarly strong, positive relationship with outcomes. On the other hand, factors related to business licensing and regulations in the zones (e.g., one stop shop services) appear to be less critical. For further details see Ibid.

[17] Lotta Moberg, "The Political Economy of Special Economic Zones," *Journal of Institutional Economics* 11, no. 1 (2015): 167-190.

opportunity for a vast number of overseas Pakistanis to return home and participate in nation building activities, helping reverse the effects of the 'Brain Drain' that has taken place over years of underdevelopment. In 2017, the size of the Pakistani Diaspora residing abroad was about 9.1 million, comprising of almost 5% of Pakistan's total population.[18] These SEZs, if carefully planned, would greatly help in luring this segment of the population, bringing in both investors and skilled workers from abroad.

Chinese investors are also aware of these dynamics, based on China's own experience of the decisive impact of such a transition. Surging economic growth in China over the last few decades played a huge part in allowing the Chinese Diaspora residing overseas to invest and bring their skills back to China, helping fuel greater growth. Considering how these SEZs under CPEC are aimed at emulating the Chinese growth model, Chinese investors planning to participate in these SEZs are aware of the huge potential of such an opportunity with respect to Overseas Pakistanis.

Furthermore, Pakistan considerably lacks in its ability to innovate and indigenously employ cutting edge technologies. This has contributed to a large degree in decreasing its international competiveness while also adversely affecting its total factor productivity. With foreign companies being lured by these SEZs into setting up operations in Pakistan, there is a unique opportunity for Pakistan to benefit from the transfer of technology and expertise across the wider industry. By promoting research and development (R&D) activities and allocating resources within these SEZs accordingly, industries within Pakistan can themselves contribute to innovation and technological advancement on an international scale. Of course, this will only be made possible if policymakers properly plan and engage with world leading companies in such activities from the very outset of planning and laying out these SEZs.

---

[18] Rashid Amjad, "Introduction: an Age of Migration," in *The Pakistani Diaspora: Corridor of Opportunity and Uncertainty*, ed. Rashid Amjad (Lahore: Lahore School of Economics, 2017), 7-9.

Based on these opportunities, these SEZs should also provide a valuable opportunity to local workers to further improve and develop their skills. As successful international firms within these SEZs come to be increasingly integrated with the domestic labor market, there will be a positive spillover effect of developed skills and expertise, to other firms and segments of the economy as well.

All of the above factors combined would thus provide a unique opportunity for the country to further expand its exports and tap into even greater markets. This can be achieved on the back of better quality products and greater price competiveness through innovation and more efficient production. This would directly contribute to improving Pakistan's trade balance while also shoring up fast depleting foreign exchange reserves.[19] All in all, SEZs as a key component of CPEC would help bring in FDI, enhance the labor market through greater skills and innovation, and boost productivity all with the potential of creating a series of multiplier effects for the Pakistani economy.

Challenges Resulting from SEZs

Pakistan's experience with existing domestic industrial estates however remains unsatisfactory to a large extent. This can be attributed to a number of reasons, the most salient of them being: (a) unsuitable locations; (b) lack of connectivity to domestic and foreign markets; (c) high trade and business costs; (d) low quality infrastructure; (e) lack of skilled workers; (f) lack of modern technology; and (g) lack of complementarity with firms located in other parts of the country. While establishing new SEZs to attract foreign investment, Pakistan needs to ensure that it does not repeat such policy mistakes from the past.

Furthermore, the imposition of these newly planned SEZs are also likely to create policy distortions alongside market distortions (market failures). Foreign investors will not be attracted to Pakistani SEZs if a better work environment and fiscal incentives stemming from the right

---

[19] Some other aspects of opportunities emanating from SEZs can also be noted from my earlier paper. See Zafar Mahmood, "Opportunities and Challenges of Special Economic Zones under CPEC for Pakistan," in *The International Academic Seminar on Industrial Cooperation and Construction of Industrial Zones, CPEC: Center for Pakistan Studies of Peking University, and China Three Gorges International Corporation*, January 5-7, 2018.

policies are not offered to them as compared to what is on offer in other countries. Pakistani local investors, who are afraid of competition from foreign companies are conveniently demanding from the government to provide a level playing field. However, in light of the current economic situation this demand seems highly unrealistic because it is Pakistan who is in desperate need of opening up its economy to foreign capital. Therefore, it has to offer competitive incentives.

Moreover, given the paucity of financial resources at hand, the second-best policy option for the government would be to cope with such policy distortions for some time and allow foreign investors to first firmly plant themselves within Pakistan. During this phase however, it would be a real challenge for the Pakistani government to ensure that the country draws benefits from these policies in terms of economic growth, increased export earnings, transfer of technology and the skill development and employment for its educated youth as outlined in the previous section. Only such benefits that commensurate with the country's infrastructure investment and its cost of incentives will result in a win-win outcome, thus allaying the fears of critics.

Pakistan should also ensure that it has in place the relevant safeguards and regulations to ensure its economy against adverse trade practices that may result from the imposition of SEZs. This is because numerous international companies have been known to exploit certain loop-holes with regard to local labor and tax laws in developing countries. For example, the practice of transfer pricing where such companies under-invoice exports and over in-voice imports (from their parent company normally based in their home country), can lead to direct losses for the host country. This arises from the loss of potential export revenues as well as from potential import tariffs that are being waived off to lure such companies. Such companies have thus been known to siphon profits away to their home country by avoiding taxes in the host country in this manner.

Both of these practices, instead of improving the BoP worsens it, going against the very rationale for which these SEZs are being established for in the first place. Thus, a challenge for Pakistani policymakers is to be watchful and counter any such trends and practices. This would require Pakistan to devise smart and innovative ways to maintain regulation and oversight over such practices. Otherwise the preferential treatment meted out to foreign companies at the expense of indigenous companies would then work against the economy, where maintaining a level playing field would have been better.

Specifically with regard to potential Chinese companies, it is worth noting that these companies are used to the business environments and incentives on offer in African and East Asian countries. Therefore, to attract Chinese investment in these SEZs, Pakistan will have to offer at least a comparable business environment and incentives. Anything less would deter Chinese investors from investing in Pakistani SEZs. In this context, long-term government commitment and consistency in harmonized policies would be crucial for the success of its SEZs.

Another major challenge could arise from the fact that, due to the lack of education and proper skills, Pakistani workers may not fulfill the requirements of international companies. This would result in less than expected jobs for the domestic population, limiting the impacts of these SEZs in generating greater employment. The Government may have to allocate sufficient resources to developing training and vocational institutions, to help bring local labor up to international standards.

For the success of these export-oriented SEZs, international connectivity is extremely important. At the present, Pakistan is virtually disconnected from global value and supply chains that have in turn become the key to ensuring greater efficiency and competitiveness in international markets. While the entire CPEC initiative is geared towards directly addressing this challenge with respect to the BRI, the proposed SEZs need to be aligned in sync with the broader goals of the BRI and CPEC for them to be able to fully partake in these global value and supply chains. The achievement of CPEC's core objectives as outlined in its Long-Term Plan would thus go a long way in ensuring that these SEZs are able to contribute meaningfully to global trade and production.

In summary, with international firms expected to draw all sorts of benefits from these SEZs, it is expected that they too contribute to economic growth, export development, increased employment, the transfer of technology, and greater skill development of the local population to help Pakistan achieve its objectives. Disagreements between these firms and the host government would arise only when either side starts violating their commitments and obligations. Hence, the overall challenge would be to jointly and cooperatively devise the rules of business and establish a fair and speedy disputes resolution system, as part of the overall regulatory framework aimed at providing oversight and direction to the success of these SEZs.

Policy Directions

In order to successfully bring about the required paradigm shift within its Economy, the Pakistani government must take into consideration the numerous opportunities and challenges that have been pointed out in this chapter thus far. By ensuring that the planning and implementation of these SEZs (as part of CPEC) are in tune with the unique political, economic and social requirements of Pakistan's development agenda, Pakistan can successfully set the stage for a new phase of industrialization within the country. Thus, building on the above discussion, the following points offer a set of specific policy recommendations that can help utilize these planned SEZs to their maximum potential.

First and foremost, both the Pakistani and Chinese governments need to develop agreed 'rules of business' and 'rules of engagement' with regard to the specific outcomes being envisioned by each side. During this process they would also need to take on board key representatives from the provincial governments as well as from the local community. This is to ensure that all stakeholders take ownership and are accountable to the success of these SEZs as they all have a shared interest in their success. Therefore, all of them should be engaged in the decision making process right from the beginning.

At the present, the Board of Investment in Pakistan (BOI) has been made responsible for providing the required fiscal incentives under its

Revised Special Economic Zones Act 2012[20] (amended up to 31st December 2015). Under this act, international firms willing to establish themselves within these SEZS are offered, "A one-time exemption from customs duties and taxes for all capital goods imported for the development, operations, and maintenance of a SEZ (both for the developers and the zone enterprises) and exemption from all taxes on income for a period of ten years."

The Act assumes that additional benefits offered to SEZs investors will be the same as those given to existing SEZs in Pakistan. It does not however, explicitly state the exact additional incentives for these investors. Hence, the Board of Investment (BoI) needs to make its incentive package at least as consistent as what Chinese investors are receiving in other foreign destinations for their investments. Besides, the BoI should also make it clear what additional benefits are being offered in Pakistan in terms of the overall ease of doing business.

To overcome the above and similar governance problems it is necessary to decentralize the decision making process as much as possible with the involvement of the private sector. This is essential because the vast majority of the companies to be based in these SEZs are likely to be private enterprises. Therefore, a market-based approach should be adopted that includes both the delegation of traditional functions to private agents and the introduction of market style management practices.

Given the size of certain domestic Small and Medium Enterprises (SMEs) however, it would be difficult for them to establish themselves in these SEZs jointly or independently because of a lack of financial and technological resources. Therefore, the government needs to devise incentivizing schemes, such as *offset* programs, to link such domestic, private SMEs with foreign SEZ firms.

---

[20] "Special Economic Zones Act 2012," *Board of Investment, Government of Pakistan*, December, 2015, http://boi.gov.pk/UploadedDocs/Downloads/Modified%20SEZ%20Act%202012.pdf (accessed August 2, 2018).

This emphasis on private investment can also be fostered by recognizing overseas Pakistanis as the potential champions and drivers of these SEZs. They should be encouraged to participate by offering specific incentives to be able to spearhead entrepreneurship within these SEZs. By promoting widespread stability and security the State should create the sort of environment that inspires confidence in it, while assuring such potential investors that their investments and skills would be not only protected, but extremely useful in helping develop the country.

Another major caveat that needs to be carefully addressed is to ensure that entrepreneurs and businesses do not exploit these SEZs by resorting to rent-seeking activities. This is because the country will then be forced to distort its very own markets and policy environment. This should be discouraged and stringent regulations and oversight should be placed to disallow investors from exploiting policies and circumventing the very objectives of establishing SEZs. For instance, this would include preventing the exploitation of tax and tariff exemptions against certain imports, ensuring that the government does not lose out on potential revenues.

All in all, this next phase of CPEC which is focused on the establishment of SEZs is unlikely to be an easy one and may not please everyone. As tough decisions need to be taken in order to restructure the economy, the Pakistani government needs to ensure that all stakeholders (Chinese and Pakistani) are on board and are ready play their respective roles for the success of these SEZs. This is all the more important since international experience suggests that it takes about a decade before SEZs are considered a success. Furthermore it has also been noted that about 50 percent of SEZ firms underperform as compared to companies based in the DZs.[21] Therefore, in order to make Pakistan's economic restructuring a reality, a concerted and sustained effort is required from the diverse range of stakeholders that are involved in this initiative.

---

[21] "Pham Minh Chinh, t of the CPV Central Committee, and His Party Visit CCSEZR," *China Center for Special Economic Zones Research*, February 6, 2018, http://www.ccsezr.org/enews/news_detail.php?newsid=3986 (accessed August 2, 2018).

Conclusion

Summing up this chapter, SEZs are established in a country to counter certain market failures present in the economy. Thus, the SEZs being envisioned under the CPEC initiative serve as a lifetime opportunity for Pakistan to establish modern and efficient industries across the country. These SEZs are expected to be a major source of innovation and technical expertise along with a highly valuable source of Foreign Direct Investment. They are expected to stimulate economic growth, improve the BoP and generate much needed jobs for the educated youth of the country.

It needs also to be understood however here that there are large financial and other risks associated with this initiative. The end-result and thus potential success of this initiative hinges directly on how these costs and risks are managed by the Pakistani government as well as the numerous foreign and local investors and stakeholders.

Thus, while the establishment of these SEZs presents the next logical step in consolidating and further multiplying the gains being envisioned under CPEC, there is a lot more work that needs to be done for them to truly represent a win-win outcome for all.

Part IV: CPEC as Part of a New Global Paradigm

Chapter 9: Ensuring the Economic Viability of CPEC - A Security Perspective

Dr. Shabana Fayyaz*

Introduction

The China–Pakistan Economic Corridor commonly known as CPEC, is a sum total of multiple infrastructural projects worth $62 billion[1] that are currently underway throughout Pakistan. The upshot of CPEC is to bring in peace and prosperity in the region by laying a mix of road networks, railways and pipelines in this area. It will transform Pakistan by upgrading its economic profile, reviving its industry, augmenting its connectivity with adjacent regions, addressing energy shortfalls, improving public infrastructure and expanding societal links between Pakistan and China. Pakistan's share in this game changer project thus ranges from economic to human domains.

Parallel to this, there are key domestic and international challenges facing both states in order to materialize this road map of security interdependence. This chapter aims to understand the core risks and opportunities associated with the implementation of this crucial project. In doing so it focuses on the security dimensions of CPEC viewed from the perspective of a more integrated concept of international security. It

---

* Dr. Shabana Fayyaz is Assistant Professor in the Defence and Strategic Studies Department at the Quaid-i-Azam University, Islamabad.
[1] For details please refer to Appendix 'A' on page 265.

thus attempts to visualize CPEC as a safety valve not only for Pakistan but for the broader region as well.

Contextual Overview

The China Pakistan Economic Corridor (CPEC) is being hailed as a fate-changing investment in Pakistan as part of China's all-encompassing vision for its Belt and Road Initiative (BRI). It has been portrayed as a potential life-line for fostering sustainable economic growth within Pakistan.

The corridor comprises of over 2,000 kilometers of road and rail links between Western China and Pakistan, as well as a number of massive infrastructure projects centered on enhancing the country's Energy, Agriculture, Trade and Industrial sectors.[2] These in turn are backed by a massive drive towards greater socio-cultural integration between both countries.

The BRI initiative of which CPEC is a key component encompasses the population of more than 4 billion people and an economic output of US$ 21 trillion. Its vision for peace through greater regional integration straddles across Eurasia, Africa, the Persian Gulf, South and South-East Asia.[3] Within this context, the BRI can be further considered as a reflection of regional integration amidst a more humanized form of economic development. This in turn is characterized by bringing about a marked improvement in trade relations, the up gradation of key economic infrastructure and the promotion of greater political flexibility. The BRI is an unfolding plan that would thus interlace Asia, Europe, Africa, Oceania and the Middle East through vehicles of diplomacy, new infrastructure and free trade zones.

Within this framework, CPEC has far-reaching implications not only for China and Pakistan but also for Iran, Afghanistan, the Central Asian

---

[2] Adam Hodge, "Karakoram Highway: China's Treacherous Pakistan Corridor," *The Diplomat*, July 30, 2013, https://thediplomat.com/2013/07/karakoram-highway-chinas-treacherous-pakistani-corridor/ (accessed November 16, 2017).

[3] James Griffiths, "Just what is this One Belt, One Road Thing Anyway?," *CNN*, May 12, 2017, https://edition.cnn.com/2017/05/11/asia/china-one-belt-one-road-explainer/index.html (accessed August 20, 2018).

Republics and India. It holds the key to the broader region's ability in moving towards sustainable peace and prosperity. CPEC thus requires a commitment by all its stake holders. It requires all of them to work towards a shared vision of enhanced geographical connectivity with improved road, rail and air links alongside new-found social links between societies and cultures. It is hoped that this would lead to greater economic cooperation and joint business ventures in a win-win cooperation framework of integrated development throughout the region.[4]

However, things are not as smooth and friction free as they look on the surface. There exist credible security threats, both traditional and non-traditional in nature, that are directly linked to CPEC. In order to mitigate and address these security challenges nation states such as Pakistan need to adopt a more integrated and sustainable approach to mitigating these threats. Before elaborating on these security dilemmas and the way they have been responded to, it is necessary to firstly clarify the concept of security employed throughout this chapter.

CPEC within the Contemporary International Security Framework

The world today does not comprise of a more military dominated era where one can simply ignore the non-traditional aspects of security. Today, threats to security can emanate just as much from water scarcity, intense population growth, famine, climate change, terrorism, poverty, the proliferation of drugs/mafia/armaments and the numerous maladies associated with failing states. These in turn define the international security landscape alongside the more conventional military threats to state security. This reality has thus given rise to new challenges to state security and policy formulation, particularly within the overall landscape of global geo-politics. Formulating new economic priorities and plans that take in to account these new security threats, thus serves as one of the biggest challenges to policymakers within the contemporary international framework. This holds especially true for all those involved in the planning and implementation of CPEC.

---

[4] Ibid.

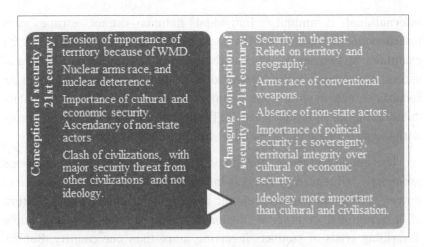

Figure 9.1- Paul D. Williams, "Changing Concept of Security," in *Security Studies: An Introduction* (New York: Routledge, 2008), 1-10.

Under the auspices of the United Nations and based on the above dynamics, this focus on security has further shifted from a state-centric to a more human centric-approach to international security.[5] This notion of Human Security is for instance evident within the agendas of the UN's numerous component organizations, and has been incorporated into the studies of the academic security community further widening its definition. Sadly, it is worth noting however that since the 9/11 attacks and the US's global 'War on Terror', this definition of security has once again been narrowed down to a more militarized, state-centric approach towards international peace and stability.

Within the context of the BRI and CPEC, the ensuing discussion postulates security as a relational phenomenon that is synonymous with the accumulation of power. It subsequently involves the capabilities, desires and fears of all interacting states in relation to CPEC and the BRI. This obviously carries with it a series of implications for the broader regional and international environment as well.

In the globalized world of nuclear weapons and interdependence, the security of one country is often equated with the security of the entire

---

[5] Schafer P.J, "The Concept of Security," *Human and Water Security in Israel and Jordan Springer Briefs in Environment, Security, Development and Peace* 3 (2013): 113.

international community. Individual nations cannot escape such interdependence within an increasingly complex world. This can be examined at two levels: first at the level of the individual State, and second at the level of the International System. Each State examines its security threats in view of the stability of the state and its society, and its vulnerability to external threats. At the second level it operates and deals with the structure and nature of the International System as a whole.

This entire pattern of International Security and its related problems are mostly influenced by changes in key variables such as the balance of power, technological and economic advances, and the changing pattern of international commerce. Regional labels can be used in simply describing crisis or conflicts involving more than one country. But for security in an interdependent world, these hold more importance than a situation involving two countries or a particular war or crisis in a specific region. These deeper understandings highlight the fact that there are security groupings between states at the sub-regional level, which are determined by the geographical proximity of states.[6]

The model on the next page gives a visual overview of the above discussion, summarizing the underlying framework of Contemporary International Security:

---

[6] Barry Buzan, "A Framework for Regional Security Analysis," in *South Asian Insecurity and the Great Powers* (London: Palgrave Macmillan, 1986), 3-33.

The International Contemporary Security Paradigm

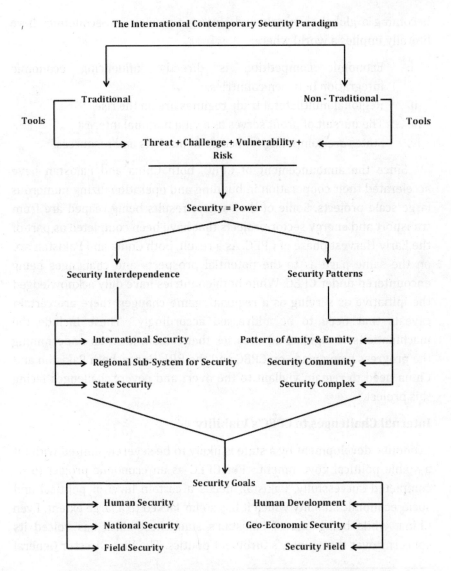

Figure 9.2- A Model of the International Contemporary Security Paradigm.

Applying this framework to the theme of this book, China's pursuit of the BRI and CPEC as its flagship project, is a reflection of its firm belief in using geo-economics as a vehicle to connect the world. This relates directly to China's ambitions towards achieving its much coveted goal of becoming a global economic and strategic power. Geo-economics here literally implies a world where:

i.   Economic competition is directly influencing economic integration between countries.
ii. Regional multilateral trade regimes are on the rise
iii. The pursuit of profit serves as a vital national interest
iv. States are competing for access to markets and resources.[7]

Since the announcement of CPEC, both China and Pakistan have accelerated their cooperation in building and operationalizing numerous large scale projects. Some of the earliest results being reaped are from transport and energy sector projects that have been completed as part of the Early Harvest phase of CPEC. As a result, both China and Pakistan are on the same page as to the potential prospects and challenges being encountered under CPEC. While both countries have duly acknowledged the initiative as serving as a regional 'game changer' there are certain caveats that need to be addressed accordingly.[8] These include the machinations of regional adversaries that remain keen on undermining the progress being made on CPEC and the BRI. Hence, both Pakistan and China need to remain vigilant to the overt and covert challenges facing this project.[9]

Internal Challenges to CPEC's Viability

Economic development by a state is likely to be severely limited without a stable political government. For CPEC as an economic project to be completed successfully, Pakistan needs a certain level of political and socio-economic stability which it has so far lacked to a large extent. Even China, while being one of Pakistan's staunchest allies has voiced its concerns over the country's turbulent politics. The Vice Director General

---

[7] "Geo-Economics with Chinese Characteristics: how China's Economic Might is Reshaping World Politics?," *World Economic Forum*, January 2016, http://www3.weforum.org/docs/WEF_Geoeconomics_with_Chinese_Characteristics.pdf (accessed November 20, 2017).
[8] "CPEC, OBOR Game-Changer for Entire Region," *Express Tribune*, December 13, 2017, https://tribune.com.pk/story/1582585/1-cpec-obor-game-changer-entire-region/ (accessed September 11, 2018).
[9] Zafar Nawaz Jaspal, "Challenges to CPEC," *Pakistan Observer*, April 20, 2017, https://pakobserver.net/challenges-to-cpec/ (accessed May 6, 2017).

of the Policy Research Office at the International Department of the Central Committee Communist Party of China, Mr. Luan Jian Zhang has raised these concerns directly with his counterparts in Pakistan. He is of the view that with the successful completion of CPEC, Pakistan would become a center of economic activities. This however is only likely to come about by first eliminating the risks posed by political instability, nepotism among key administrations and institutions, and terrorism.[10] Hence, with regard to CPEC, the Pakistani government is currently confronting a number of internal challenges that are limiting the full potential of CPEC projects.

Building on this context of internal threats, the following arguments provide a more detailed overview of some of the most salient challenges being posed from within Pakistan to ensuring the economic viability of CPEC:

Politico–Economic Challenges
Recent discord amongst Pakistan's major political parties is emerging as a major challenge to the implementation of CPEC projects in Pakistan. Their concerns are mostly related to the different proposed routes of the corridor, the allocation of investment funds, and the proposed dividends and rewards to be reaped from it. These concerns have emerged from the chequered history of political-economic and federation-provincial relationship during the past seven decades of Pakistani politics. It is often argued that the Center has always asserted greater control over the allocation of resources, consequently further politicizing the process of development.[11]

This was evident for instance in the past disagreements between the Federal and KPK governments. During the initial planning and negotiation stages of CPEC, the provincial governments of both KPK and Punjab had raised reservations regarding the proposed routes and projects of CPEC. This situation arose when the Federal government of

---

[10] Massarrat Abid and Ayesha Ashfaq, "CPEC: Challenges and Opportunities for Pakistan," *Journal of Pakistan Vision* 16, no. 2 (2015): 142-169.
[11] Rafiullah Kakar, "Making Sense of the CPEC Controversy," *Express Tribune,* January 21, 2016, https://tribune.com.pk/story/1031850/making-sense-of-the-cpec-controversy/ (accessed September 11, 2018).

Pakistan had revised the expected route of CPEC. The political parties of KPK had opposed these alterations arguing that this would divert the potential economic benefits more towards Punjab. They had demanded that the Federal Government rescind these alterations.

Commenting on these developments, Wu Zhaoli, an Assistant Research Fellow at the National Institute of International Strategy, Chinese Academy of Social Sciences, has stated that "It is largely security concerns that have remained critical in helping determine the path of this corridor".[12] This implies that changes were made more due to the security apprehensions of policymakers, as opposed to any political goals.

Dr. Ahmad Rashid Malik, Senior Research Fellow at the Institute of Strategic Studies Islamabad (ISSI), concurs with this view, stating that the route controversy is "baseless and an unfounded reality."[13] The larger problem here perhaps lies in the absence of political consensus between the provinces which remains crucial to the smooth functioning and implementation of the entire CPEC initiative.

The case of Baluchistan too provides an interesting example with respect to this complex interconnection between security, politics and economic development. Despite its huge development potential and abundant natural resources, Baluchistan has remained a hotbed of ethnic tensions and violence. Local insurgents and political feudal leaders have long raised concerns over the under-development of the province and exploitation of its resources. However these same feudal politicians have been blamed for limiting the state's writ over development as it undermines their own authority over this vast region. As a result, the security dynamics in the region despite considerable improvements have created a perception of uncertainty owing to previous kidnappings and deaths of foreign workers as well the sabotage of civil infrastructure and communication lines. This situation, while certainly improving, still

---

[12] Wu Zhaoli, "Economic Corridor will be Lever for all of South Asia," *Global Times*, May 30, 2013, http://www.globaltimes.cn/content/800223.shtml (accessed November 29, 2017).
[13] Rashid Malik, "Route Alignment Controversy," *The Nation*, February 20, 2015, https://nation.com.pk/20-Feb-2015/route-alignment-controversy?show=blocks?version=amp (accessed November 29, 2017).

holds considerable risks for both local and Chinese investors working to develop the region to its full potential.

Localized Socio-Economic Challenges

Some major segments of society including Baloch nationalists, civil society leaders and residents of Gwadar city are raising concerns over the impact of CPEC projects being implemented within their locales. The Head of Gwadar's Fishermen Association stated in an interview with international news channel (NBC) that "Development is good, China is our great friend, this CPEC thing sounds amazing, but don't forget that this is our land, first."[14] While some residents doubt they will see any of the benefits promised by CPEC, others fear that they will be evicted from their homes in order to make way for infrastructure works.

In response to such concerns raised by the local residents and community, the government and security officials need to give constant assurances that locals will not be deprived of the benefits of CPEC and that it is them who have the first right on employment opportunities. Furthermore, they should be also assured that existing residents will not be displaced as a result of the development process, dispelling the notion that such development would bring along riches only for the more empowered classes.

External Challenges to CPEC's Viability

As an economic and trade initiative, CPEC faces major challenges from both intra and extra regional competitors. These include a number of challenges being posed by rival states as well as non-state actors all of which pose a number of threats to the economic viability of CPEC.

For instance, the United States has for quite some time been expressing its concerns over the growing Chinese footprint in the region. It had initially suggested that Pakistan refrain from handing over Gwadar port to China. Washington had instead called for handing over the

---

[14] Wajahat S. Khan, "Gwadar Port Project Reveals China's Regional Power Play," *NBC News,* April 30, 2016, https://www.nbcnews.com/news/world/gwadar-port-project-reveals-chinas-regional-power-play-n558236 (accessed September 11, 2018).

management of the port to Singapore Port Authority.[15] Despite increasing tensions, the US still holds a major a stake within the wider region. As the world's leading economic and military power, its presence and interests in the region have made it increasingly difficult to ignore despite its frayed relations with Pakistan. Thus, there is an urgent need to diplomatically engage with the United States and other countries for discussing their apprehensions regarding CPEC and to insulate it from such external limitations.

Building on these concerns the following arguments provide a more detailed overview of the various threats and risks being posed to CPEC by key actors outside of Pakistan. These more or less comprise as subsets of the key challenges being faced by the country across a broad range of foreign policy issues moving beyond just CPEC.

CPEC and Afghanistan

The uncertainty within the Region's security environment poses one of the most significant threats to CPEC particularly with respect to Pakistan's border areas. The ongoing war in Afghanistan thus currently serves as the primary challenge to CPEC. The huge investments which the Chinese are making through CPEC in the region greatly depend on the maintenance of enduring peace and stability in Pakistan, Afghanistan and Western China respectively. Beijing is trying its best to play a more stabilizing role within the region as evident in its past efforts in bringing the Taliban to the negotiating table within the quadrilateral agenda between China, Pakistan, US and Afghanistan.

CPEC and Xinjiang

Due to various socio economic reasons including poverty, underdevelopment and ethnic tensions, the Western Chinese province of Xinjiang has been categorized as the soft underbelly of China. It is a Muslim majority region comprising of largely the native Uyghur population. The East Turkestan Islamic Movement (ETIM) in particular is confronting the Chinese government with the three evils of terrorism,

---

[15] "Gwadar Port Handed over to China," *Express Tribune*, February 18, 2013, https://tribune.com.pk/story/509028/gwadar-port-handed-over-to-china/ (accessed September 11, 2018).

extremism and separatism. It is widely perceived that ISIS is providing the ETIM its full support and training, due to which these groups have come to pose a significant threat. This is evident from a number of, instances where Uyghur belligerents have been noticed being trained in their camps.[16]

In recent years the Xinjiang Uyghur Autonomous Region (XUAR) has seen increasing tensions with regard to the local socio-political environment. Riots and terrorist assaults within Xinjiang, Kunming and Beijing have taken place occasionally. In order to confront these challenges, Beijing has responded via a two-pronged approach. First, the Chinese government initiated a firm crackdown on terrorist activities, resulting in widespread arrests and prosecutions. Secondly, Beijing coupled its uncompromising approach with earlier promises of economic development in the region as a means of addressing racial rigidities.[17]

Considering how Xinjiang serves as a key component of CPEC across the Chinese border, any threats or risks emanating from it would adversely affect the success of the entire initiative greatly limiting its full potential.

CPEC and India

India being Pakistan's age old strategic rival is widely perceived as having vested interests in the failure of CPEC. These perceptions are further grounded in the fact that both India and China while boasting serious economic growth over the last two decades have been competing for regional supremacy and security particularly with respect to their maritime interests in the Indian Ocean.

Pakistan's South Western port of Gwadar which holds the key to CPEC's success, has thus, been propelled to the forefront of the emerging security dynamics of the South Asian region. The situation has been further complicated with Indian support to the South-Western Iranian

---

[16] Nodirbek Soliev, "How Serious is the Islamic State Threat to China?," *The Diplomat*, March 14, 2017, https://thediplomat.com/2017/03/how-serious-is-the-islamic-state-threat-to-china/ (accessed September 12, 2018).

[17] Sudha Ramachandran, "CPEC Takes a Step Forward as Violence Surges in Baluchistan," *Asia Times*, November 16, 2016, http://www.atimes.com/cpec-takes-step-forward-violence-surges-balochistan/ (accessed November 29, 2017).

port of Chabahar which is being perceived as a direct competitor to Gwadar. For India, access to Chabahar is crucial to forming a direct maritime link with landlocked Afghanistan and Central Asia by bypassing Pakistan. If successful, Chabahar would effectively serve as a transit port for energy and trade imports coming from the Gulf region destined for Afghanistan and Central Asia, hence offering an alternate to the Gwadar linked CPEC route.

Additionally, India has also expressed concerns over the disputed nature of the Gilgit Baltistan and AJK region, expressing doubts over the true motives of Chinese interests in this region. Taken under the broader context of the BRI, India remains highly skeptical of China's growing interests throughout the Asian region which it views as Beijing's attempts at encircling India thus limiting its own potential to project power across the wider region.

Arc of Militancy

Rooted in decades of regional conflict, militancy in all its forms within the surrounding region also poses grave challenges to the successful implementation of CPEC. There exists a wide arc of extremist militant groups ranging from Xinjiang to Gwadar. These comprise of the East Turkestan Islamic Movement (ETIM), Tehreek-e-Taliban Pakistan (TTP), Lashkar-e-Jhangvi (LeJ), Daesh (ISIS), Baluchistan Liberation Army (BLA), Baluchistan Liberation Front (BLF) and numerous militant organizations straddling the boundary between political action groups and full blown insurgencies. Even though most of these groups do not hold any direct animosity towards the Chinese government their intentions to harm Chinese interests in the form of CPEC are intended to limit Pak-China cooperation while fomenting turmoil and instability within the region.

During the past decade Pakistan has faced a prolonged Islamist insurgency which emerged in full force in the Post 9/11 era. The outlawed Tehrik-i-Taliban Pakistan (TTP) has been widely attributed as leading the insurgency as it has repeatedly claimed responsibility for a string of terrorist attacks. Consequently, Chinese analysts have since expressed their concerns over the safety of Chinese nationals within

Pakistan, and have engaged with the Pakistani government over implementing improved security measures for foreigners. Chinese authorities have also been concerned that these varied groups could potentially join hands with activists in Xinjiang, leading to new instances of cross-border terrorism between the Pak-China border.[18]

These concerns however have held little weight since 2014 when the Pakistan military launched a series of offensives under its Operations *Zarb-e-Azb,* and *Radd-ul-Fasaad.* These operations have since severely limited the scope of terrorist activities throughout the country, leading to a marked improvement in the country's security situation.

While perceptions of insecurity still remain widespread, particularly among foreign observers, Pakistan remains resilient and battle hardened in its resolve to combat both internal and external threats to its economic potential. Areas that still require improvement involve eliminating risks arising from sectarian conflicts, as well as the maintenance of law and order in its sprawling urban centers to secure the dividends being earned from the economic growth and development emanating from CPEC.

Pakistan's Response to These Challenges

Internal
Internal security in Pakistan has shown visible improvement as a result of various military operations against terrorist organizations. However, the overall security landscape still poses formidable challenges for the secure implementation of massive development projects under CPEC. Despite the formation of a special security force to ensure the security of project sites and Chinese personnel, terrorism emanating from Afghanistan and the difficult terrain in Baluchistan still continue to pose certain challenges, requiring round the clock vigilance

In the maritime security domain, Pakistan and Chinese naval forces have jointly collaborated to guard trade convoys in international waters. This is helping Pakistan expand its maritime footprint in the Arabian Sea.

---

[18] "Pakistan says will Help China Fight Xinjiang Militants," *Reuters,* November 8, 2014, https://www.dawn.com/news/1143134 (accessed November 29, 2016).

In December 2016, Pakistan's Navy announced the formation of a special taskforce "TF-88" to ensure maritime security for CPEC sea-bound trade.[19] Reports suggest, that in total around 15,000 Pakistani security personnel have been assigned the task of ensuring the security of Chinese workers in Pakistan.[20]

In order to specifically address security challenges to Pakistan, the federal government has also formed a 'Special Security Division' which is also overseeing the implementation of security operations directly pertaining to CPEC. As a result Pakistani security agencies have conducted counter-insurgency operations against a number of suspected ETIM and TTP militants.

While these efforts have been successful in mitigating a significant proportion of the overall threat to CPEC, there are still certain caveats that can be addressed to eliminate potential risks. These for instance include local dissidents in Baluchistan who need to be engaged with in a more inclusive dialogue process. This would help bring them back into the national mainstream while addressing their concerns.

External

Pakistan has always advocated that without expanding economic and trade linkages between regional nations of Central and South Asia, their economic challenges cannot be resolved. Regional organizations such as the South Asian Association for Regional Cooperation (SAARC) and the Economic Cooperation Organization's (ECO) primary objective is to promote trade and economic cooperation among the members of these regional bodies.

Islamabad has proposed that its regional neighbors also take part in CPEC projects. This would greatly enhance the significance of these development projects and also boost investor confidence. On April 21, 2015, former Prime Minister Nawaz Sharif stated that: "CPEC is a catalytic project that will help us combine the geo-economic streams of

---

[19] "TF-88: Pakistan Navy Special Task Force for CPEC Security Inaugurated," *Times of Islamabad*, December 13, 2016, http://timesofislamabad.com/tf-88-pakistan-navy-special-task-force-cpec-security-inaugurated/2016/12/13/ (accessed January 29, 2016).

[20] Syed Irfan Raza, "15000 Military Personnel Protecting CPEC," *Dawn*, February 21, 2017, https://www.dawn.com/news/1316040/ (accessed August 31, 2018).

our countries. The corridor symbolizes our commitment to creating win-win partnerships which threaten none and benefit all."[21] This points towards how CPEC can play a key role in greatly de-escalating regional tensions on the back of greater cooperation for trade and economic development.

With specific regard to the risks emanating from both locally based militant groups (particularly the Tehrik-i-Taliban Pakistan-TTP and the Balochistan Liberation Army-BLA), and international Jihadi organizations (such as al-Qaeda and the Islamic State), it is worth noting however that such groups still hold the potential of adversely affecting CPEC, based on the immense economic and political costs these would lead to for the Pakistani state. This holds particularly true if there was to be a major terrorist attack targeting Chinese companies, and workers within Pakistan.

The attempted attack on the Chinese Consulate in Karachi in November 2018[22], serves as a cogent example of such attempts at derailing Pak-China cooperation over CPEC. However, as evident in the swift response of security forces in repelling the attack, Pakistan remains steadfast and every-ready in its resolve to combat all forms of terrorist threats. Pakistan duly recognizes the strategic importance accorded to its relations with China, and remains committed to defending these in solidarity with its age-old strategic partner. Islamabad further views CPEC as a mutually advantageous in terms of not only its long-term economic development, but also from a National Security perspective.

In this context the formation of Apex Committees at the federal and provincial levels, was geared towards enhancing civil-military coordination to improve the internal security situation and counter-terrorism. Former Chief of the Army Staff (COAS) General Raheel Sharif

---

[21] Zafar Nawaz Jaspal, "CPEC's Potential to Revolutionize Regional Cooperation and Make Pakistan Pivotal," *Global Village Space,* March 17, 2017, https://www.globalvillagespace.com/cpecs-potential-to-revolutionize-regional-cooperation/ (accessed July 29, 2017).

[22] "Karachi Attack: China Consulate Attack Leaves Four Dead," *BBC News,* November 23, 2018, https://www.bbc.com/news/world-asia-46313136a-46313136 (accessed December 4, 2018).

had emphasized that the country has no other option than to eliminate "all manifestations of extremism and terrorism at the grass roots level". He had also emphatically stated that, "we [Pakistan's security forces] will not stop unless we achieve our end objective of a terror-free Pakistan." The measures by which Pakistan's security forces are dealing with such future threats are provided in detail in Appendix (H).[23]

Conclusion

Considering how the purported benefits of CPEC are likely to take a few years to be fully witnessed, it becomes difficult to exactly predict how things will shape up in the future. On the security front, despite repeated assurances by the Pakistani government and its armed forces there are still certain caveats that pose real risks to the entire enterprise. Given the magnitude of the project, Pakistan's fractious relations with its immediate neighbors, and its chequered history of conflict and terrorism; strict vigilance is required to ensure that both Pakistan's and China's interests are not made hostage to the machinations of its enemies.

As things stand, there are still pockets of militancy with which the armed forces are engaged in. Suspicions over civil military distrust and federal-provincial tensions are also likely to pervade despite a series of improvements during successive governments. As the project progresses, envious neighbors and outside interferences are also likely to increase in magnitude and frequency further compounding these challenges. Unless multi-pronged measures are stringently implemented such as those envisaged in the country's National Action Plan, the security dimensions of CPEC are likely to further increase in complexity.[24]

There are a number of important measures that have been taken to secure CPEC from internal, regional and international threats. Based on this experience so far, securing CPEC from terrorism has remained as one of the toughest challenges for both China and Pakistan. CPEC has a

---

[23] See Appendix "H" at page 278.
[24] Dr. Maqsudul Hasan Nuri, (Former President IPRI, in discussion with the author, November 2017.

long route of 3,000 km from Gwadar to Kashgar, defending which requires an unprecedented level of security and massive counter-terrorism measures at the highest level. To be sure, Pakistan has taken significant steps to develop and deploy a number of land, air and sea-based military assets in order to combat the risks associated with these more asymmetrical security threats being posed to CPEC. Indeed, China has also supported these and broader efforts by Pakistan by enhancing its overall conventional military capabilities.

However, this has also led to concerns that increased China-Pakistan military cooperation is still taking place against the backdrop of intensifying competition within the context of the broader region. This includes rising India-Pakistan tensions and certain disagreements between China and India as to the preferred trajectory of growth within the South Asian region. Thus, the very measures ostensibly aimed at tackling the discussed non-traditional security challenges could inadvertently heighten threat perceptions and fuel interstate rivalry. This in turn accentuates the security risks being posed to CPEC rather than ameliorating them across a broader regional scale.[25]

Also, any instances of violence targeted specifically against Chinese personnel or assets would further lead to a serious escalation of these concerns and pose a huge setback to the immense progress that has been made so far. This would in turn adversely affect investor confidence in Pakistan, greatly tarnishing its standing both at the regional and international levels.

The current premise behind CPEC is still that it would fundamentally transform Pakistan's economy. In the long-term it is expected to address these challenges being posed by extremism and terrorism in Pakistan and the wider region. Both China and Pakistan view economic development as a means to addressing these issues in turn fostering peace and stability in the region. China is fully cognizant of the fact that these myriad political, cultural and socio-economic challenges limiting

---

[25] John Calabrese, "The China-Pakistan Economic Corridor (CPEC): Underway and Under Threat," *Middle East Institute*, December 20, 2016, http://www.mei.edu/content/map/china-pakistan-economic-corridor-cpec-underway-and-under-threat (accessed July 29, 2017).

the economic viability of CPEC cannot be left unaddressed. It is well aware of the fact that these threats pose direct risks to the success of the entire BRI initiative and cannot be allowed to negatively impact its vision. China thus remains committed in its resolve of standing by Pakistan and helping eliminate these challenges.

Thus, by jointly working together, both countries can surmount these obstacles, provided that they are given the due care and attention required of them. By continuing to believe in its shared vision of regional peace and prosperity, a robust response to CPEC's security challenges now can greatly reduce the potential security risks to the broader region over the long run. This in itself would serve as direct evidence of how an emphasis on combating more non-traditional risks to regional security can bring about such a massive transformation within the overall international security framework.

Chapter 10: Emerging Dynamics of the Race for Regional Integration

Dr. Shabbir Ahmad Khan*

Introduction

The implosion of the former Soviet Union created a vacuum in Central Asia that was once a part of the Communist bloc. In its aftermath, the Central Asian Republics (CARs) became vulnerable to considerable pressure owing to several internal and external factors. At the same time, the major powers sought to penetrate and fill this vacuum and force certain developments in a direction that was more advantageous to their own economic and strategic interests. The Central Asian region has been contested for influence among major powers since the nineteenth century. During this era, this intense rivalry that was played out mainly between the Russian and British Empires for establishing greater influence over the Central Asian region was popularly framed as the 'Great Game'. This same Great Game saw its resurgence following the collapse of the Soviet Union.

The term Great Game was coined by Arthur Connolly (1807-1848) in describing the political maneuverings between Tsarist Russia and Imperial Great Britain for dominating Central Asia. This concept was further immortalized by British novelist Rudyard Kipling (1865-1936) in his famous novel 'Kim' (1901).

---

* Dr. Shabbir Ahmad Khan is Associate Professor at the Area Study Centre, University of Peshawar, Peshawar.

Within the more contemporary study of International Relations, the renewed geostrategic competition in Central Asia, albeit with newer players, has been described as a 'New Great Game' by several analysts. It was the New York Times that coined the term for the first time in 1996 when referring to the newly emerging web of power relations within the International System.[1] The New Great Game however is based more on establishing key spheres of influence for the implementation of trans-continental trade-corridors, key energy pipelines, military bases and other related contingencies.

The current major players of the New Great game are Russia, China and the US; each of whom is pushing for certain developments to take shape in a direction benefiting their interests.[2] Each of these contesting States has their own grand strategy for regional integration and stability. Likewise, their conflicting interests and competitive approaches are further based on exclusionary tactics of denying their rivals access to their proposed regional setups.

Russia is an old player of the game as a result of its geographical proximity, historical leverage and politico-cultural influence on the Central Asian States. Since the post-Soviet era, Russia has been faced with numerous internal and external challenges that have greatly diminished its hold on these former Soviet bloc countries. However, over the last few decades a growingly assertive Russia has shown that it is not afraid to flex its economic and military might within the region. It is thus within this context that Russia plans to integrate the region through its concept of the 'Eurasian Union'.

China's geographical proximity along with its economic rise has also allowed it to integrate and project its own interests across Central Asia. Its overarching BRI initiative that has been discussed at length

---

[1] "New Great Game in Asia," *New York Times*, January 2, 1996, https://www.nytimes.com/1996/01/02/opinion/the-new-great-game-in-asia.html (accessed April 4, 2017).
[2] Shabir Ahmad Khan and Saima Kyani, "Pipeline Politics in Central Asia: Paradox of Competitive/Cooperative Relations between the United States, Russia and China," *Central Asia*, no. 73 (Winter 2013): 57-83.

throughout this book has been arguably planned and implemented to a great extent against the backdrop of this 'New Great Game'.

The US too has a plan under the New Silk Road Initiative to integrate the region under the Central Asian Regional Economic Cooperation framework (CAREC). However, US current engagements in the Middle East and Afghanistan along with the recent shift in its foreign policy have cast uncertainty on its seriousness and willingness to see this through.

For Pakistan, the China Pakistan Economic Corridor (CPEC) as a key component of the BRI plays a key role in re-shaping power relations within the region. With the warm-water port of Gwadar at the heart of the CPEC initiative, Pakistan has once again been propelled back into the Great Game, harking back to the days when American fears of the 'Domino Effect' and the Soviet occupation of Afghanistan had served as a major turning point for the prevailing International System during the Cold War.

At the present however, it is China's immense stake in Gwadar as part of the BRI that has led Pakistan to play a defining role within this complex web of power relations. Based on their long history of mutually beneficial bi-lateral relations, both China and Pakistan have joined together to secure the route between Central Asia and the Indian Ocean running through Pakistan and Western China. It is thus within this present multipolar context of the South Asian, as well as the broader Asian region, that CPEC has been termed as a 'Game-Changer', significantly tilting the balance of power in China's favor within the region.

New Dimensions to the Old Heartland

The inner crescent of the Eurasian Landmass broadly defined as Central Asia, has served as the historic site of contestation for the Great Game. This area includes present day Kazakhstan, Kyrgyzstan, Tajikistan, Turkmenistan, Uzbekistan and to a certain extent Afghanistan as well. While the present day territorial dimensions are vastly different from when the idea of the Great Game was first presented nearly two centuries ago, the broader region still holds immense significance in terms of the current web of power relations being played out both at the regional and international levels. Before setting out on an examination of these current power relations however, it is important to first outline the theoretical framework under which the Great Game for Central Asia has been enshrined within international relations discourse throughout its history.

The ideological premise of the Great Game throughout can be attributed largely to Mackinder's Heartland Theory. In this theory formulated around 1919, Mackinder presented Central Asia as 'the geographical pivot of history.' This can be summarized in his highly popular corollary in which he states that: "…he who rules Eastern Europe commands the heartland; he who rules the heartland commands the world islands (i.e. Eurasia) and he who rules the world islands commands the world".[3]

Nicholas J. Spykman further expanded on this theory and stated that the Power which controls the Eurasian landmass controls the destiny of the world.[4] The former National Security Advisor to the US Government from 1977 to 1981 Zbigniew Brzezinski, while echoing Spykman's sentiments also emphasized the significance of Eurasia. According to his theory, control over Central Asia and Afghanistan was key for maintaining control over Eurasia.[5]

It has been argued that the US has long attempted to use Afghanistan as a springboard to enter Central Asia and ultimately establish its influence over the Eurasian landmass.[6] Over the last two decades, the US's declared agenda has been framed against combating terrorism and promoting democracy, human rights and economic reforms in Central Asia. However its operational policy has pointed more towards

---

[3] Halford J Mackinder, "The Geographical Pivot of history (1904)," *Geographical Journal* 170, no. 4 (December 2004): 298 321.

[4] Shabir Ahmad Khan, "Dynamics of Trade Corridors and Energy Pipeline Politics," in *Pakistan's Strategic Environment; Post 2014*, ed. Mushir Anwar (Islamabad: Islamabad Policy Research Institute, 2014), 71-90.

[5] Zbigniev Brzezinski, *The Grand Chess Board* (New York: Basic Books, 1998), 39.

[6] Shabir Ahmad Khan and Saima Kyani, "Pipeline Politics in Central Asia: Paradox of Competitive/Cooperative Relations between the United States, Russia and China," *Central Asia*, no. 73 (Winter 2013): 80.

minimizing Russian influence and to pursue a policy of non-Russian, non-Chinese and non-Iranian routes for its proposed energy pipeline.[7]

China in its 'Go West' policy, initially settled its border issues with the Central Asian Republics through the Shanghai Five mechanism, which later became the Shanghai Cooperation Organization (SCO). This has allowed China to further develop extensive diplomatic and economic relations with the Central Asian Republics over the last few decades. The stability and development of Xinjiang (Western China) is also closely related to its energy and trade relations with Central Asia. During the last decade, China has more or less replaced Russia as the major trading partner with the region. Hence, it can be argued that Chinese influence is waxing while Russian influence is waning. China however has had to tread carefully over security issues in the region which is a sensitive issue for Russia. China is thus supporting local regimes in the region for the sake of regional security and stability.[8]

Russia on the other hand, after a span of ten years has been resurging in the region particularly after 2001. Its objectives in the region include; using the CARs as a buffer against the Islamic South, political stability, creation of a single economic space and the protection of ethnic Russians in the region.[9] Russia in comparison to the US and China is extensively linked to the region on account of deep seeded historical, political, socio-cultural and economic ties. Moscow still considers Central Asia as its backyard and has sought a more privileged role in the region based on more traditional and historical linkages.

In light of the differing strategies of regional integration being promoted by each of these powers, there have arisen a number of far-reaching consequences for a number of states linked with the Central Asian region. This also includes states in the South Asian region that are directly affected by the power politics of Russia, China and the US being played out in Central Asia.

---

[7] Ibid.
[8] Alexander Cooley, *Great Games, Local Rules* (New York: Oxford University Press, 2012), 75-95.
[9] Ibid., 51.

For instance, the US continues to view both Chinese and Russian influence within the region from a highly strategic vantage point, focusing on their containment. Russia while remaining critical of US interference has its own vision of regional integration, as it expands its sphere of influence along the historical boundary lines of the former Soviet Union. China while wholly conscious of its rise as a global power is looking for new markets and secure supply chains to help fuel its growing economy; the very economy that serves as the underlying basis of its power.

With respect to Pakistan and the South Asian region, China is seeking to balance India regionally and the US globally. The US on the other hand is expanding its strategic partnership with India to balance China regionally and globally as well. An increasingly assertive Russia is looking to challenge US supremacy and is deeply concerned with how US actions have played out in the Middle East and Persian Gulf.

These geo-strategic alliances, alignments and re-alignments are still evolving and will likely play a key role in shaping the policies of all countries within the Eurasian and South Asian regions. With each power's attempts at regional integration spilling beyond the Central Asian region, the scope of this New Great Game has extended far beyond the Eurasian heartland onto South Asia and South-East Asia. This is reflected in the vast scope and ambition of China's Belt & Road Initiative with its proposed vision for the Asian continent borne out of these very realities.

The Central Asian Republics – A Domestic Overview

The Central Asian Republics, being institutionally weak and economically underdeveloped hold little leverage against this troika of world powers i.e. Russia, China and the US. Yet despite their size and influence, they are however aware of their wealth and potential significance with respect to the interests of each of these powers. The Central Asian arena has long been contested for its strategic and economic significance. Rather than being passive pawns within this framework, the Central Asian Republics are actively pursuing policies with the aim of balancing and playing the great powers off one another. Their actions have been thus primarily based on maximizing their own national interests that have been more or less defined by their ruling elite.

According to Alexander Cooley, domestic politics within Central Asia is to a large extent characterized by regime security and the personal benefits of the ruling class.[10] While these same dynamics are evident in most developing countries, they have taken on a greater significance within contemporary Central Asia, as a result of the broader politics of the above mentioned global powers.

With each of these powers vying for influence amongst the local leadership, these leaders have been known to quickly switch their alliances and preferred patrons, based on the ebb and flow of both domestic and international politics. This has enabled the CARs to shirk their individual commitments to any patron, weakening the overall control of the objectively more powerful actors.[11] This has resulted in a relatively stronger position for the CARs than what may appear at first glance.

However, the leverage these CARs maintain over the great powers does vary from state to state depending upon their respective institutional structures and the extent of their resource endowments. For instance, Uzbekistan tried to pursue an independent policy during the 1990s and forged closer ties with Washington. After the 'Tulip Revolution' in neighboring Kyrgyzstan and the Andijan episode, Tashkent accused the US Embassy for promoting social unrest in the Andijan region. Consequently, it gave a deadline of 90 days for the evacuation of US personnel from the Karshi-Khanabad military base under the umbrella of SCO in 2005.[12] Moscow and Beijing supported the Uzbek official stance on the crises while Washington demanded a probe into the event. As a result, Uzbekistan soon distanced itself from Washington and embraced the Russian security role, thus relinquishing closer ties with the US for closer relations with Russia.

---

[10] Ibid., 16-29.
[11] Ibid., 9.
[12] Shabir Ahmad Khan, "Tashkent in November 2005," *Central Asia*, no. 58 (Summer 2006): 167-176.

Similarly, Kazakhstan due to its long border and demographic and economic linkages with Russia has historically remained close to Moscow. However it has also developed relations in other directions pursuing a 'multi vector' policy. During the last decade, economic revival and political stability has enabled Kazakhstan to pursue a more prudent policy having political and economic relations in all directions.

Turkmenistan has pursued a more or less independent foreign policy by emphasizing its preference of neutrality. This policy has earned some concrete rewards in the form of gas pipelines to China and greater internal stability. Unlike its more involved neighbors such as Uzbekistan and Kazakhstan, Turkmenistan does not appear to have any ambitions to take on a more leading and influential role in the broader region.

Kyrgyzstan due to its relative lack of hydrocarbon resources and mountainous terrain has had to deal with a number of developmental challenges that has led it to rely extensively on the help of global financial institutions. These economic challenges have been further exacerbated by political turmoil in the form of multiple revolutions and civil strife. The case of neighboring Tajikistan too is of a similar nature. These factors have led both Kyrgyzstan and Tajikistan to represent the most impoverished parts of Central Asia that have relied extensively on global powers for both economic support and political security.

Relations between these Central Asian Republics are influenced by a number of factors comprising of border disputes, water issues, inter-ethnic issues and endemic corruption. Nevertheless, the oil and particularly gas pipelines from Turkmenistan via Uzbekistan and Kazakhstan, and via Kyrgyzstan and Tajikistan to China present some of the most recent and salient examples of regional cooperation between these countries.

At present, the Central Asian economies are heavily dependent on commodity exports. As a result the current export basket, as well as the underlying economic structure needs to be diversified. Turkmenistan exports mainly gas, Kazakhstan oil and Uzbekistan exports cotton and gold. As a result of fluctuating commodity prices, the economies of these states are vulnerable to shocks due to a glaring lack of diversification. If for instance, gas supply from Turkmenistan to China was disrupted; its impact could prove detrimental to its politico-economic stability. Likewise, both Tajikistan and Kyrgyzstan are heavily dependent on remittances and aid particularly from Russia. Any tensions between the global powers on the international stage are likely to negatively affect their economies leading to increased political instability.

There are also other issues that mar relations within the region. For instance, drug trafficking from Afghanistan through Tajikistan's porous border is yet another problem particularly for Russia. This adds an added dimension to the immense risks associated with the region. If for example Tajikistan becomes politically and economically unstable like it did during the 1990s, it is unlikely that the 7000 Russian troops stationed there would idly standby. Similarly, this scenario holds equal importance for China which borders Tajikistan and Afghanistan to its West.

Owing to their proximity both Russia and China have genuine stakes in regional stability and are playing important roles to keep 'their backyard' politically stable and economically developed. The US based on its continued presence in Afghanistan, its subsequent role in the global War on Terror, and its policy of containment of both the rise of China and Russia; also cannot afford the disintegration of the CARs, which have so far acted as a buffer against these very issues.

It is worth noting that the CARs being well aware of these dynamics are more inclined towards Russian and Chinese interests owing to their geographical and socio-cultural proximity. Based on their requirements of regime security and internal stability discussed above, they are relatively more suspicious of US interests than Chinese and Russian interests especially when considered via the economic rationale of greater regional integration.

Hence, based on this complex web of both internal and external power dynamics, the Central Asian region serves as a major potential flashpoint for the global powers, and is in turn highly dependent on the internal stability of the CARs. That is why the CARs themselves are the real stakeholders in the security and economic sustainability of the wider region. Hence, a regional approach is needed to address these important issues.

While considerable effort has been made to foster greater regional integration, there is a lot more that can potentially benefit these states as well as the surrounding region. For instance, going ahead the CARs need to simplify procedures for border crossings in terms of time, service delivery and profitability to make continental modes of transport more competitive; hence, attracting more traffic. If for instance the CARs are unable to address such basic issues related to ungoverned border crossings from both security and trade perspectives, then the development of trade corridors may not attract the required growth in traffic.

The US Plan for Regional Integration: The New Silk Road Initiative

The American 'New Silk Road Initiative' was announced in 2011 by former US Secretary of State Hilary Clinton during her visit to India.[13] The US initiative has been supported by the Asian Development Bank (ADB) through the CAREC program. The plan has been to provide assistance to Afghanistan and link it intra-regionally. The main objective of the initiative is to integrate Central and South Asia via Afghanistan for the benefit of the US backed government in Afghanistan. However, it has been stated that an important objective of the New Silk Road initiative is to also serve as an exit strategy for the US from Afghanistan, and to thus fill the void left by its departing military.[14]

The declaratory policy of the US has been to develop cross-border infrastructure for regional economic development and cooperation, promotion of international trade, greater space for civil society groups, the promotion of human rights and the development of a robust democracy.[15] However it's this very support to civil society groups at the cost of deteriorating state institutions, and regime change policies

---

[13] Vladimir Fedorenko, "The New Silk Road Initiative in Central Asia," *Rethink Paper* 10 (August 2013): 9-20.
[14] Erica Marat, "Following the New Silk Road," *The Diplomat*, October 22, 2014, http://thediplomat.com/2014/10/following-the-new-silk-road/ (accessed April 19, 2017).
[15] Vladimir Fedorenko, "The New Silk Road Initiative in Central Asia," *Rethink Paper* 10 (August 2013): 9-20.

disguised as democracy development, that have led to a growing suspicion of US motives amongst the CARs.

Throughout the post-Soviet era, the region's geo-politics have been framed against the competing interests of two prime groups that have been contesting each other for the natural wealth of the region. These comprise of the US-EU bloc on the one side and the Sino-Russian bloc on the other. Both groups are competing for access to Central Asia's vast untapped energy reserves in the form of pipeline politics.

According to Zhao Huasheng, Central Asia is the only place where the conflicting interests of all the great powers converge, despite their declared inclinations towards greater cooperation. This contest has more recently greatly intensified due to the strategic distrust particularly between these two groups.[16]

Initially under its operational policy, the US has tried to diversify the energy supply of its NATO partners in the EU by reducing its dependence on Russian energy sources. By linking Caspian and Central Asian energy reserves with Europe, the idea was to bypass the Russian controlled energy supply chain.[17]

Furthermore, based on its foreign policy stance on South Asia and the Persian Gulf, the US also did not support Iran and China for its proposed energy pipeline routes. Iran despite being a major supplier of oil was particularly left outside of the US's New Silk Road initiative owing to deteriorating Iran-US relations. The Central Asia-South Asia electricity transmission project CASA 1000 and the Trans-Afghan-Pakistan-India (TAPI) gas pipeline are all projects under this 'New Silk Road initiative' and are supported through the World Bank and the Asian Development Bank. However, the lack of trust between the US and Pakistan, and continued instability in Afghanistan still present major hurdles in their materialization as both these projects have to pass through Afghanistan.

---

[16] Zhao Huasheng, "Central Asia in Chinese Strategic Thinking," in *The New Great Game: China and South and Central Asia in the Era of Reform,* ed., Thomas Fingar (USA: Stanford University Press, 2016), 181.

[17] Shabir Ahmad Khan and Saima Kyani, "Pipeline Politics in Central Asia: Paradox of Competitive/Cooperative Relations between the United States, Russia and China," *Central Asia*, no. 73 (Winter 2013): 77.

The US's prolonged involvement in Afghanistan and the lack of any serious policy for the region under the new Trump administration adds to the difficulties of the US pursuit of its New Silk Road Initiative. Furthermore, the US has a natural disadvantage of being physically thousands of miles away from the region, having no direct links in contrast to Russia and China. Hence, it is apparent that US capability of projecting its power the world over is diminishing as a result of 'imperial overstretch'. US authority and capacity seems to have been reduced to coerce or persuade other major and minor players whereas these same players are increasingly resorting to pursuing independent foreign policies.[18]

During this phase, the US 'New Silk Road Initiative' was also perceived with great skepticism in China. Based on its assessment of waning US influence, Beijing has serious misgivings on the US's political and economic commitment to supporting these major projects.[19] This is evident from the fact that TAPI and CASA 1000 are still more or less stalled projects.

China also appears to see little or no benefit from coordinating its efforts in the region with those of the US. This is because Beijing perceives American political and strategic maneuvers within the region as being aimed at containing its rise as demonstrated by US-India collaboration. At the same time, China is highly concerned about American efforts in the region aimed at discouraging its allies from joining the Chinese led Asian Infrastructure Investment Bank.[20] Critics argue that the US unnecessarily politicized its New Silk Road initiative by deliberately excluding important regional states like Russia, China and Iran.[21]

---

[18] Bobo Lo, *Axis of Convenience* (London: Chatam House, 2008), 24.

[19] Thomas Zimmerman, "The New Silk Roads: China, the US and the Future of Central Asia," *Centre on International Cooperation*, October, 2015, http://cic.nyu.edu/sites/default/files/zimmerman_new_silk_road_final_2.pdf (accessed April 17, 2017).

[20] Ibid.

[21] Erica Marat, "Following the New Silk Road," *The Diplomat*, October 22, 2014, http://thediplomat.com/2014/10/following-the-new-silk-road/ (accessed April 19, 2017)

At the present, the US initiative seems to be less focused on capital-intensive projects. In fact more attention has been paid to addressing the regulatory and technical challenges faced by the region. For instance, the US established a Border Management Staff College in Dushanbe, Tajikistan and a Customs Training Staff College in Bishkek, Kyrgyzstan as key projects under the New Silk Road Initiative.[22] Likewise the re-framing of the Afghanistan-Pakistan Transit Trade agreement (APTTA) and the facilitation of a Cross Border Trade Agreement between Afghanistan, Kyrgyzstan and Tajikistan are other examples of US actions taken under its New Silk Road initiative. The US State Department has emphasized the importance of establishing more efficient customs and border management systems by overcoming administrative and technological challenges, as part of its sponsored bilateral and multilateral trade arrangements across the region.[23]

However the overall scope of the US integration plan has been limited to such ad-hoc measures that have hardly brought about any real change at the ground-level. This has been attributed to the US's more geo-strategic as opposed to geo-economic focus on regional integration. The same argument is made by Eurasian expert Michal Romanovski who points out that, "the US New Silk Road Initiative is a misfire because it is poorly financed and totally Afghanistan-oriented".[24]

Russia's Eurasian Union

Russia in the immediate aftermath of the post-Soviet period pursued a policy of band-wagoning with the US led West under Boris Yeltsin. During this time, Russia was facing severe transitional issues. As a result of its ravaged economy it was in a limited position to shape and implement any effective policy towards the broader Central Asian region. After Washington's refusal of Yeltsin's fantasies of equality, Moscow

---

[22] Vladimir Fedorenko, "The New Silk Road Initiative in Central Asia," *Rethink Paper* 10 (August 2013): 9-20.

[23] "U.S. Support for the New Silk Road," *US Department of State*, 2017, https://2009-2017.state.gov/p/sca/ci/af/newsilkroad/index.htm (accessed April 23, 2017).

[24] Michał Romanowski, "Decoding Central Asia: What's Next for the US Administration?," *Diplomat*, February 28, 2017, http://thediplomat.com/2017/02/decoding-central-asia-whats-next-for-the-us-administration/ (accessed April 19, 2017).

started framing a policy of balancing the US. The thrust for shaping a multipolar world order made China the natural option for Moscow.

Likewise, the US led Western presence in Central Asia made the region Putin's first destination for an official visit in 2001 and a major focus of Russian foreign policy since then. Russia considers Central Asia as its backyard and its traditional zone of influence. At present it is asserting itself in the region through a number of bilateral and multilateral approaches such as the 'Union Treaty' with Uzbekistan signed in 2005[25], the Eurasian Economic Union, the Customs Union, the Collective Security Treaty Organization (CSTO), the SCO and the Eurasian Union.

The Eurasian Economic Community group, founded in the year 2000, comprises of Russia, Belarus, Kazakhstan and Tajikistan as a successor to the Central Asian Economic Cooperation Organization.[26] The Customs Union was announced in 2010, the CSTO in 2002, and the SCO in 2001. The current Russian plan for regional integration is to create a common economic framework within Eurasia including the CARs. This was done through the development of the Eurasian Union the formation of which was announced in 2012. The Eurasian Economic Community was dissolved on January 1, 2015 and replaced by the Eurasian Economic Union including Russia, Armenia, Belarus, Kazakhstan and Kyrgyzstan.[27]

The main building blocks of the contemporary era which the Russians call the "New International Architecture" are based on these cooperative frameworks.[28] Based on these proposals, Russia's current foreign policy objective can be termed as being dominated by this sense of 'Eurasianism'. The emergence of the Eurasian Union is strategically important for Russia to successfully compete globally.[29] Russia considers

---

[25] Shabir Ahmad Khan, "Tashkent in November 2005," *Central Asia*, no. 58 (Summer 2006): 167-176.

[26] Alexander Cooley, *Great Games, Local Rules* (New York: Oxford University Press, 2012), 59.

[27] Evgeny Vinokurov, "Eurasian Economic Union: Current State and Preliminary Results," *Russian Journal of Economics* 3, no.1 (March 2017): 54-70.

[28] Igor Torbakov, "Managing Imperial Peripheries: Russia and China in Central Asia," in *The New Great Game*, ed. Thomas Fingar (USA: Stanford University Press, 2016), 251.

[29] Ibid., 252.

itself as a Eurasian civilization that is neither Western nor Eastern. Hence, this Project of the Eurasian Union is not only important economically but is also closely related to Russia's identity. At the same time Russia desires to use the Eurasian Union as a major power bloc within the contemporary world serving as a link between Europe and Asia.[30]

The Eurasian Union Project is a reflection of Russia's prized geographical location and its bi-continental (Euro-Asian) dimension which is essential for Russia if it has to be reckoned as a major global power. This requires having a strong influence in Central Asia that would in turn help realize Russia's political, strategic and economic objectives throughout the region.[31]

Within the more recent regional context, Russia desires to achieve three primary aspects within Central Asia:

i.   A leading role with a supportive China particularly in the security realm.

ii. An absent or disinterested West.

iii. Reduced threats from Islamic fundamentalism.

Russia also recognizes that there are limitations to its power in terms of achieving these objectives. Owing to the rising strength of China and its growing leverage over the region, any frontal assault on China-Central Asia deals can be detrimental or counterproductive for Russo-Sino relations, as well as Russia's relations with the CARs. Hence, Central Asia still holds the potential of being a major source of tensions between Russia and China in the long-term.

As Stephen Blank points out, "with China eclipsing Central Asia, Russia presented its plan for the Eurasian Union as a Customs Union to inhibit Chinese economic penetration. Without these regional states who are members of the Eurasian Union, Russia cannot effectively operate as

---

[30] Vladimir Putin, "New Integration Project for Eurasia: Future in Making Today," *Izvestia*, October 3, 2011, http://www.rusemb.org.uk/press/246 (accessed April 19, 2017).
[31] Igor Torbakov, "Managing Imperial Peripheries: Russia and China in Central Asia," in *The New Great Game*, ed. Thomas Fingar (USA: Stanford University Press, 2016), 251.

a major Asian power."[32] Kazakhstan has thus become more important to Russia as it controls the southern border of this Customs Union with the other CARs. It has since become an indispensable member of the Eurasian Union attracting over $118b in Foreign Direct Investment since 1993.[33]

However Central Asia also has the potential of leading to a lasting convergence of interests between Russia and China. This is presented by the possibility of integrating the Eurasian Union with the BRI for a win-win situation for all. Framed against the backdrop of declining US influence, this partnership further carries a measure of stability and predictability in the form of offering some semblance of balance amidst the emerging multipolar world order.

Despite China's emergence as a major player in Central Asia, the region still lies at the root of the age-old strategic rivalry between Russia and the US. As established earlier in this chapter, Russia considers its role within the Central Asian region as emanating from its historic ties dating back to even before the formation of the Soviet Union. The US on the other hand explicitly rejects this notion along with Russia's right to dominate the region.[34]

This is evident from the recent pipeline politics being played out in the region. When Georgia helped the US led West diversify its energy supply by constructing more oil and gas pipelines while bypassing Russian territory (via the. Baku-Tiblisi-Cehan (BTC) pipeline), its leadership was overthrown in a coordinated attack by Russian separatists in 2008, which many claim was directly carried out by Russia.[35] Likewise, the Crimean peninsula in Ukraine which serves as

---

[32] Stephen Blank, "The Intellectual Origin of the Eurasian Union," in *Putin's Grand Strategy: Eurasia and its Discontents*, ed. S. Frederick Starr and Svante E. Cornell (Washington: Central Asia-Caucasia Institute, 2014), 14-28.

[33] "Invest in Kazakhstan, 10 Reasons to Invest in Kazakhstan," *Embassy of the Republic of Kazakhstan Qatar*, n.d., http://www.kazembqatar.com/addme/1365694309/ (accessed April 24, 2017).

[34] Bobo Lo, *Axis of Convenience* (London: Chatam House, 2008), 24.

[35] Mikhelidze Nona, "After the 2008 Russia-Georgia War: Implications for the Wider Caucasus," *International Spectator* 44, no. 3 (2009): 27-42.

one of the main conduits of Russian energy to Western Europe was directly annexed by Russia for similar reasons.[36]

However, this is not the case within the Russia-China bi-lateral framework, especially with respect to the Central Asian context. China has already built a number of oil and gas pipelines from Central Asia which are currently operational for the last few years. Yet, Russia has far from responded with the same heavy handedness as it has done in the case of Crimea and Georgia.

It is argued that there are three probable reasons for Russia's acceptance of Chinese engagement in Central Asia:

i.   This collaboration being beneficial to the CARs ultimately coincides with Russian interests of maintaining regional stability.

ii.   Russia has chosen to collaborate with China to counter the US in the region as Russia single handedly cannot do this.

iii. The eastward movement of Central Asian energy diminishes the chance of Central Asian energy competing with Russia for access to the larger European markets to the West.[37]

In all, the unipolar world since the breakup of former Soviet Union has become more anarchic, instable and dangerous. In a unipolar world system, unless a hegemon protects and respects the sovereignty of other states, it is more likely to give birth to greater dissatisfaction within the world system as states resort to expanding their capabilities and directly challenging the writ of the hegemon.[38] This appears to be the case with Sino-Russian cooperation particularly in the context of Central Asia as both countries are moving closer to jointly countering US maneuvers within the region.

---

[36] "Crimea Profile," *BBC News*, January 17, 2018, https://www.bbc.com/news/world-europe-18287223 (accessed August 10, 2018).

[37] Shabir Ahmad Khan and Saima Kyani, "Pipeline Politics in Central Asia: Paradox of Competitive/Cooperative Relations between the United States, Russia and China," *Central Asia*, no. 73 (Winter 2013): 73.

[38] Michael O. Slobodchiko, *Strategic Cooperation: Overcoming the Barriers of Global Anarchy* (UK: Lexington Books, 2013), 6.

Russia at the same time values Pakistan's geographical location and desires to assist Pakistan in its peaceful integration into the multipolar Eurasian framework being constructed by Sino-Russian strategic cooperation. Within this framework, the multimodal CPEC currently provides the best opportunity to link Eurasia with South Asia.[39]

BRI as a Corollary to the Rise of China

China being a close neighbor has made Central Asia a major focus of its foreign policy. Under its 'Go West' policy, China has naturally been inclined towards maintaining close and cordial relations with Central Asia. For instance, China resolved its border issues with three of the CARs through the Shanghai Five Mechanism in the mid-1990s by offering concessions in the form of withdrawing certain territorial claims to the region.[40] More recently, stability and development in Xinjiang remains crucial for having smooth trade and economic relations with Central Asia. As a whole, China also views Central Asia as its strategic rear and Chinese interests will obviously be well served if the region remains stable.[41] US presence in the region and the need to counter it is also a major determinant of China's policy towards Central Asia.

China being a world leading energy consumer is attracted by the region's surplus energy resources. The vast hydrocarbon reserves available at its doorstep have made Central Asia a natural choice for China. The Russian factor also remains important in China's policy towards Central Asia as Beijing first went to Moscow and then to Central Asia, i.e. China first improved its relations with Russia by recognizing Russia's historical role in the region.

Based purely on trade relations however, China has replaced Russia as the CARs major trading partner with several gas and oil pipelines leading to China becoming operational. China has so far pursued a policy

---

[39]Andrew Korybko, "Pakistan a Zipper to Eurasian Integration," *Russian Institute of Strategic Studies*, 2015, https://en.riss.ru/analysis/18882/ (accessed April 11, 2017).

[40] Shabir Ahmad Khan and Nadeem Akhtar, "China's Policy towards Central Asia since 1991: An Overview," *Central Asia*, no. 69 (Winter 2011): 65.

[41] Zhao Haasheng, "Central Asia in Chinese Strategic Thinking," in *The New Great Game: China and South and Central Asia in the Era of Reforms,* ed. Thomas Fingar (USA: Stanford University Press, 2016), 181.

of non-intervention in the region and is playing according to the local rules i.e. regime security and personal interests of the ruling class.[42] Hence, it can be rightly inferred that China has been pursuing a pragmatic and economy oriented policy towards Central Asia since 1991 and has been following that in its Belt & Road Initiative.

China also remains cautious of the previously discussed Russian objectives and maintains political neutrality amongst the CARs. As a result it also refrains from investing in any disputed projects. For instance, China announced that it won't invest in the Rogun Dam Project until and unless Tajikistan and Uzbekistan resolve their dispute over this issue.[43] Nonetheless, Central Asia remains at the core of the BRI as Central Asia provides overland connectivity to European markets which is a major precursor of the BRI's success.

The reality that Central Asia is a landlocked region however cannot be ignored. It desperately needs investment in cross-border connectivity infrastructure development which China offers.[44] China's strategic partnership with Russia is important to develop its cooperation with Central Asia. The emerging dynamics of this relationship can be surmised by the sense that Russia acts as a security provider to Central Asia while China acts as a banker to the region's development. Chinese investment in CARs has passed over $30.5 billion during 2005 to 2014 while Chinese trade volume with the region reached $50 billion in 2014.[45] This sort of relationship between Russia and China is highly valuable to the CARs and is evident in the positivity they have maintained with their giant neighbors. Furthermore, China does not intend or try to directly involve itself in the intra-regional politics of

---

[42] Alexander Cooley, *Great Games, Local Rules* (New York: Oxford University Press, 2012), 79.

[43] Vladimir Fedorenko, "*The New Silk Road Initiative in Central Asia*," *Rethink Paper* 10 (August 2013): 9-20.

[44] Lim Tai Wei, "China's Pivot to Central and South Asia," in *China's One Belt One Road*, ed. LIM Tai Wei, *Henry Chan Hong Lee and others* (London: Imperial College Press, 2016), 272.

[45] Tao Wang and Rachel Yampolsky, "Will China and Russia's Partnership in Central Asia Last?," *The Diplomat*, September 21, 2015, http://thediplomat.com/2015/09/will-china-and-russias-partnership-in-central-asia-last/ (accessed April 11, 2017).

Central Asia. Rather than opposing Russia's Eurasian Union it seeks to instead complement it through its own initiatives.[46]

China's Belt & Road Initiative (BRI)

The BRI was announced by the President of China in September 2013 with the aim of developing connectivity infrastructure to integrate the Asian, African and European continents on the basis of 'Open Regionalism'. More than 68 countries around the globe have expressed their interest in the BRI. These comprise of around 4.4 billion people, (70 percent of the global population) generating 55 percent of global GNP and holding 75 percent of known energy reserves.[47] Six corridors have been planned to be developed under the BRI framework. These include the China Pakistan Economic Corridor (CPEC), China-Mongolia-Russia corridor, the New Eurasian Land Bridge, the China-Bangladesh-India-Myanmar Corridor and the China-Indochina Corridor.

The Chinese Ministry of Foreign Affairs has declared three interconnected geo-economic and geopolitical objectives of the BRI; (i) to develop China's western interior and turn it into a frontier for opening up to the world, (ii) to enhance the status of Asia in the world through the development of connectivity infrastructure and enhanced productivity, and (iii) to form a community of shared destiny for China's relations with the wider region.[48]

The BRI can also be viewed as having two major components. These comprise of the Silk Road Economic Belt and the 21st Century Maritime Silk Road, as shown in Figure 1. The 21st Century Maritime Silk Road originates from the Eastern ports of China via the South China Sea and the Straits of Malacca, continues on through the Indian Ocean towards the Persian Gulf, and moves onwards to Europe through the Suez Canal.

---

[46] Zhao Haasheng, "Central Asia in Chinese Strategic Thinking," *The New Great Game: China and South and Central Asia in the Era of Reforms,* ed. Thomas Fingar (USA: Stanford University Press, 2016), 184.

[47] Manzoor Ahmad, "China's Role and Interests in Central Asia," *Dawn,* October 6, 2016.

[48] Lim Wen Xin, "China's Belt and Road Initiative: A Literature Review," in *China's One Belt One Road,* ed. LIM Tai Wei, Henry Chan King Lee and others (London: Imperial College Press, 2016), 115.

Figure 10.1- China's Proposed New Silk Roads. "The BRI - China's Big Bet on Soft power," *Council on Foreign Relations*, https://www.cfr.org/backgrounder/chinas-big-bet-soft-power/ (accessed April 11, 2017).

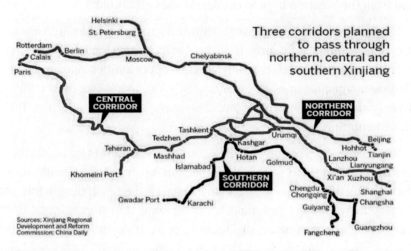

Figure 10.2- Three Routes of Silk Road Economic Belt. Cui Jia, "China studying new Silk Road rail link to Pakistan," *China Daily*, June 28, 2014, http://www.chinadaily.com.cn/business/2014-06/28/content_17621525.htm (accessed April 27, 2017).

The Silk Road Economic Belt is the overland connectivity route emanating from China via Kashgar to Central Asia and then on to Europe in two corridors. The Northern Corridor starts from Beijing and passes through northern Xinjiang, Kazakhstan and Russia up to Helsinki and Rotterdam. The Central Corridor passes from central Xinjiang to Tashkent, Tehran and then on to Paris.

The Southern Corridor which passes through southern Xingjian via the Kashgar Special Economic Zone, crosses through Pakistan to its port of Gwadar where it links with the 21st Century Maritime Silk Road depicted above. It is obvious that the Northern and Central Corridors pass through a number of countries while the Southern Corridor i.e. China-Pakistan-Economic-Corridor (CPEC) involves only Pakistan in which China has placed immense trust. These two components of the BRI fill the infrastructure gap in Asia and connect markets across the Asian, African and European continents by overland routes as well as through the Sea Lanes of Communication. The two financial institutions, Asian Infrastructure Investment Bank (AIIB) and Silk Road Fund (SRF) have been established by China to fund the BRI, allowing it to be financially free from the Western backed Bretton Woods institutions.

Some observers argue that the BRI is framed to further increase and augment Beijing's influence over the Central Asian region.[49] That it is instead aimed more at creating greater opportunities and access for Chinese companies in overseas markets.[50] Yet, the espoused benefits to these states are still evident even in these early stages of the BRI's implementation.

For instance, according to The Economist "for Chinese manufactured goods, the journey to Europe by sea takes up to 60 days while trains from South-West China to Germany only 14 days.[51] Hence, while the development of such large-scale, trans-regional, transport infrastructure will benefit the movement of Chinese goods, it would also benefit the

---

[49] Ibid., 113.
[50] Ibid.
[51] "The New Silk Road Hardly an Oasis," *The Economist*, November 18, 2014, http://www.economist.com/news/asia/21632595-kazakhstan-turns-geography-advantage-china-builds-new-silk-road-hardly-oasis (accessed April 27, 2017).

people of those regions from which these goods and services pass through. This presents a key element of the widespread benefits of China's vision for greater regional integration.

Hence, based on these arguments Central Asia still remains crucial to China's plans to provide overland connectivity to African and European markets. The region is important for China not only due to its energy resources, but also for serving as a conduit between Europe and Asia.

The Geo-Strategic Potential of CPEC vis-à-vis the BRI in South Asia

CPEC is a significant leg of the Chinese BRI initiative which starting from the Kashgar Special Economic Zone in Southern Xinjiang reaches Gwadar Sea Port in Baluchistan, via the Karakoram Highway (KKH). Based on this key route, CPEC is to play a vital role in both the sea and land based components of the BRI. This is to be achieved via overland connectivity between Kashgar and Gwadar, and maritime connectivity from Gwadar onwards. Currently, 95 percent of the goods moved between Asia and Europe takes place via Maritime routes leaving 2 to 3 percent of trade to continental routes.[52] In this context CPEC is of crucial importance as it has to play a key role in expanding Maritime trade through the Gwadar Sea Port. As a result, CPEC offers the shortest distance vis-à-vis the other six corridors to be developed under the BRI initiative. It does so by bypassing the 13000km maritime route between eastern China and the Persian Gulf (from where China imports 80 percent of its energy) to about 2500 km via Gwadar. This reduces transportation times from an average of 20 days to around 48 hours.

This would thus end the Malacca Dilemma for China, reducing its reliance on the South China Sea which has become a potential flashpoint vis-à-vis the USA and ASEAN countries. Based on the immense level of trust between Pakistan and China, CPEC would in effect also allow China to be a 'Two Oceans' power, in the same vein as the US's Western and Eastern Coasts allow it to exert its influence across both the Pacific and Atlantic respectively.

---

[52] Sebastien Peyrouse and Gael Raballand, "Central Asia: the New Silk Road Initiative's Questionable Economic Rationality," *Eurasian Geography and Economics* 56, no. 4 (2015):405-420.

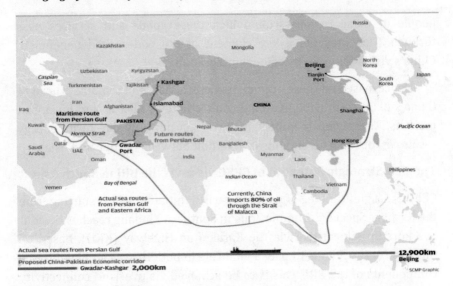

Figure 10.3- CPEC and 21ˢᵗ Century Maritime Silk Road. Shabir Ahmad Khan, "China-Pakistan Economic Corridor (CPEC) in a Multipolar World", in *Pak-Army 'Green Book'* 2015 (Rawalpindi: GHQ, September 2016), 19.

According to an Indian source, Chinese strategic interests in Central Asia and Afghanistan revolve around the BRI of which CPEC is a subsidiary project in the context of South Asia.[53] China has been developing the Silk Road high-speed railway linking the CARs with Xinjiang, ultimately linking Gwadar with the CARs via Kashgar. CPEC provides an essential outlet to the landlocked regions of Central Asia and Western China towards the Indian Ocean and beyond. This forms one of the key outcomes of how Pak-China strategic cooperation centered at Gwadar has the potential to alter the entire regional geo-strategic configuration.

CPEC would thus be instrumental in accelerating the emergence of the new centers of power within Asia that were discussed in the earlier sections of this chapter. Surrounded by resource laden countries on one side and resource deficit states on the other, CPEC can serve as a key supply chain for these emerging markets. Each region's growth path is a

---

[53] Vikram Sood, "The New Great Game: An All Asian Game?," *Observer Research Foundation*, April 6, 2017, http://www.orfonline.org/expert-speaks/new-great-game-all-asian/ (accessed April 27, 2017).

function of many factors unique to it and the resource endowment factor cannot be overlooked in the case of Central Asia. The resource rich countries of Central Asia can benefit from their edge in natural resource endowment by linking efficiently to markets through overland connectivity as well as through Sea Lanes of Communication. Undoubtedly, both the inter, and extra-regional connectivity that CPEC offers to Central Asia could greatly expedite their economic rise.

India too acknowledges the geographic significance and future potential of Pakistan based on this evolving framework. According to M.K. Bhadrakumar, "Pakistan, due to its strategic location, is a pivotal state which impacts the regions of Central Asia and South Asia".[54] He acknowledges the importance of how CPEC would end the Malacca Dilemma for China with Gwadar providing a platform for China to protect its interests in the Indian Ocean.

This does not bode well for India's US backed domination of the Indian Ocean though. Similarly, both Japan and Australia too have expressed their reservations against China's increasing presence along key maritime routes passing through the Indian Ocean. The formation of this quadrilateral alliance referred to as the Quad, thus presents a key challenge for Pak-China cooperation particularly with respect to Gwadar.[55]

Amidst continuing instability in Afghanistan, CPEC serves as a strategically viable alternative to linking Pakistan with Central Asia. In contrast, the strategic and economic implications of the tri-partite agreement of India-Iran-Afghanistan remain limited as neither state is a major player in the New Great Game for influence in Central Asia.[56] As is, India's current plans to marginalize or sideline Pakistan in its attempts to access Central Asia has made India uncompetitive in the Central Asian

---

[54] M.K. Bhadrakumar, "Pakistan, China, Iran and the Remaking of Regional Security," *Pakistan Defence,* April 18, 2015, https://defence.pk/pdf/threads/pakistan-china-iranand-the-remaking-of-regional-security.371759/ (accessed April 19, 2017).

[55] Gurmeet Kanwal, "Pakistan's Gwadar Port: A New Naval Base in China's String of Pearls in the Indo-Pacific," *CSIS,* April 2, 2018, www.csis.org/analysis/pakistans-gwadar-port-new-naval-base-chinas-string-pearls-indo-pacific (accessed October 23, 2018).

[56] Munir Akram, "The New Great Game," *Dawn,* June 12, 2016, https://www.dawn.com/news/1264242 (accessed October 23, 2018).

markets vis-à-vis China and other players like Turkey. It is only CPEC that currently provides the best opportunity to Central Asia for greater regional integration as the converging interests of Russia, Pakistan and China shape a new potential power troika that is bonded by the changing politico-economic paradigm across the wider region.[57]

The regions of Central and South Asia are the least integrated in the world. The economic weaknesses of regional countries owes in large part to this lack of inter, intra and extra-regional integration mainly due to poor cross-border connectivity infrastructure. These regions face multiple and almost identical economic, political and security issues. CPEC as part of the BRI offers a model of integration that is based on open regionalism in contrast to closed regionalism which favors more protectionist measures against non-member or non-regional states. This in turn presents a sectorial project based approach to regional integration where any regional or extra regional state can join a particular bi-lateral, tri-lateral or multilateral arrangement in accordance with its own priorities. Since developing regional countries lack the capacity to develop such cross-border infrastructure on their own, China while taking the lead has put forth a grand vision, based on which it is developing the required cross-border connectivity infrastructure in the region.

Conclusion – Building on the Open Regionalism of the BRI

Central Asia is undergoing significant geo-strategic and geo-economic changes as a consequence of the integration plans of the major powers i.e. Russia, China and the US. Russia is better prepared to assert itself in its traditional sphere of influence after the Crimean episode, while Chinese influence is growing and the US more or less retreats from the region. Russia is the major player in the hard security realm, having close defense ties particularly under the CSTO. In the post Crimea period, Russia is looking East towards Asia and particularly China for strategic and economic cooperation. Thus, Central Asia can be viewed as both a source of tension as well as a source of lasting convergence of interests

---

[57] Sabena Siddiqi, "Reconnecting Central Asia," *Katehon*, February 2, 2017, http://katehon.com/article/reconnecting-central-asia (accessed April 27, 2017).

between Russia and China depending upon how Russia and China manage their relations vis-à-vis the region.

The US New Silk Road initiative has hardly materialized on the ground. The anomalies of Eurasian Union and BRI need to be addressed and can be addressed on a project/sectorial basis. The Eurasian Union seems to evoke a kind of closed regionalism with protectionist measures in form of uniform tariffs against non-member states. The BRI and CPEC instead offer greater regional integration based on the tenets of open regionalism. In this case, the Eurasian Union can serve as an institutional check on Chinese goods moving through and to the Central Asian members of the Eurasian Union. Likewise, the Eurasian Union has been planned to be governed by supra-national institutions while the BRI and CPEC is based on the principles of open regionalism where governance of the project is a joint responsibility of the signatory groups pertaining to specific projects. Open regionalism in fact integrates markets with flexible relations to address the weaknesses of closed regionalism. Open regionalism is outward oriented, where a country can join different regional arrangements simultaneously and need not surrender its sovereignty.

It is thus in this context that CPEC through its combination of maritime and land routes, is key to promoting the open regionalism enshrined within the overall vision of the BRI. Its implications for the Central Asian Republics and the New Great Game are immense as it offers the most pragmatic and economic solution to the region's current geo-strategic challenges. While the multi-polar dynamics of the international system have once again led to diverging US, Chinese and Russian interests in Central Asia, the growing success of the BRI backed by the world's second largest economy has tipped this balance quite considerably in China's favor. Amidst declining US influence, and growing convergence on issues between Russia and China, the BRI remains well poised to fulfill its grand vision of regional connectivity based on the principles of openness, non-interference and economic competitiveness.

This emphasis on openness thus perhaps offers the most interesting development to have been borne out of a region, which has historically remained as a site of contestation between world powers for centuries.

Chapter 11: Maximizing the Regional Potential of CPEC

Lt. Gen (R) Naeem Khalid Lodhi* & Brig (R) Abdul Rehman Bilal**

Introduction

In this chapter, it has been argued that CPEC while being a potential game changer for Pakistan, and the region beyond would require additional steps for the realization of its full potential. Prudent financial modeling, overcoming political impediments and controlling strategic fall outs are of utmost importance to ensuring its success. Within this context, CPEC's political, economic and strategic impact on the region has been dealt with in detail in this chapter. Based on these broad ranging implications, a series of recommendations are presented focusing on how to better prepare the people of Pakistan, its society and state to optimize this great opportunity from a security perspective.

As has been presented in detail throughout this book, CPEC is the flagship project of the Belt and Road Initiative (BRI) with respect to the South Asian region. It binds China and Pakistan together in a strong enduring relationship at a time when free trade and globalism is being challenged by the forces of discrimination and protectionism elsewhere. Indeed, a growing number of ultra-nationalists in the West have vitiated the global atmosphere, with hard-line and hawkish leaders presently gaining ground across the major powers. As political forces of the far right currently make headway in Europe, NATO members are still pondering over the implications of spending not even 2% of their GDP on

---

* Lt. Gen (R) Naeem Khalid Lodhi is the Former Defense Secretary of Pakistan.
** Brig (R) Abdul Rehman Bilal is the former Rector of Fauji Foundation University, Islamabad.

defence.[1] Simultaneously, the US, India, Australia and Japan under the new quadrilateral framework have allied together in a bid to contain the economic rise of China. All of this is happening during a time when Afghanistan is still struggling to regain stability.

Within this context it is important to consider that CPEC, based on its great vision has a number of important regional and global geostrategic implications that cannot be ignored. While many regional and global powers view CPEC as a genuine opportunity for economic growth, there are others that are highly apprehensive of its motives. Meanwhile the Pakistani narrative, that has termed it as a game changer for the region, has drawn considerable flak from its opponents who are highly apprehensive of the security implications of this initiative.[2]

The Belt and Road Initiative (BRI) – A Brief Recap

The BRI is in its essence a Chinese concept for the region which is intended to promote a global environment in which trade flourishes bringing prosperity to all. There is no doubt that it visualizes an era of peace and prosperity for the world with a win-win situation for all. However, an incisive analysis will reveal that it is infrastructure that forms the most salient features of the Belt & Road Initiative. While the BRI does envision connectivity across multiple levels and sectors i.e. physical/geographical connectivity, IT connectivity through high speed integrated communications networks, supply chain connectivity based on energy and fuel supply lines, industrial connectivity via SEZs and FTAs and people to people connectivity aimed at greater socio-cultural integration; it aims to achieve these objectives primarily through the development of large-scale infrastructure.

---

[1] "NATO Countries are Not Spending Enough on Defence, the Alliance's Chief Says," *The Independent*, http://www.independent.co.uk/news/uk/politics/nato-jens-stoltenberg-military-spending-gdp-target-countries-not-enough-a7384236.html (accessed October 17, 2017).
[2] Muzaffar Hussain, "China Pakistan Economic Corridor (CPEC): Challenges and the Way Forward,"
Naval Postgraduate School Monterey, California, June 2017,
https://calhoun.nps.edu/bitstream/handle/10945/55626/17Jun_Hussain_Muzaffar.pdf?sequence=1 (accessed October 17, 2017).

This infrastructure is in turn honeycombed with smart business deals and partnerships that will lend strength to the entire initiative. Its greatest attraction is currently for the lesser developed countries that lack the requisite capital for progress and development. China has become the world's manufacturing engine of growth and a role-model for lesser developed countries. It has accumulated surplus reserves exceeding $3.5 trillion.[3] China believes that this money has to be wisely invested and is thus planning and implementing a large number of projects in pursuit of this goal. Besides internal growth, China requires materials as well as markets for its fast growing economy, all while seeking the most competitive costs for its manufactured goods and services. For realizing the latter purpose, China is investing heavily across the world in an unprecedented manner.

Presently, there has been a production glut of Chinese commodities, with a clear understanding that promoting growth abroad would increase foreign demand for Chinese goods. Furthermore, infrastructural linkages would provide easier access to raw materials and cheaper labor for Chinese offshore companies. The 'Belt' in essence also symbolizes the importance of sea trade within the Chinese policy framework. One cannot deny the fact that the proposed sea ports along the BRI are of utmost importance when it comes to redefining trade and economics at the international level. Since new trends in shipbuilding aim at bigger and cheaper ships of EEE (economy, energy efficient, eco-friendly) category, deep sea ports are required. The world is on the threshold of the next generation of sea trade with EEE category. This includes ships with the capacity to carry 18000 or more twenty-foot equivalent unit (TEUs) containers.[4] For this purpose, China is pursuing a policy wherein it visualizes deep sea ports at locations suitable for hinterland connectivity or transit in Asia, Europe and Africa.

---

[3] "Government Productivity Unlocking the $3.5 Trillion Opportunity," *McKinsey Center for Government*, April 2017, http://www.astrid-online.it/static/upload/f140/f140e4621680e1977b08ffe0945e5e9f.pdf (accessed October 17, 2017).

[4] "Engine Selection for Very Large Container Vessels," *Winterthur Gas & Diesel Ltd.*, September 2, 2016, 2https://www.wingd.com/media/1756/wingdpaper_engine_selection_for_very_large_container_vessels_201609.pdf (accessed October 17, 2017).

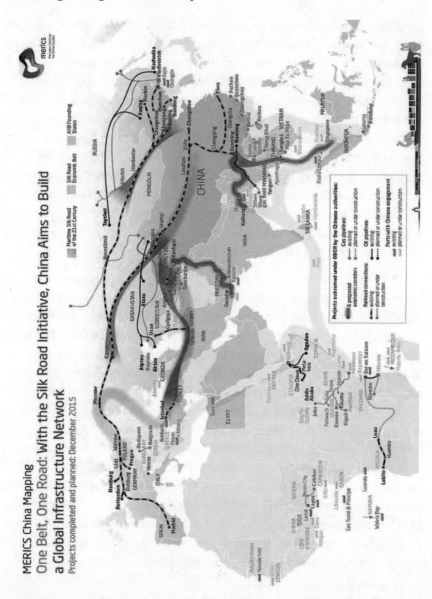

Figure 11.1- MERICS C. "The One Belt One Road," *Agricultural Research*, https://
par.com.pk/news/cpec-to-be-featured-in-one-belt-one-road-obor-summit
(accessed October 17, 2017).

Furthermore, the BRI also visualizes bold projects aimed at expanding the world's shipping and maritime waterways such as the Suez Canal in Egypt. China has also signed an MOU with the Thai Government to construct a canal through the Kra Isthmus in Thailand as a shortcut to the Strait of Malacca.[5]

With such dreams and resolute execution, the writing on the wall is clear. The US has been replaced by China as the global sponsor for development.

CPEC as the South Asian Component of the BRI

China is no longer considered as an Asian continental power with a Pacific coastal navy. With the growth of Chinese maritime trade, the Chinese Navy is also undergoing rapid expansion and modernization.[6] CPEC has provided a trade outlet to China on the Indian Ocean with strong security overtones. Resultantly, China is no longer merely a low-technology hinterland power, crouched on the Western Pacific shores. Nor is it hedged in by a chain of strong economic pro-US ramparts including Japan, South Korea, Taiwan, Philippines, Australia and New Zealand. China is now actively involved in Indian Ocean trade. Indeed, Gwadar is being planned as an Indian Ocean Rim outlet of goods for the Middle East and East Africa.

In contrast to the regional maritime overview, a brief glimpse of the Eurasian hinterland picture reveals that China and Southeastern Europe are connected to Mainland Europe through the Eurasian land bridge. China also has access to the Mediterranean Sea through the Rim-Land route which passes through or around the Caspian Sea. Another prong of its western routes runs south towards Gwadar and Chabahar. Chinese

---

[5] Rhea Menon, "Thailand's Kra Canal: China's Way around the Malacca Strait," *The Diplomat*, April 6, 2018, https://thediplomat.com/2018/04/thailands-kra-canal-chinas-way-around-the-malacca-strait/ (accessed December 05, 2018).

[6] Ronal O' Rourke, "China Naval Modernization: Implications for US Navy Capabilities: Background and Issues for Congress," *Congressional Research Service*, August 1, 2018, https://www.everycrsreport.com/files/20180801_RL33153_1036f8edb5271519e9bd80690adce95f6e5bcbc6.pdf (accessed December 5, 2018).

use of the latter port however is inhibited by an all pervasive Indian presence.

In this continental setting, Pakistan is the only country currently providing a friendly, single window operation to China. The Central Asian Republics (CARs) are still in the process of resolving their internal and international problems, hence China's economic assistance can be of great value in this regard. Presently, in the southern neighborhood, the Kabul government is maintaining its partial but weak writ due to large infusions of the coalition's development and military aid. In view of emerging symptoms of western donor fatigue,[7] Chinese influence will continue to increase. In realpolitik terms, this may be tenaciously contested by India through covert and overt means.

The establishment of CPEC is thus not only an economic game changer, but a geostrategic coup that has demolished the last vestiges of the traditional Cold War concepts of containing China. It transcends simple trade connectivity and lays down the basis for mutually beneficial relations between unequal powers resulting in win-win situations.[8] CPEC is the model being closely watched by the world for the solution of Pakistan's economic problems. A large number of countries want to be associated with it, with the extent of inclusion being open to discussion. This may lead to a pride and prejudice situation where success of the CPEC will be a gratifying moment for the well-wishers and perceived as a snub by its detractors.

Geography suggests that a significant proportion of trade extending from the Arctic Ocean in the North, and the regions between the Volga in the West and the Yenisey River to the east will be attracted to Gwadar. What could not be achieved by the Soviet invasion of Afghanistan will be possible now through economic development. There could not be a

---

[7] Tamim Asey, "The other Drawdown -Why Donor Fatigue is Threatening to Derail Afghanistan," *Foreign Policy*, November 10, 2014, http://foreignpolicy.com/2014/11/10/the-other-drawdown-why-donor-fatigue-is-threatening-to-derail-afghanistan/ (accessed October 17, 2017).

[8] Daniel S. Markey and James West, "Behind China's Gambit in Pakistan," *Council on Foreign Relations (CFR)*, May 12, 2016, https://www.cfr.org/expert-brief/behind-chinas-gambit-pakistan (accessed October 17, 2017).

better application of the words of Sun Tzu, the great Chinese military sage who said that 'the supreme art of war lies in victory without bloodshed'. In this environment, for how long can shrinking pockets of Kabul based US dominance survive amidst a geopolitical sea of change is anyone's guess.

All of these developments present a highly interesting scenario as to the possible trajectory of geo-politics within the South Asian and surrounding regions. For instance, due to the close Sino-Pakistan nexus, Russia may feel a strong pull towards Gwadar enabling it to realize those trade aims that could not be achieved by the Soviet invasion of Afghanistan. Therein also lies the potential of linking a geographically isolated Afghanistan with the rest of the world. The Central Asian Republics are yearning for a sniff of the sea. Iran, too, requires a transit corridor to China for its hydrocarbons. In addition, the Gulf too can be linked with China through Pakistan. Thus, the entire Middle Eastern and East African region would be able to gain considerably from CPEC. This perhaps could finally enable the visualized conflict-free areas of Asia and Africa to make progress, and close the gap with the West which continues to suffer from domestic demographic decline. On the wider plane, it will enable China and its allies to emerge on the global scene as more powerful states.

The following section presents these scenarios in greater detail with respect to the potential benefits to be reaped by each of these countries.

What Would a 'Win-Win' Scenario for the Region Look Like?

Tajikistan

The country which is perhaps most keenly looking forward to the success of this venture is Tajikistan.[9] It is a landlocked state with high mountains and limited resources. After acquiring independence, the ethnic Russians realized that without Moscow's financial infusions, there would be a rapid decline in living standards. On the other hand, the rapid decline of Russia's population called for immigration. Due to civil war,

[9] Mir Sherbaz Khetran, "PM Nawaz Sharif's Visit to Tajikistan: Prospects of Cooperation," *Institute of Strategic Studies Islamabad*, July 20, 2017, http://issi.org.pk/wp-content/uploads/2017/07/IB_Khetran_dated_20-7-2017.pdf (accessed October 17, 2017).

ethnic Russians left Tajikistan rapidly. In addition, a large number of Tajik people also left their country to seek employment in Russia by legal as well as illegal means. Presently, more than one million Tajiks work in Russia.[10] This amounts to more than ten percent of Tajikistan's population.

Figure 11.2- Political Map of the Caucasus and Central Asia. "Political Map of the Caucasus and Central Asia," *CIA*, n.d., https://commons.wikimedia.org/wiki/File:Caucasus_central_asia_political_map_2 000.jpg (accessed October 17, 2017).

Framed against this scenario, access to the sea would enable Tajikistan to progress more rapidly and explore new options for the prosperity of its people. Presently, the 108th Russian Motorized Division is based there along with a sizable Indian presence at the Farkhor and Ayni Air Bases. However, Tajikistan's relations with Pakistan are cordial. China has now connected Tajikistan with the CPEC through the Kolma Pass. At present limited trade is taking place between Tajikistan and Pakistan via the Karakoram Highway as a result of this newly developed pass. Going ahead Tajikistan has expressed its desire to further expand

---

[10] Mikhail Denisenko, "Migration to Russia and the Current Economic Crisis," *E-International Relations*, May 5, 2017, http://www.e-ir.info/2017/05/05/migration-to-russia-and-the-current-economic-crisis/ (accessed October 17, 2017).

these links with Pakistan through the Ishkashem – Dorah Pass - Chitral route and through the Bandar Sher Khan–Kunduz-Salang Tunnel–Kabul–Torkhum route.

Kyrgyzstan
Kyrgyzstan is a land locked mountainous country located between Tajikistan, Uzbekistan, Kazakhstan and China. It has a population of 6 million with limited opportunities.[11] Despite being a tourist paradise, it has not fully lived up to its potential due to pervading political instability. On the domestic front, there have recently been bloody riots with clashes between the ethnic Uzbek and Kyrgyz populations in the Osh and Jalalabad regions of the Ferghana Valley. There has also been widespread discontent in the country which has been further attributed to the 2005 Tulip Revolution and a series of subsequent changes.[12]

CPEC provides Kyrgyzstan with the ideal economic opportunity to escape from this vicious cycle of violence. Presently, China is linked with Kyrgyzstan via the Irkeshtum and the Torugart Passes. It is estimated that 70 percent of its trade is with China and the remainder with Russia. Kyrgyzstan's trade with Pakistan however is quite limited at the present, with trade more or less limited to a small portion of the pharmaceutical industry.

Kazakhstan
Kazakhstan is the territorial giant amongst the Central Asian Republics. As part of its inherited legacy from the Soviet Union, the Baikanoor Cosmodrome and the Semipalatinsk nuclear testing ground both fall under Kazakh territory. It had numerous ICBMs deployed in silos on its territory near Karaganda which were later shifted to Russia.[13] It has large agricultural resources, considerable mineral wealth, sizeable hydrocarbon resources and a 22.8 percent ethnic Russian population

---

[11] "An Overview of the World Bank's Work in the Kyrgyz Republic," *The World Bank in the Kyrgyz Republic Country Snapshot*, April 2017, http://pubdocs.worldbank.org/en/835161493272763879/Kyrgyz-Republic-Snapshot-April-2017.pdf (accessed October 17, 2017).
[12] Alexander Cooley, "Kyrgyzstan on the Brink," *Current History* 109, no. 729 (October 2010): 301-307.
[13] Robert S Norris & William M. Arkin, "Russian (C.I.S.) Strategic Nuclear Forces: End of 1994," *Bulletin of the Atomic Scientists* 51, no. 2 (March 1995): 78-79.

that binds it closely with Russia.[14] A section of the Trans-Siberian Railway also passes through northern Kazakhstan. Its vast spread from the Eurasian steppes in the north, the Caspian Sea in the southwest and China to the east, has positioned it as a key geo-strategic transit point.

The main Chinese border crossing point is at Khorgas. It has excellent highways and railways along with an efficiently operated crane service which can shift containers from Chinese trains to the different gauge Russian trains. China has planned to develop an industrial zone in the area. There is a lot of excitement that Khorgas is going to emerge as a Eurasian land hub for trade.[15] Chinese trains to Iran and Afghanistan have already passed through Khorgas. Its 2,729 feet height ensures that it remains permanently open. CPEC will enable Kazakhstan to diversify its trade relations even more by further building on the above initiatives.

Turkmenistan
Turkmenistan is a vast desert country endowed with tremendous hydrocarbon wealth.[16] It has close relations with the US and Turkey. However, it also maintains strong ties with the Russian energy giant, Gazprom.[17]

Its capital Ashgabat has also served as an important center for the Northern Distribution Network (NDN) supplying coalition forces based in Afghanistan. When Pakistan had stopped the flow of the coalition's supply and logistics through its territories after the American bombing of Salala Post, it was Ashgabat that had served as an alternate route.

At present, there are two railway routes directly linking Turkmenistan with Afghanistan up to Turghundi and Aqeena. However, there is no rail link between Turkmenistan and Gwadar, which would

[14] Muhammad Asif Noor & Farhat Asif, "20 Years of Diplomatic Relations between Kazakhstan & Pakistan," *Diplomatic Insight*, 2012, http://ipd.org.pk/wp-content/uploads/Book-Kazakhstan-Pakistan-20-Years-of-Diplomatic-Relations.-Final.pdf (accessed October 17, 2017).

[15] Richard Pomfret, "Trade and Transport in Central Asia," *Global Journal of Emerging Market Economies* 2, no. 3 (2010): 237-256.

[16] Erika Weinthal and Pauline Jones Luong, "Energy Wealth and Tax Reform in Russia and Kazakhstan," *Resources Policy* 27, no. 4 (2001): 215-223.

[17] Oleh Havrylyshyn, "Economic Dependence on Russia," in *the Political Economy of Independent Ukraine* (Palgrave Macmillan: UK, 2017), 223-247.

have to pass through Afghanistan. There is a road link to Gwadar port that passes through the Chaman border crossing between Afghanistan and Pakistan. However, there is still no road linking Farah in Western Afghanistan with Nokundi in Baluchistan, to complete this proposed route between Turkmenistan and Pakistan via Afghanistan. The governments of Pakistan as well as Turkmenistan are keen to establish both road and rail links along this route including a gas pipeline.[18]

Uzbekistan
Uzbekistan is a centrally located country within the region featuring an elongated northwest-southeast layout. It shares a common border with all the other Central Asian countries located east of the Caspian Sea.[19] It is also the most powerful amongst these countries.

Uzbekistan is extremely important for the North-South connectivity of the region.[20] The city of Termez, located on the Amu Darya serves as one of the key entry points for Central Asia, which could also serve as a potential transport hub linking CPEC with the rest of the Central Asian region. The railway track passing through the bridge on the Amu Darya has been extended southward from the Hairatan border crossing between Afghanistan and Uzbekistan up to Mazar-e-Sharif. If linked with the Torkhum border crossing in Pakistan, it can provide a very useful offshoot of CPEC linking together Pakistan and Central Asia. This could further help in alleviating tensions between Uzbekistan and its neighbors promoting greater regional cooperation and connectivity.

Afghanistan
Afghanistan being a landlocked country shares a 1500 mile long border with Pakistan. Capitalizing on its long history and common heritage with Pakistan it has an opportunity to reap early fruits from the entire CPEC

---

[18] Shazia Mehmood Khan, "Turkmenistan-Pakistan Bilateral Relations: From Strength to Strength," *Defence Journal* 20, no. 10 (2017): 37.
[19] Edward Allworth, "Uzbekistan," *Encyclopedia Britannica*, n.d., https://www.britannica.com/place/Uzbekistan (accessed October 17, 2017).
[20] "Ministerial Conference on Transport Third session, Strengthening South Asia –Central Asia connectivity," *UNESCAP*, December 2016, 2-10, http://www.unescap.org/sites/default/files/Strengthening%20Connectivity%20South%20Asia%20new%20note.pdf (accessed October 17, 2017).

enterprise.[21] Besides the Chaman and Torkham crossing points, numerous other crossing points like the Dorah Pass, the Nawa Pass, Wana, Kamber Ali Karez, Noshki and many other routes along the West link it with Pakistan.

While Afghanistan's eastern and central regions can continue to benefit from Karachi, its Southern and Western regions are better poised to be linked via Gwadar. The construction of a road network south of Farah can be immensely useful not just for the people of Afghanistan but also for Turkmenistan, Kazakhstan and Russia.[22] The ensuing mercantile activity would facilitate the funneling of trade from the adjoining Eurasian landmass through Afghanistan on to Gwadar, Pakistan. With two thirds of the Pakhtun population living in Pakistan and a third in Afghanistan, there is hope that natural affinity would defeat Indian designs of driving a wedge between the two brotherly countries.[23]

Iran

Iran would also greatly benefit from CPEC if it were to link its infrastructure with China via Pakistan. This holds particular importance when considering the potential of a robust transport corridor for the supply of oil and gas.

However, the current geo-political scenario within the South Asian region has been more or less characterized by India attempting to exclude Pakistan in the South Asian region's proposed integration with the Persian Gulf.[24] This is evident from the numerous MOUs India has

---

[21] Zahid Hussain, "Sources of Tension in Afghanistan and Pakistan: A Regional Perspective," *CIDOB Policy Research Project*, December, 2011, https://www.cidob.org/en/publications/publication_series/stap_rp/policy_research_papers/sourc es_of_tension_in_afghanistan_and_pakistan_a_regional_perspective (accessed October 17, 2017).

[22] Khalid Manzoor Butt &Anam Abid Butt, "Impact of CPEC on Regional and Extra-regional Actors," *Journal of Political Science* 33 (2015): 23-44.

[23] "Afghanistan: The Challenge of Relations with Pakistan," *Parliamentary Information and Research Service Publication*, January 9, 2008, https://lop.parl.ca/content/lop/ResearchPublications/prb0733-e.pdf (accessed October 17, 2017).

[24] Robert M. Hathaway, "Asia Program Special Report: The Strategic Partnership between India and Iran," *Woodrow Wilson International Center for Scholars*, April 1, 2004, https://www.wilsoncenter.org/sites/default/files/asia_rpt_120rev_0.pdf (accessed October 17, 2017).

recently signed with Iran for the development of the Chabahar port along with its accompanying hinterland connectivity infrastructure.[25] The Indian funded construction of the road network linking the Zaranj border crossing between Afghanistan and Iran is aimed at creating a similar link between the Iranian Chabahar port and the rest of Central Asia. This competing route for providing landlocked Central Asia with a link to Maritime Trade via the Indian Ocean is widely believed to be the reason why India is fanning separatist sentiment in Pakistani Balochistan; thus competing directly with the CPEC funded Gwadar port.[26]

Nepal

Nepal is a relatively small landlocked Himalayan country dependent upon India for its sea trade.[27] If its road infrastructure is connected with Pakistan through China, it would have a viable alternative to supplement its links to the sea. It would also help facilitate Pak-Nepal trade, promote tourism and add a new color to the CPEC initiative.

Oman

Oman can also gain immensely from CPEC based on its proximity to Gwadar. The ports of Muscat, Sur and Rasul Had can greatly benefit from ferry services while also serving as major trade hubs for Chinese goods shipped to and from the Gulf region. Presently, Oman is well-connected with other GCC countries through road networks while extensive rail links are also being developed.[28] The close affinity between the Omani

---

[25] Rick Rowden, "Understanding Foreign Relations between India and Iran," *Sheffield Political Economy Research Institute,* July 12, 2017, http://speri.dept.shef.ac.uk/2017/07/12/understanding-foreign-relations-between-india-and-iran/ (accessed October 17, 2017).

[26] Muhammad Khurshid Khan, Asma Sana and Afifa Kiran, "Balochistan Unrest Internal and External Dimensions," *NDU Journal (2012)*: 104.

[27] Y P Pant, "Nepal-India Trade Relations some Recent Trends," *Economic Weekly* 14, no. 8 (February 1962): 161.

[28] Wang Jian, "One Belt One Road: A Vision for the Future of China-Middle East Relations," *Al Jazeera Centre for Studies,* May 9, 2017, http://studies.aljazeera.net/mritems/Documents/2017/5/10/9034672c6c8945d1b52014fe6dbcb7c4_100.pdf (accessed October 17, 2017).

and Gwadari populations add further credence to the possibility of successfully integrating CPEC with the Middle East and Gulf regions.[29]

Dubai

Initially, there existed a belief that Gwadar was in competition with Dubai.[30] Actually, both ports are complementary to each other in the sense that while Dubai primarily serves the Gulf region, Gwadar is more geared toward serving the northern Asian hinterland and China.[31] The first few months of commissioning of Gwadar have proved that there is no clash of interests between the two sister ports. Indeed, a healthy trade relationship can easily be developed between these two ports to the mutual benefit of all parties.[32] In addition, Arab oil pipelines can pump oil through CPEC to China. In view of decreasing American dependence on imported oil and an increase in Chinese consumption, futuristic diplomacy suggests a cordial relationship between the 'Belt' Gulf Arabs and CPEC for regional prosperity and stability.

India

India wants that Pakistan should allow its trade through the Wagah border to pass through Pakistan onwards to the Afghan border.[33] This would open a key Indian trade route with Central Asia and Russia. However, Pakistan has linked such concessions with the resolution of the Kashmir issue. Additionally, the transit of goods through Pakistan is considered a major security hazard within the current state of tensions in the region.

---

[29] Sehar Kamran, "Pak-Gulf Defense and Security Cooperation," *Center for Pakistan and Gulf Studies*, January 2013, 15, http://cpakgulf.org/documents/Pak-Gulf-Security-Ties-final.pdf (accessed October 17, 2017).

[30] Naveed Ahmad, "Gwadar, Chabahar and Dubai," *Express Tribune*, March 14, 2017, https://tribune.com.pk/story/1354422/gwadar-chabahar-dubai/ (accessed October 17, 2017).

[31] Dr. Shabir Ahmad Khan, "Geo-Economic Imperatives of Gwadar Sea Port and Kashgar Economic Zone for Pakistan and China," *IPRI Journal* 13, no. 2 (Summer 2013): 87-100.

[32] Ashis Biswas, "Can Pakistan Handle CPEC Impact?," *Dhaka Tribune*, October 7, 2017, http://www.dhakatribune.com/world/south-asia/2017/10/07/can-pakistan-handle-cpec-impact/ (accessed October 17, 2017).

[33] Elke Grawert, Rabia Nusrat & Zulfiqar Ali Shah, "Afghanistan's Cross-border Trade with Pakistan and Iran and the Responsibility for Conflict-Sensitive Employment," *BICC Working Paper- Bonn International Center for Conversion* 4 (September 2017): 1-48.

It is thus mainly due to these reasons that India is investing in Chabahar port to bypass Pakistan and isolate it by developing a direct route to Afghanistan via Iran.[34] With the emerging of the quadrilateral alliance between the US, India, Japan and Australia, India may be further emboldened to rope in other regional actors in an attempt to limit the impacts of CPEC as well as growing Chinese influence. For this purpose, it could further escalate tensions based on the disputed status of Kashmir and Indian sponsored violence in Baluchistan as major weaknesses in CPEC.

However, the initiation of such economic warfare by India can open a Pandora's Box that can in turn risk a major conflagration with China. While communal fanaticism permeating the incumbent Indian government may goad on its current political helmsmen along a reckless path, it is hoped that more pragmatic and sane voices prevail in order to deescalate such rising tensions.

In addition, Western interests in the region in general, and the Gulf in particular would further help in limiting such a move that could impede the smooth outflow of oil from the region. Given the present and projected trends, China, Pakistan, the Middle East's oil exporting countries and its trade partners are all highly reliant on regional stability. However, the recent US sponsored Indo-pacific quadrilateral alliance comprising of India, Japan and Australia are likely to further coalesce together on the strategic plane without prejudice to the free flow of oil from the Gulf.

Maximizing CPEC to its Full Geographic Potential

Moving on from the broader regional challenges and opportunities, it is also worth discussing the more specific geographical challenges currently limiting the full potential of this initiative. Specifically with regard to the location of the Pakistan-China Border crossing, the high-altitude and mountainous terrain of the Karakorams has presented its own list of technical engineering challenges that have largely been overcome by both countries. However, these challenges may need to be

---

[34] NK Bhatia, "India, Chabahar, and the Changing Regional Dynamics," *CLAWS Journal* (Winter 2016): 103.

revisited if present road links were to be expanded to provide alternative routes and to later directly link these areas with the Central Asian Republics and Russia.[35]

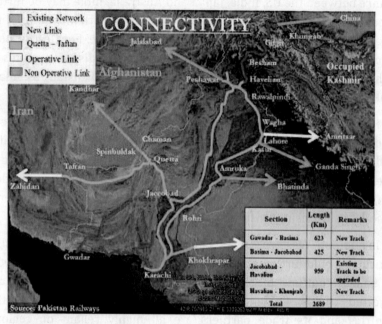

Figure 11.3- Proposed Routes of CPEC. "Proposed Routes of CPEC," *Pakistan Railways,* https://www.google.com/search?q=Proposed+Routes+of+CPEC+by+pakistan+railway&rlz=1C1CHBD_enPK813PK813&source=lnms&tbm=isch&sa=X&ved=0ahUKEwjTtPCUwLrgAhVCXhoKHZgMAT0Q_AUIDigB&biw=1366&bih=625#imgrc=0Z52ChSu6kdYfM (accessed October 17, 2017).

For instance, at present there are highly limited alternatives to the Khunjerab – Gilgit route. The Mintaka Pass provides an excellent secondary route where a well-constructed road can link Mintaka with Khudabadon via the Karakoram Highway. In addition, a three kilometer long tunnel near Misgar can further link this route with the Chapursan Valley. An additional tunnel of about 8.5 kilometers near Chilinji Pass can link this area with Chilinji Glacier and further south with Gilgit and

---

[35] Afzal Ali Shigri, "An Alternate Route for CPEC," *Dawn,* August 23, 2016, https://www.dawn.com/news/1279254 (accessed October 17, 2017).

Chitral through Ishkoman Valley which further opens into Ghizar Valley. An additional, northern tourist route and bypass can further branch off the north and link it with Karambar Pass, Baroghil Pass and Mastuj. This would in turn directly link the main CPEC route with Afghanistan and Tajikistan via Pakistan's Northern territories. It would also allow the Karakoram Highway's current length to be shortened and the areas of Mansehra – Abbotabbad hills and conurbations bypassed by linking Thakot Bridge with Buner, Swabi and the M-1 Motorway at Colonel Sher Khan Interchange.

No doubt, the most important component of CPEC as part of the BRI is Gwadar. Indeed, providing the most direct access to the Arabian Sea is the raison d'être for CPEC.[36] In order to maximize Gwadar's full potential, there are a number of potential routes and junctions that can greatly complement existing road links. One such example is the key road junction of Hoshab, located along the edge of the Makran coastline. This area holds tremendous potential for development and can be further linked with the Pasni and Ormara ports which are also located along the Arabian Sea. This would provide a viable bypass for Turbat and decrease the dependence of these two strategic ports on Karachi via the lone Coastal Highway.

After developing this fully robust transport network, the next challenge would be to enhance the economic viability of CPEC by developing offshoots that link the Eurasian hinterland with Gwadar. As discussed earlier, the Indian sponsored port of Chabahar in Iran and its accompanying link to Afghanistan via the Zaranj-Dilaram Road have been set up as a key alternative to CPEC. In a free market global economy, Pakistan must offer better facilities to the hinterland countries which include Central Asian countries and Russia. These could be provided by offering multiple routes connecting Central Asia with both China and Pakistan as discussed above. Furthermore, CPEC as part of the BRI can also be ultimately linked to Mongolia and Nepal via China further boosting the Gwadar port's competitiveness against the Chahbahar port.

---

[36] Jialing Sun, "Gwadar Port from the Perspective of Xinjiang Province of China," *Erasmus University Rotterdam*, October 20, 2011, https://thesis.eur.nl/pub/33110/ (accessed October 17, 2017).

Chapter 12: Progress Report on CPEC

S. Sadia Kazmi*

CPEC is a model of economic development through connectivity and dividend sharing as the preferred policy agenda. Under the same premise President Xi Jinping's ideals of "community of common destiny" and "shared future"[1] are being practically demonstrated by China through massive investment of its financial resources around US $9 tn in the BRI project.[2] Belt and Road Initiative visualizes developing interdependence through building network of infrastructure, transport, and energy and trade cooperation for enhanced social and economic interaction across the globe. Sixty five countries as part of BRI make up for almost half of world's population i.e. 60% and almost 40% of world GDP.[3] By undertaking this initiative China hopes to enhance its GDP by 25% and reap huge economic dividends of more than US $21 tn shared by all.[4] Hence BRI emerges as the only yet massive initiative of its kind to enhance global connectivity and plans to be the manifestation of "building a community of shared destiny for common progress and win-win cooperation for a mutually bright future" as is proclaimed by President Xi Jinping.

* Ms. Syedah Sadia Kazmi is Senior Research Associate at the Strategic Vision Institute (SVI), Islamabad

[1]Hujjatullah Zia, "Towards a Community with Shared Future", *China Daily,* (June 21, 2018), http://www.chinadaily.com.cn/a/201806/21/WS5b2b73c6a3103349141dd98e.html (accessed Nov 8, 2018).

[2] Philippa Brant, "One Road, One Belt? China's Community of Shared Destiny", *Lowy Institute*, (March 31, 2015), https://www.lowyinstitute.org/the-interpreter/one-belt-one-road-chinas-community-common-destiny (accessed October 5, 2018).

[3]Hujjatullah Zia, "Belt and Road, A Unique Platform for Exchanges", *China Daily,* (August 29, 2018).http://www.chinadaily.com.cn/a/201808/29/WS5b867952a310add14f3887ec.html (accessed Nov 10, 2018).

[4]Joshua P. Meltzer, "China's One Belt One Road Initiative: A view from the United States", *The ASEAN FORUM,* Brookings, (June 19, 2017), https://www.brookings.edu/research/chinas-one-belt-one-road-initiative-a-view-from-the-united-states/ (accessed September 11, 2018).

It was first time in 2013 when Chinese PM Li Keqiang paid a two day visit to Pakistan on 22-23 May and the MoU for the long-term plan on CPEC was signed by China National Development and Reform Commission's Chairman Xu Shao Si and Advisor to the PM Shahid Amjad Chaudhry in presence of then Pakistani President Asif Ali Zardari, PM Nawaz Sharif and Chinese Premier Li Keqiang.[5] The MoU was signed in 8 different areas including:[6]

1. Long-term plan on CPEC,

2. Maritime cooperation,

3. Boundary management system between Xinijang and Gilgit-Baltistan area,

4. Management of border ports,

5. Agreement on economic and technical cooperation,

6. Cooperation in the field of marine science and technology,

7. Agreement of cooperation between China Satellite Navigation Office (CSNO) and Pakistan Space and Upper Atmospheric Research Commission (SUPARCO),

8. Agreement on establishing Confucius Institute at Karachi University,

The two sides also set up a Joint Coordination Committee (JCC) on CPEC which until Dec 2018 has convened 8 meetings.[7] There are further five Joint Working Groups (JWGs) under JCC for long-term planning, infrastructure development, energy, industrial development, and development of Gwadar port. It was also decided to hold a meeting on

---

[5]"Pakistan, China Sign Eight Agreements, MoUs", *The News*, (July 6, 2013). https://www.thenews.com.pk/archive/print/631527-pakistan,-china-sign-eight-agreements,-mous (accessed Nov 8, 2018).
[6]"Pakistan, China Ink Accords on Economic Corridor Plan, Maritime Cooperation", *Pakistan Today*, (May 22, 2013), https://www.pakistantoday.com.pk/2013/05/22/pakistan-china-ink-accords-on-economic-corridor-plan-maritime-cooperation/ (accessed August 10, 2018).
[7]"JCC Meeting: Pakistan-China Finalize MoU on Industrial Cooperation", *The Express Tribune*, (December 21, 2018).https://tribune.com.pk/story/1871431/2-jcc-meeting-pakistan-china-finalise-mou-industrial-cooperation/ (accessed December 30, 2018).

newly set up JWG for the socio-economic matters under CPEC.[8] The 8th JCC meeting was specifically important as it focuses the orientation of CPEC future aims toward the socio-economic development of people of Pakistan, their health care, and poverty alleviation by launching small scale livelihood projects. China laid more stress on agriculture cooperation to help Pakistan improve agricultural technology, product efficiency, and value added agricultural industry. The JCC looks after the planning and coordination while the JWGs are responsible for the implementation of the plans. After the signing of initial plan on CPEC, it was in 2015 that President Xi Jinping visited Pakistan and penned a historical MoU with 51 Agreements related to energy and infrastructural development of Pakistan under the ambit of CPEC.[9]

It is significant to note that while in 2013 the idea for CPEC was discussed and deliberated upon, the formal launching of the economic corridor worth US $46 bn as per the initial estimates took place on 20th April 2015.[10] Today the total agreed investment from China for CPEC has reached US $62 bn.[11] The two countries reached a consensus to cooperate in 4 major areas under CPEC, also known as '1+4': development of Gwadar port, energy, transport infrastructure, and industrial cooperation.[12]

The whole project is divided into two terms i.e. Early Harvest Program (EHP) (2015-2019) and Long-Term Plan (LTP) (2017-2030).

---

[8]"Bakhtiyar Expresses Complete Satisfaction Over 8th Meeting of CPEC JCC Outcome", *APP*, (December 21, 2018, https://www.app.com.pk/bakhtyar-expresses-complete-satisfaction-over-8th-meeting-of-cpec-jcc-outcome/ (accessed December 25, 2018).
[9]"Agreement Signed between Pakistan and China", *The Express* Tribune, (April 26, 2015). https://tribune.com.pk/story/876286/agreements-signed-between-pakistan-and-china/ (accessed Nov 20, 2018).
A detailed list of Agreements is available in Appendix K on pg 284.
[10]Katherine Houreld, "China and Pakistan Launch Economic Corridor Plan Worth $46billion", *REUTERS*, (April 20, 2015), https://www.reuters.com/article/us-pakistan-china/china-and-pakistan-launch-economic-corridor-plan-worth-46-billion-idUSKBN0NA12T20150420 (accessed Nov 13, 2018).
[11]Salman Siddiqui, "CPEC Investment Pushed from $55b to $62b", *The Express* Tribune, (April 12, 2017), https://tribune.com.pk/story/1381733/cpec-investment-pushed-55b-62b/ (accessed October 5, 2018).
[12]"Backgrounder: China-Pakistan Economic Corridor", *China Daily*, (April 22, 2015), http://www.chinadaily.com.cn/world/2015xivisitpse/2015-04/22/content_20503693.htm (accessed Nov 8, 2018).

These two terms are divided into four stages of project completion making CPEC fully functional by the year 2030 i.e. over the period of 15 years from 2015 to 2030.[13] The LTP is further divided into three phases of project completion. The short term projects under LTP will be completed by 2020, medium term by 2025, and the long term by 2030.[14] Each phase of development spans roughly over the period of 5 years i.e. 2015-2020 is the Early Harvest phase and is the first stage of project completion along with the beginning of Long-term Plan; 2020-2025 is the Medium phase and the second stage in which the LTP short term project completion will be achieved during the year 2022; and the third phase spans over 2025-2030. It is during the final third phase that the third and fourth stages of LTP project completion are expected to be achieved with most of the medium term projects to be completed by 2025 and the long term projects culminating to fruition in 2030.[15] At the moment CPEC has entered the second term with the unveiling of 26 page LTP Plan on 18th Dec 2017,[16] while most of the Early Harvest projects have been completed in just 32 months.[17]

CPEC is a 3,000km long corridor comprised of railways, roads, and pipelines that will carry goods, oil and gas through Gwadar port in Pakistan to Kashgar city in north China's Xinjiang Uygur region.[18] Out of 51 agreed upon projects 21 projects are related to energy sector development and cooperation through coal, gas, wind, and solar power plants and 30 are dedicated for the infrastructural development including railways, roads, industrial zones, agricultural sector, and fiber

---

[13] Col. M. Hanif, "CPEC: A Win-Win Project for Region", *Pakistan* Observer, (May 25, 2016), https://pakobserver.net/cpec-a-win-win-project-for-region/ (accessed September 9, 2018).
[14] Ahmed Rashid Malik, "CPEC's Long Term Plan", *The* Nation, (December 22, 2017). https://nation.com.pk/22-Dec-2017/cpec-s-long-term-plan (accessed Nov 9, 2018).
[15] Dr. Ishrat Hussain, *CPEC & Pakistani Economy: An Appraisal*, (Islamabad: Centre of Excellence for CPEC, 2018), p.20, http://cpec.gov.pk/brain/public/uploads/documents/CPEC-and-Pakistani-Economy_An-Appraisal.pdf (accessed December 8, 2018).
[16] "CPEC Long Term Plan: Complete Document", *The* News, (December 19, 2017), https://www.thenews.com.pk/latest/258078-cpec-long-term-plan-complete-document (accessed November 8, 2018).
[17] Ahmed Rashid Malik, "CPEC's Long Term Plan", *The* Nation, (December 22, 2017). https://nation.com.pk/22-Dec-2017/cpec-s-long-term-plan (accessed October 18, 2018).
[18] "Backgrounder: China-Pakistan Economic Corridor", *China Daily*, (April 22, 2015), http://www.chinadaily.com.cn/world/2015xivisitpse/2015-04/22/content_20503693.htm (accessed Nov 8, 2018).

optics etc.[19] The energy projects once completed are expected to generate 16,400MW of electricity to the national grid. Accor٬ ੍ੋ to Pakistan Ministry of Planning, Development and Reform, so fɛ 22 projects worth US $28 bn have been completed in a short span of oɪ.ly 4 years.[20] This figure alone shows that CPEC is the fastest moving and most effective project of BRI.

Some of the financial facts about CPEC worth mentioning here are that out of total US $62 bn, the major portion of funds worth US $35 bn is dedicated for energy projects. The funds for this portion are entirely being looked after and financed by the foreign investors who will get 17% return on their equity investment.[21] These energy projects are planned to be completed by 2020. While the US $27 bn is for infrastructure, Gwadar port development, airport and industrial zones etc. which is expected to be completed by 2025-2030.[22] These funds will be made available through government to government loan provided by the Government of China at the concessional rate of 2% loan to be paid back by Pakistan over the period of 20-25 years.[23] The disbursement of loans is being looked after by Exim Bank of China, China Development Bank and the ICBC.[24] Recently on 2nd Nov 2018, the Asia Infrastructure Investment Bank (AIIB) President Jin Liqun met PM Imran Khan on the sideline of China international Import Expo and announced to invest in CPEC projects.[25]

---

[19]Ibid.

[20]"CPEC Projects Worth $28bln completed in 4 Years", *The News*, (October 13, 2018), https://www.thenews.com.pk/print/380059-cpec-projects-worth-28bln-completed-in-4-years (accessed Nov 14, 2018).

[21]Ahmed Ali Siddique, "Choosing the Right Financing Option for Pakistan", *Pakistan Economist*, (November 26, 2018), http://www.pakistaneconomist.com/2018/11/26/choosing-the-right-financing-option-for-cpec/ (accessed December 8, 2018).

[22] Ishrat Hussain, *CPEC & Pakistani Economy: An Appraisal*, (Islamabad: Centre of Excellence for CPEC, 2018), p.20.

[23]Ahmed Ali Siddique, "Choosing the Right Financing Option for Pakistan", *Pakistan Economist*, (November 26, 2018), http://www.pakistaneconomist.com/2018/11/26/choosing-the-right-financing-option-for-cpec/ (accessed December 15, 2018).

[24]Ishrat Hussain, "Financing Burden of CPEC", *DAWN*, (February 11, 2017), https://www.dawn.com/news/1313992 (accessed Nov 8, 2018).

[25] "AIIB President Meets PM Imran, Announces to Invest in CPEC Projects", *ARY News*, (November 2, 2018), https://arynews.tv/en/aiib-president-meets-pm-imran-announces-to-invest-in-cpec-projects/ (accessed December 1, 2018).

Details of projects included under CPEC are given below along with the status of progress as per the official government sources. The information below not only present progress on the CPEC project but also mentions number of Pakistanis involved in these projects, this indeed helps in cultivating more trust in the CPEC as it is generating sufficient employment opportunities for Pakistanis helping them with their socio-economic challenges.

Energy projects details:

Seven Energy Projects have been completed[26]

Sr. No.	Name	Financing Model	No. of Pakistani Staff
1	50MW Dawood Wind Power Project	US $115 million, invested by Chinese comp.	117
2	100MW Pakistan Jhimpir UEP Wind Power Phase-I	US $262 million, invested by Chinese comp.	192
3	Sachal 50 MW wind Power Project	US $110 million, invested by Chinese comp.	162
4	Zonergy 900 MW solar Project	US $460 million, invested by Chinese comp.	3755
5	Port Qasim 2x660MW Coal fired power project	US $2085 million, invested by Chinese comp.	532
6	Sahiwal, 1320 MW Coal fired power plant	US $1800 million, invested by Chinese comp.	3246
7	Three Gorges Second Wind power project (100MW)	US $42.3 million, invested by Chinese comp.	447

---

[26] Zhao Lijian, "Press Briefing by Chinese DCM", *Embassy of People's Republic of China in Pakistan*, October 26, 2018.

Five under construction Energy Projects are:[27]

Sr. No.	Name	Financing Model	No. of Pakistanis Employed
1.	720MW Karot Hydro Power Project	US $1650 million, invested by Chinese comp.	3505
2.	660MW HUBCO Coal Power Plant	US $2100 million, invested by Chinese comp.	2525
3.	Suki-Kinari Hydro Power Project	US $1962 million, invested by Chinese comp.	6323
4.	2x330MW Coal fired power plant at Thar Block-II Sindh	US $1108 million, invested by Chinese comp.	1362
5.	3.8Mta Open Cast Lignite Mine at Thar Block-II, Sindh	US $845 million, invested by Chinese comp.	1098

Eight Energy Projects are in the Pipeline:[28]

300MW Imported coal-based power project at Gwadar
Thar Block I Coal Fired Power Plant
Engro Thar Block II 2x330MW Coal fired Power Plant
SSRL Thar Coal Block-I 6.8 mtpa & SEC Mine Mouth Power Plant (2x660MW)
Matiari to Lahore ± 660KV HVDC Transmission Line Project
Kohala Hydel Project, AJK
Cacho 50 MW Wind Power Project
Western Energy (Pvt.) Ltd. 50 MW Wind Power Project

Details of Industrial Projects:

One industrial project is completed, and one is under construction. Before 2018, Pakistan's only fiber cable outlet was a submarine cable

---

[27] Ibid.
[28] Ibid.

through the Indian Ocean. The China-Pakistan Cross Border Fiber Cable Project opened up a new information channel for Pakistan, which will benefit IT industry and strengthen bilateral information link. Hence it has led to strengthening of information connectivity.

Sr. No.	Name	Financing Model	No. of Pakistani staff
1.	Laying of Optical Fiber Cable (OFC) From Rawalpindi to Khunjrab	US $144 million Funded by Chinese govt soft loan **(completed)**	505
2.	Digital terrestrial Multimedia Broadcasting	US $23 million Aided by Chinese govt.	138

Details of Infrastructural Projects:
Out of three ongoing infrastructure projects, one is completed[29]

Sr. No.	Name	Financing Model	No. of Pakistani staff
1.	KKH Phase-II (Havelian-Thakot)	US $1.3 billion funded by Chinese govt soft loan **(completed)**	8424
2.	Karachi-Lahore Motorway (Sukkur-Multan)	US $2.8 billion funded by Chinese govt soft loan	33333
3.	Metro Rail Transit System on the Orange Line in Lahore	US $1.6 billion, funded by Chinese govt soft loan	2349

---

[29] Zhao Lijian, "Press Briefing by Chinese DCM", *Embassy of People's Republic of China in Pakistan*, October 26, 2018.

Five Infrastructural projects are in the pipeline[30]

KKH Thakot-Raikot N35 remaining portion (136 Km)
Khuzdar-Basima road N-30 (110km)
Upgradation of DI Khan (Yarik)-Zhob , N-50 Phase-I (210 Km)
Expansion and reconstruction of existing Line ML-1
Havelian Dry Port (450 M. Twenty-Foot Equivalent Units)

Details of Gwadar projects:
Out of four projects, one is completed.

Sr. No.	Name	Financing Model	No. of Pakistani staff
1	China-Pakistan Friendship School	US $0.399 million Aided by Chinese govt **(completed)**	More than 400 Pakistani students are enrolled
2	Gwadar Port operation and Development of Free zone	US $114.7 million invested by Chinese company	630
3	Expressway on east bay of Gwadar	US $143 million Free-interest loan by Chinese govt.	4222
4	Gwadar smart port city master plan	US $4 million Aided by Chinese govt.	8

Status of Early Harvest projects:

Ten have been successfully completed while twelve are under construction with total contract amount of around US $19 billion.

---

[30] Ibid.

Details of ten completed Early Harvest projects:

1.	10 Early Harvest Projects completed 500MW Dawood Wind Power Project	6.	Sahiwal 1320MW Coal-fired Power Plant
2.	100MW Pakistan Jhimpir UEP Wind Power Phase-I project	7.	China-Pakistan Friendship School, Exp Colony
3.	Sachal 50MW wind power project	8.	Laying of Optical Fiber Cable (OFC) from RWP to Khunjerab
4.	Zonergy 500MW solar project in Punjab	8.	Feasibility study for upgradation of ML-1 and Establishment of Havelian Dry Port
5.	Port Qasim 2x660MW Coal fired power project	9.	Three Gorges Second Wind power project (100MW)

Details of twelve under construction Early Harvest Projects:

1.	KKH Phase-II (Havelian-Thakot)	7.	Gwadar port operations and development of Free Zone
2.	Karachi-Lahore Motorway Suukkur-Multan section (392KM)	8.	SUKI KINARI hydro Power project
3.	Metro Rail Transit System on the Orange Line in Lahore	9.	Gwadar smart port city Master Plan
4.	Expressway of east bay of Gwadar	10.	DTMB Demonstration project
5.	720MW Karot Hydro Power project	11.	2x330MW Mine mouth coal-fired power plant at Thar Block-II, Sindh
6.	660MW HUBCO Coal power plant	12.	3.8Mta Open cast Lignite Mine at Thar Block-II, Sindh

Development of Special Economic Zones (SEZs) is the main area of priority in the Long-term Plan. Total 27 SEZs are planned to be constructed out of which 9 have been earmarked as priority projects.

Chinese experts have held three expert group meetings for China-Pakistan industry cooperation and visited most of the proposed SEZs. The Chinese Export Group also provided consultations and suggestions on the incentives and preferential policies for PSEZs and offered Pakistan the future reference on SEZs policy making.

Priority list of SEZs

Province	Location
KPK	Rashakai & Hattar Economic Zone
Sindh	Dhabeji
Baluchistan	Bostan Industrial Zone
Punjab	Punjab-China Economic Zone, M-3
Northern Areas	Moqpondass, Gilgit SEZ
Northern Areas	Bhimber Industrial Zone
Federal Government	Development of Industrial Park on Pakistan Steel Mill Land in Port Qasim near Karachi
Federal Government	ICT Model Industrial Zone, Islamabad
FATA	Mohmand Marble City

A Brief Roundup:

CPEC has contributed in the increased energy supply. 7 energy projects under CPEC have been installed with capacity of 3240 MW in only 3 years, since the first energy project groundbreaking ceremony in 2015. These projects accounted for 11% of total electricity generation in Pakistan.

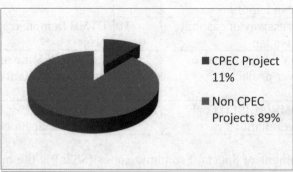

Figure12.1 Pakistan's National Installed Capacity: 29000MW
Source: Embassy of the People's Republic of China in Pakistan
https://pk.chineseembassy.org/eng/zbgx/t1626097.htm

Pakistan's Energy optimization has been one of the major agendas of the CPEC. The charts below show how the energy supply is expected to increase from 2013 till 2022 when all the energy projects under CPEC will be completed.

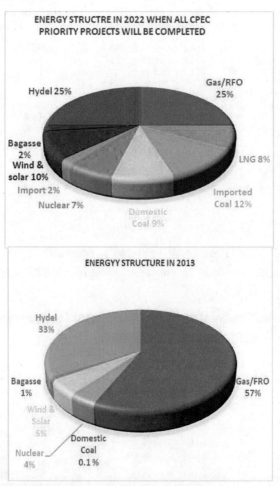

Figure12.2 Pakistan's Energy Structure. Existing and Projected
Source: Embassy of the People's Republic of China in Pakistan
https://pk.chineseembassy.org/eng/zbgx/t1626097.htm

CPEC has considerably promoted investment in Pakistan. There has been an increase in the foreign investment since the launch of the CPEC while China has become the largest investor for the last 5 years. CPEC has not only attracted much more Chinese investment in Pakistan, but also made Pakistan a popular destination for investment as is evident from the details provided below:

Country	Before the Launch of CPEC				After the Launch of CPEC				
	2009-10	2010-11	2011-12	2012-13	2013-14	2014-15	2015-16	2016-17	2017-18
China	-3.6	47.4	126.1	90.6	695.8	319.1	1,063.60	1,211.70	1,585.80
UK	294.6	207.1	205.8	63.3	157	169.6	151.6	215.8	278.7
USA	468.3	238.1	227.7	227.1	212.1	223.9	13.2	44.6	92.3
Hong Kong	9.9	125.6	80.3	242.6	228.5	136.2	93.3	17.2	140.8
Switzerland	170.6	110.5	127.1	149	209.8	-6.5	58	101.8	88.1
U.A.E.	242.7	284.2	36.6	22.5	-47.1	213.6	109.7	120.5	5.4
Italy	4	7.9	200.8	199.4	97.6	115.4	105.4	60.5	56.6
Netherlands	278.6	-48.5	22.1	-118.4	5.5	-34.5	29.9	457.6	70
Austria	56.8	32.4	68.8	53.3	53.8	24.8	42.7	21.7	27.7
Japan	26.8	3.2	29.7	30.1	30.1	71.1	35.4	57.7	56.9
Turkey	0.8	1.8	0.3	0.5	7.9	43.4	16.8	135.6	29.8
Other	601.3	625.1	-304.6	-73.2	47.6	-288.2	585.7	301.9	3335.3
Total	2,150.8	1,634.80	820.7	1,456.50	1,698.60	987.9	2,305.30	2,746.80	2,767.60

CPEC Launched

CPEC has also Promoted Pakistan's economic growth and the ongoing projects are likely to contribute 9% to 10% of GDP in FY2018-19.

Gross Domestic Product (GDP) (Billion Rupees)

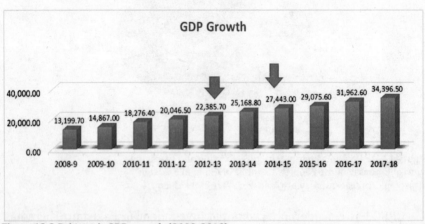

Figure12.3 Pakistan's GDP growth (2008-2018)

CPEC aims to strengthen physical connectivity of important cities across Pakistan and ultimately develop a link to China through Gwadar-Kashgar corridor. CPEC ongoing projects will promote Pakistan's North-South interconnection and help Pakistan's coastal areas strengthen ties with the northern areas, promoting the coordination and development in depth and breadth. CPEC ongoing infrastructure projects will significantly reduce the time cost of transportation. After the completion of KKH-II (Havelian-Thakot), the travel time between the two places will be reduced from 4 hrs to 1.5 hrs, which will promote commercial development and exchanges.

Karachi-Lahore Motorway
(Sukkur-Multan)

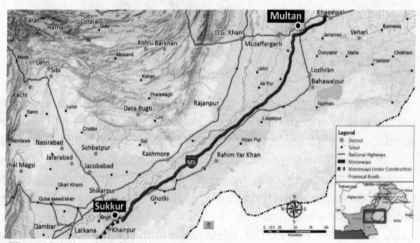

Figure12.4 Karachi-Lahore Motorway
Source: CPEC China-Pakistan Economic Corridor (Official Website)
http://cpec.gov.pk/project-details/29

KKH Phase-II
(Havelian-Thakot)

Figure12.4 Karachi-Lahore Motorway
Source: CPEC China-Pakistan Economic Corridor (Official Website)
http://cpec.gov.pk/project-details/28

Another significant contribution of CPEC is that it has been quite instrumental in creating job opportunities for Pakistani people. As per the official data 22 projects directly hired more than 75000 Pakistani local staff. CPEC also promotes relevant upstream and downstream industries including catering, raw material processing, cargo transportation, manufacturing etc. which have provided more employment opportunities for the local people. Similarly, the CPEC Centre of Excellence CPEC-CoE could assist in the creation of 1.2 million jobs under its presently agreed projects.

It is important to note that of all the CPEC projects only KKH Phase-II, Karachi-Lahore Motorway (Sukkur-Multan), Orange Line, and laying of Optical fiber cable used the Chinese government soft loan, which were granted by Pakistani government, the total amount was around US $6 tn. According to the statistics of Ministry of Finance of Pakistan, the external debt of Pakistan and liabilities reached 595 trillion by October 2018. Chinese govt. soft loans for CPEC projects accounted for only 6.3% of Pakistan total foreign debt. The payment time of the 4 projects starts from 2021, repaying US $300 mn - 400 mn annually. All CPEC projects are funded by commercial loans which are borrowed and repaid by the Chinese. There is no foreign debt on Pakistani government brought about by CPEC.

However, despite all the available data and information on CPEC from the Chinese and Pakistani official sources, it has largely remained embroiled in controversies with regards to CPEC preferred vs. feasible route and its finances, loans and debts. There is often misreporting about halting of funds from China which in fact never has been the case as is evident from the official statement by Pakistani Foreign Office spokesperson[31] as well as from the Chinese side.[32] As a matter of fact in November last month, China showed firm commitment to move forward to the CPEC project and also agreed to bail Pakistan out of its current financial crisis.[33] Nevertheless, finances remain the lingering and recurring controversy. Recently a local newspaper reported a detailed breakdown of payable loans to China over the period of 20 years.[34] However, the very next day the Ministry of Planning, Development and Reform issued a rebuttal on the CPEC debt news article having mostly incorrect information and analysis.[35] Soon after, the Chinese Embassy issued its official stance condemning the misreporting of facts and offered the factual details of investment on the 22 completed projects and the loan repayment details.[36] The timely and prompt refutation

---

[31] "Chinese Funding for CPEC Dispersed: FO Refutes Reports of Halts", *Dunya News*, (December 14, 2017), http://dunyanews.tv/en/Pakistan/419167-Chinese-funding-for-CPEC-projects-dispersed-FO-refutes-reports-of-halt (accessed September 17, 2018).

[32] Mian Babar, "China Rules Out Halting of Funds for CPEC", *Pakistan Today*, (December 16, 2017), https://www.pakistantoday.com.pk/2017/12/16/china-rules-out-halting-of-funds-for-cpec/ (accessed September 17, 2018).

[33] "China Agrees to Bailout Pakistan", *Pakistan Today*, (November 4, 2018), https://www.pakistantoday.com.pk/2018/11/03/more-talks-needed-on-economic-aid-for-pakistan-says-china/ (accessed Nov 8, 2018).

[34] Shahbaz Rana, "Pakistan to Pay China $40b on $26.5b CPEC Investment in 20 Years", *The Express Tribune*, (December 26, 2018), https://tribune.com.pk/story/1874661/2-pakistan-pay-china-40-billion-20 years (accessed December 29, 2018).

[35] "Planning Ministry Clarifies News Article on CPEC Debt", *The News*, (December 26, 2018). https://www.thenews.com.pk/latest/411030-ministry-clarifies-news-report-on-cpec-debt (accessed December 29, 2018).

[36] "Chinese Embassy Clarifies False Report on CPEC Debt", *The Nation*, (December 29, 2018). https://nation.com.pk/29-Dec-2018/report-regarding-pak-s-40bn-debt-under-cpec-termed-false (accessed December 29, 2018).

while has helped in mitigating the doubts and confusion, it has curbed yet another propaganda hurled at the CPEC. One cannot deny that Pakistan is under a serious threat of "hybrid warfare" which is spewing all kind of venom and wrong information against CPEC, with the sole aim of rendering it futile prompting enough distrust in China's true motives. The recent article shows a sorry state of affairs wherein the local media could so easily be made to play a pawn of ill-wishers to propagate incorrect information. This also raises serious concerns about the vulnerabilities that the CPEC is often exposed to. Nonetheless, Pakistan and China are quite vigilant and have been collectively putting up a fight against such malicious agendas. Referring to the article appeared in local press "Pakistan to Pay China $40b on $26.5b Investment in 20 years", it has been reported that "out of $39.83 billion the debt repayments of energy and infrastructure projects amount to US $28.43 bn. The rest of US $11.4 bn will be paid in shape of dividends to the investors. These low figures are because the outflows have been worked out on the basis of only $26.5 billion investment. The article maintains that unlike the claimed $62 billion CPEC investment, the actual investment will remain half of the initially announced investment figures. It goes on to state that the only major project that can materialize in the next few years is $8.2 billion Mainline-I Project of Pakistan Railways".[37] The Chinese DCM Zhao Lijian was quick to respond to this through his twitter account maintaining that "the so-called claims of $40billion debt to be paid to China by Pakistan under CPEC, is a mere counterfeit, forged & misleading. Though Ministry of Planning issued a clarification, documents of Chinese Embassy have further broken facts from fiction".[38]

---

[37] Shahbaz Rana, "Pakistan to Pay China $40b on $26.5b CPEC Investment in 20 Years", *The Express Tribune*, (December 26, 2018).
https://tribune.com.pk/story/1874661/2-pakistan-pay-china-40-billion-20-years (accessed December 29, 2018).
[38] Yasir Masood, "Stop Spinning CPEC Finances", *Center for Research and Security Studies*, (December 30, 2018).
https://crssblog.com/2018/12/30/stop-spinning-cpecs-finances-yasir-masood/?fbclid=IwAR1eeDJbm9InSJ6LU-BdzppmNnCB738vfVwDNm522C-BxYWZgycd9RT13cA (accessed December 30, 2018).

He has also provided a detailed financial run down of 22 projects under CPEC[39] which can be found in Appendix L[40].

According to the official statements issued by Chinese embassy, Pakistan only has to pay US $6.017 bn plus interest to China over the period of 20-25 years. So far US $18.9 bn have been invested for the energy and infrastructural projects by the Chinese government. US $5.874 bn is exclusively for transport infrastructure at 2% interest rate, the repayment of which will start around2021. US $12.8 bn is invested by Chinese companies and their partners for the energy projects in Pakistan. Out of this US $3 bn comes from companies' own equity and US $9.8 bn is provided by commercial banks at 5% interest rate. The repayment period is 12-18 years. It is also mentioned that Pakistan doesn't have to repay these loans under CPEC; instead the companies are independently responsible for the repayments of the loans, profits and losses. Simultaneously, the second phase of CPEC expands its domain further to include projects including Gwadar International Airport, Gwadar vocational training center, and hospital etc. Financial details of these new projects are being deliberated upon and will be shared at a later stage.

However, in a further positive development recently China expressed interest in expanding CPEC to new stage of expansion and broadening of bilateral ties. In this regard China on its part has time and again firmly stood by the mutual interests and has voiced the promotion of bilateral industrial cooperation, expansion of China's direct investment in Pakistan, and encouraging Chinese enterprises to actively participate in the construction of SEZs. Chinese side has also proposed that SEZ under CPEC industrial cooperation will provide fair access to Pakistani domestic enterprises and encourage third party investment and that China will help Pakistan develop manufacture and export

---

[39] Zhao Lijian, "Chinese Embassy provided a financing rundown of 22 CPEC projects.This is for early harvest projects completed or under construction. We are discussing financial details of more projects such as Gwadar new intl airport. They will be shared when available.", December 29, 2018, (Tweet)
[40] See Appendix L on pg 289

oriented economy. Chinese govt has encouraged Chinese companies to increase local component in their procurement in Pakistan. On 8thSeptember 2018 State councilor and FM Wang Yi met the press together with FM Makhdoom Shah Mehmood Qureshi in Islamabad and introduced 10 important consensus reached by the two Foreign Ministers:

"The normal operation of the completed project and the smooth progress of the project under construction will be ensured. At the same time according to the next social and economic development priorities and the needs of the public of Pakistani side, the future development path and cooperation direction of the CPEC will be determined through consultation. Speeding up industrial cooperation and livelihood projects, and gradually extending to the western region of Pakistan are the main focuses".

Nonetheless, amidst all the confusion, vulnerabilities, and negative forces active in spewing controversies against the CPEC, continued and dedicated efforts should be made by both China and Pakistan to cultivate trust in this economically important project and build a positive image about its regional and extra-regional dividends. The two governments are committed to this cause and to making the CPEC a success story as is evident from the victory speech of PM Imran Khan stating "we will strengthen and improve our relationship with China. We want to work toward success of CPEC. We also want to send teams to learn poverty alleviation from China".[41]In a meeting with Chinese FM Wang Yi, PM Imran Khan reiterated the stance that "the friendship with China is the cornerstone of Pakistan's foreign policy and my government is committed to implementing CPEC".[42]Chinese Premier Le Keqiang reciprocated the sentiments by stating that "China is willing to work with Pakistan to conduct close high level contracts, deepen pragmatic

---

[41] "Chinese Experts Welcome Imran Khan's Pledge to Strengthen Bilateral Ties", *The News*, (July 29,2018).
https://www.thenews.com.pk/latest/347931-chinese-experts-welcome-imran-khans-pledge-to-strengthen-bilateral-ties (accessed Nov 8, 2018).
[42] "PM Imran Renews Commitment to CPEC", *The Express Tribune*, (September 10, 2018).
https://tribune.com.pk/story/1799438/1-pm-imran-renews-commitment-cpec/ (accessed Nov 19, 2018).

cooperation, enhance coordination on major international and regional issues, promote common development and make contributions to regional peace and prosperity".[43]President Xi voiced the similar thoughts expressing faith in Pakistan and cherishing the bilateral relations by stating that "I attach great importance to China-Pakistan relations and am willing to work together with the prime minister to strengthen the China-Pakistan all-weather strategic partnership and build a new era of China-Pakistan destiny".[44] As long as the two sides continue to have faith and understanding towards each other, there is no stopping CPEC from becoming a success story. Pragmatism demand concrete measures and concerted efforts against all the negative elements.

---

[43]"Chinese Premier Li Talks with PM Imran Khan via Phone Call", *The News*, (August 20, 208).
https://www.thenews.com.pk/latest/357815-chinese-premier-li-talks-with-pm-imran-khan-via-phone-call (accessed Nov 19, 2018).
[44]"China will not Let Pakistan Down", *Pakistan Today*, (November 2, 2018).
https://www.pakistantoday.com.pk/2018/11/02/china-will-not-let-pakistan-down/ (accessed Nov 8, 2018).

Afterword

This book has offered a broad ranging set of analyses on the many ways CPEC is set to boost Pakistan's socio-economic development, as well as its prominence as a key State within the South Asian region. It has emphasized CPEC's crucial position within the Belt and Road Initiative (BRI), and has presented it from a broader, more inclusive perspective that is deeply cognizant of the huge role CPEC is to play in the changing dynamics of international relations. This includes its role as a precursor to the region's future economic growth and stability, while fostering increased connectivity and integration amongst key emerging economies. By straddling across existing geo-economic and geo-political boundaries, CPEC as part of the BRI presents a viable vision for greater regional prosperity with far-reaching implications for the rest of the world.

These implications have sprung directly from the economic rise of China, of which the Belt and Road Initiative is a key expression and extension. Considering how the BRI is itself in its initial stages, it has been difficult to quantify its overall impact on world growth and stability. While there is widespread discussion over the extent of its purported impact, there is also considerable debate regarding its projected benefits as it continues to polarize world opinion across numerous geo-political and strategic fault lines.

However, moving beyond the more political implications of the rise of China, the BRI's current trajectory indicates that China is well set to take on a more leading role in international economic development by enhancing global trade and connectivity. This is based directly on China's supremacy as the world's largest trading nation, as a major contributor of foreign direct investment (particularly in developing countries), and as the world's fastest growing economy. Furthermore, China's emphasis on fostering win-win partnerships while adhering to the principles of non-interference in the internal affairs of nation states have characterized its approach to global economic growth and development as being wholly distinct from, for instance, the US's unilateral approach. This emphasis on greater openness and inclusivity is also evident in the BRI, representing one of the most salient hallmarks of the Chinese Development Model.

The model itself can be characterized as one that employs a more long-term and holistic view of global economic development. Its focus on massive state led investments to develop large-scale infrastructure, has so far led to widespread success both within and outside China. This is evident in the tremendous growth this model has led to within the Chinese economy over the last few decades. As this model is internationalized as part of the BRI, it aims to further help industrialize the economies of developing countries on an unprecedented scale. The immense confidence China has in this approach is evident in how it is serving as the primary investor and consumer within these developing countries that have partnered with it as part of the BRI. By helping facilitate both the supply and demand for its massive infrastructure projects abroad, China is leading the financing and construction of these development projects until domestic stakeholders within these markets develop the capacity to absorb them. This is evident in China's BRI investments across Africa, Central Asia, South Asia, the Mediterranean and South-East Asia.

CPEC too, which serves as one of the most vital components of the BRI, is being developed along these lines. The major difference being that while China's investments in for instance, Kenya, Sri Lanka, Myanmar, Egypt and Greece have all been characterized as part of its rise as a major economic power, China's unique and long-standing relationship with Pakistan has with it an added dimension of bonhomie, based on a long history of mutual cooperation. Owing to its close geographical and historical proximity, both Pakistan and China have long shared a joint vision of regional peace, stability and prosperity that has been developed over years of close ties. This admittedly forms one of the key reasons why CPEC holds such crucial importance within the BRI framework.

However, Pakistan is still facing a myriad range of challenges that have arguably been exacerbated by the last few decades' geo-politics within the South Asian region. These include a broad range of political and socio-economic challenges, which have led to a vicious cycle of poverty and insecurity throughout the country. These represent some of the foremost obstacles limiting the country's development and growth potential, which have also increasingly come to characterize its very identity on the international stage.

As a result, much of the academic discourse related to Pakistan has directly focused on such issues of security (and insecurity). Unfortunately, this has also led to the existing discourse surrounding CPEC also to be viewed through the same perceptual lens. Hence, CPEC itself has come to be increasingly securitized within existing discourse, where the focus seems to be limited to its importance and potential impact as a 'geo-strategic game changer.' While this aspect of CPEC does hold considerable weight, it is but a fraction of its true potential not only within the regional context of South Asia, but the wider context of changing trends in global economic growth and stability.

Thus, instead of just being depicted as the all-encompassing panacea to Pakistan's long-standing economic difficulties, a less securitized view of CPEC offers a broader, more inclusive vision of how Pakistan, as a key state within the South Asian region, can play a leading role in a fast changing global economy. As a key component of the BRI, which is focused exclusively on fostering greater trade and people to people connectivity, CPEC can be viewed as part of a more pragmatic and inclusive framework for promoting win-win partnerships. This perspective stands in direct contrast to the zero-sum power politics that have plagued Pakistan and the wider region for decades, while allowing for a much broader appreciation of CPEC's overall objectives.

As mentioned in the introduction, addressing this gap has been a key focus of this book. By duly analyzing the vast scope and broad ranging objectives of both CPEC and the BRI; the varied perspectives presented in this book have as a whole, presented a comprehensive discussion aimed at addressing this issue within this rich and exciting subject. The credit for this goes to its chapter contributors, who while moving beyond this distinction, have shed new light and added immense value to the overall discourse surrounding CPEC.

Nevertheless, there are still many key areas that warrant further exploration with respect to this vast and important project. For instance, while much has been said about the economic and geo-political impact of CPEC, there exists a glaring lack of research on the purported societal impacts of such a large scale plan of regional integration. This includes studies on the impact of, for instance, greater cultural integration. These could incorporate sociological and even anthropological perspectives on the rich shared history between Pakistan and China, examining how CPEC provides a renewed impetus to further build on this history. Considering how the underlying premise of the BRI has often been stated as fostering greater people to people integration as part of a 'Community of Shared Destiny,' such avenues of study remain ripe for further exploration.

Also holding immense potential are studies that can focus on poverty elimination, social development and the economic uplift of some of the most underserved areas, where much of CPEC's development is being focused on. As the next phases of development under CPEC unfold, studies focusing on these issues are to remain crucial in evaluating the efficacy of these projects while holding its planners and implementers to a more defined sense of accountability. In this way, the kind of research that has been undertaken in this book, is to continue to play a key role in ensuring the viability and success of this crucial initiative even long after its completion.

With the international system on the cusp of a major transformation, the fate of both Pakistan and the wider region remains closely intertwined with the outcome of CPEC and the BRI. Considering its vast scope and broad ranging impact, the coming years are likely to bring with them a whole host of exciting developments that are to shape the lives of millions across the region for generations to come.

M Waqas Jan

List of Appendices

Appendix A

Financial Overview of CPEC Projects Currently Underway

Projects	Estimated Cost (USD Million)
Energy	34,746
Transport and Infrastructure	
Roads	7,705
Rail Network	18,437
Gwadar Port	906
Others	
ICT Connectivity	167
Total	**61,961***

Source: "CPEC Projects," China *Pakistan Economic Corridor, Ministry of Planning, Development and Reform.*

* Cost estimates may increase in light of approved new projects

Appendix B

CPEC Social Sector Development Plans

Key Areas of Cooperation	Details
People to People exchanges	• Efforts for intensification of People to People contact, media and cultural exchanges (including movies, drama, theatre etc.) would be done through agreed yearly programs. • Both sides resolved to promote Chinese and Pakistani culture and heritage as a way of long term partnership
Transfer of Knowledge in different sectors	• Experts from industrial zones, rural & urban development, job creation & SMEs, water resource management and agriculture have been sharing their knowledge and expertise with each other. • Numerous training workshops on industrial zones have been held since October 2017.

Appendix C

List of Energy Projects under CPEC

Name of project	Status / Time line
SINDH	
Port Qasim Electric Power Company (2X660 MW) SINDH	• Civil works on site in progress since May 2015 • Energization of 1st Unit December, 2017 • Second Unit Commercial Operation Date (COD) 25th April 2018 • Project completed 67 days ahead of schedule • Current Status: Operational
SSRL Thar Coal Block-I 6.8 Mtpa & SEC Mine Mouth Power Plant (2×660MW) (Shinghai) SINDH	• Financial Close of Plant and Mine second quarter of 2017. • Mine Commercial production is expected by 2019. • Plant Expected Commercial Operation Date (COD) 2018/2019.
Sachal Wind Power 50 MW, SINDH	• Project completed in 2017
Hydro China Dawood Power Wind Power Project 50 MW, SINDH	• Project completed in 2017
UEP Wind Farm (Jhimpir, Thatta) SINDH	• Financial Closed (FC) achieved on March 30, 2015 • Commercial Operation Date (COD) : 16th June, 2017 • Current Status: Operational
Sachal Wind Farm (Jhimpir, Thatta) SIndh	• Financial Closed (FC) achieved on December 18, 2015 • Commercial Operation Date (COD)

	• attained 11 April, 2017 • Current Status: Operational
Matiari-Lahore Transmission Line SINDH-PUNJAB	• Feasibility study completed • Tariff determined by NEPRA • TSA/IA initialed in December 2016 • Land acquisition for converter stations at Lahore and Matiari completed • Agreement signed between PPIB and State Grid of China on May 2018 • Expected COD in March 2021
Oracle Thar Coal Based Power Plant Mine 2x660 MW, SINDH	• Feasibility stage tariff obtained for coal. • Shareholding agreement on new equity partners in process. • Under issuance of NTP/LOI.
Engro Surface Mine in Block II of Thar Coal 3.8 metric tons per annum (MTPA), SINDH	• Financial close attained in April 2016 • IA/EA signed • Mining work in progress • 3.8 metric tons per annum (MTPA) • Thar Block II Unearths Coal on 10th June 2018 • Commercial Operation Date (COD) expected 2018/2019
Engro Thar Coal-fired Power Plant 4X330 MW, SINDH (2x 330 Approved 2x330 pending approval)	• Teams mobilized at site • Construction work in progress • Construction of Transmission line-contract awarded. Contractor mobilized • Financial close attained in April 2016 • COD June, 2019
Cacho 50MW Wind Power Project, SINDH	• Newly added
Western Energy (Pvt.) Ltd. 50MW Wind Power Project,	• Newly added

PUNJAB	
Sahiwal Power Plant 1320 MW, PUNJAB	• Project completed in 2017
Matiari-Lahore Transmission Line SINDH-PUNJAB	• Feasibility study completed • Tariff determined by NEPRA • TSA/IA initialed in December 2016 • Land acquisition for converter stations at Lahore and Matiari completed • Agreement signed between PPIB and State Grid of China on May 2018 • Expected COD in March 2021
720 MW Karot Hydropower Project, AJK-PUNJAB	• Land acquisition award done • Financial Close attained • Work initiated through equity – 25% civil works completed • COD 2020
Zonergy Solar Project, Bahawalpur 900 MW, PUNJAB	• COD of 3 x 100 MW attained
KPK	
870 MW Suki Kinari Hydropower Project, KPK	• Financial close attained. • Land acquisition award announced on 17th Nov, 2016. • Commercial Operation Date (COD) 2020/2021.
BALOCHISTAN	
CPHGC 1,320MW Coal-fired Power Plant, Hub, BALOCHISTAN	• IA/ Power Purchase Agreement Signed on 25th January 2017 • LOS issued on 12th April 2016; 1st extension to LOS issued on 24th January 2017 • Ground breaking ceremony held on 21

	March 2017 • Expected Commercial Operation Date (COD) 660 MW February 2019, 660 MW Aug 2019
Gwadar Coal Based Power Project, 300 MW, BALOCHISTAN	• LOI was issued on 26th May 2017 • Site finalized by CCCC • Land lease agreement signed by Governenment of Balochistan • NOC issued by Balochistan Enviroment Protection Agency (BEPA) on 07-07-2018. • NEPRA's tariff determination is in process
AJK	
(Actively Promoted) Kohala Hydel Power Project,1100 MW,AJK	• Feasibility Study (stage-1) Tariff Announced by NEPRA • Land Acquisition process started • Environmental NOC issued by AJ&K EPA Financial close planned in Dec 2018 • Expected Commercial Operation Date (COD) 2025
720 MW Karot Hydropower Project, AJK-PUNJAB	• Land acquisition award done. • Financial Close achieved on 22nd February 2017. • Construction of access road/bridge, concrete batching plant, diversion tunnel and spillway, etc. are in process. • Work initiated through equity – 41% civil works completed. • Expected Commercial Operation Date (COD) December 2021.

Appendix D

Western Route (Punjab, KP and Balochistan)

SECTION	STATUS
Hakla D.I Khan Motorway (285 km)	• Work in Progress • Date of Completion May 2019
D.I Khan (Yarik) –Zhob (N-50) 210 km	• PC-I Approved by ECNEC on 12th April, 2017 • Land acquisition in Progress • Frame Work Agreement forwarded to NDRC/MoT China
Zhob Quetta (N-50) 331 km	• Two lane carriageway in good condition • China-Pakistan Transport Joint Working group agreed to include up-gradation of the section as short term project. • Detail Design Completion by Mar-2018 • Land acquisition along existing road under process.
Khuzdar-Quetta– Chaman Section (N-25) 431 km (Additional Carriageway	• Feasibility Study Completed. • Detail Design completion in progress
Surab-Hoshab (N-85)	• Completed
Gwadar – Turbat – Hoshab (M-8)	• Completed and Inaugurated

Appendix E

New Infrastructural Projects after 6th JCC

Table 4: Transport Infrastructure

Name of project	Status
Khuzdar-Basima Road N-30 (110 km) BALOCHISTAN	• Feasibility and PC-I completed • LOI forwarded to Chinese side • Procedural formalities to be completed shortly (ECNEC approved the projects in May 2017) • Frame Work Agreement shared with Chinese Side
Upgradation of D.I.Khan - Zhob, N-50 Phase-I (210 km) KP-BALOCHISTAN	• PC-I Approved by ECNEC on 12th April, 2017. • Land acquisition in Progress. • Frame work Agreement Forward to MOC.
KKH Thakot-Raikot N35 remaining portion (136 Km)KP-GB	• Feasibility and PC-I completed • PC-I has been approved by ECNEC on 18-03-2017 • LOI forwarded to Chinese side • Procedural formalities to be completed shortly

New Provincial Projects

Name of project	Status
• Keti Bunder Sea Port Development Project • Naukundi-Mashkhel-Panjgur Road Project connecting with M-8 & N-85, • Chitral CPEC link road from Gilgit, Shandor, Chitral to Chakdara, • Mirpur – Muzaffarabad - Mansehra Road Construction for connectivity with CPEC route, AJK	• Studies and consultations are initiated • Project referred to JWG for implementation
• Quetta Water Supply Scheme from Pat feeder Canal, Balochistan • Iron Ore Mining, Processing & Steel Mills complex at Chiniot, Punjab	• Relevant Provincial Govts. to work out proposals on implementation of projects

Source: "CPEC New Provincial Projects," CPEC *Government of Pakistan*, n.d., http://cpec.gov.pk/new-provincial-projects (accessed March 19, 2018).

Railways

Name of project	Status
Capacity Development of Pakistan Railways (All PAKISTAN)	Focus groups be established for effective training and capacity enhancement

Rail Based Mass Transit System

Name of Project	Status
Orange Line, Lahore, Punjab	• Orange Line, Lahore project completion is planned for mid-2019
Karachi Circular Railway, Sindh	• Feasibility of Karachi Circular Railways completed in May 2017. • Groundbreaking is expected in 2019
Greater Peshawar Region Mass Transit, KP	• JCC agreed in principal for inclusion of Mass Transit System as part of CPEC component. • Transport Working Group has been asked to work on the projects based further studies and consultation. • Feasibility of Greater Peshawar Region Mass Transit is under process
Quetta Mass Transit, Balochistan	• JCC agreed in principle for inclusion of Rail Based Mass Transit Systems in Provincial headquarters as part of CPEC. • JWG on Transport Infrastructure has been asked to complete the necessary formalities. • Feasibility of Quetta Mass Transit is under process.

Source: "CPEC Rail Based Mass Transit Projects," CPEC, *Government of Pakistan*, n.d., http://cpec.gov.pk/mass-transit-projects (accessed March 19, 2018).

Appendix F
Gwadar Projects

Name of Project	Status
Gwadar East Bay Expressway	• Cost approved by ECNEC on 12-01-2015 • Contract Agreement was signed b/w GPA & CCCC on 24-09-2017 • Groundbreaking ceremony of Eastbay Expressway was held on 22nd November 2017 by Prime Minister • Construction work underway • Date of Completion October, 2020
New Gwadar International Airport	• Design and work plan agreed • Grant Agreement signed in May 2017 • Construction work to start in 2019
Provision of Fresh Water	• PC-I for 5 MGD RO plant for Gwadar cleared by CDWP • Phase-1, lying of pipelines from Swad Dam to Gwadar is under implementation. • Desalination plant establishment on BOT is floated
Technical and Vocational Institute at Gwadar	• GPA acquired 18 acres land and infrastructure of old Gwadar Degree College for establishment of Pak-China Technical & Vocational Institute • The onsite feasibility study of the project has been carried out in January 2017 by the China International Engineering Company • Minutes of onsite feasibility study has been signed with Chinese side on 09th August 2017 • LOE between EAD and MOFCOM signed in April 2018

Name of Project	Status
Pak China Friendship Hospital	• Grant request sent by EAD to MOFCOM • Feasibility study completed by Chinese team to add 100 beds from existing 50, for subsequent extension to 300 beds • LOE is signed on 10th April 2018 between EAD adn MOFCOM
Development of Free Zone	• Ground breaking done by the Prime Minister • 100% private Investment inside Free Zone. To be operated by COPHCL • 1st phase completion date completed in December 2017 • Significant progress and response from investors • Gwadar Free Zone investment guide line published • First Gwadar Expo held in January 2018
Construction of Breakwaters	• Draft business plan has been received from Chinese (COPHCL), under review by MoP&S and GPA
Dredging of Berthing Areas & channels	• Draft business plan has been received from Chinese (COPHCL), under review by MoP&S and GPA • Draft MoU for joint Technical and Commercial Feasibility has also been Prepared and being vetted by concerned Ministries
Gwadar Smart Port City Master Plan	• MoU signed in Nov 2015 • LOE signed in August 2015 • Chinese Fourth Harbour Design Institute has been nominated for Gwadar Smart City Plan • Contract Signed in May 2017 • Completion planned in 2019

Source: "CPEC Gwadar Projects," CPEC, *Government of Pakistan*, n.d., http://cpec.gov.pk/gwader/ (accessed March 19, 2018).

Appendix G

List of Approved SEZ's

Proposed sites for SEZs
• **Khyber Pakhtunkhwa** Rashakai Economic Zone on M-1 (Feasibility studies of SEZs is shared with Chinese side).
• **Sindh** Special Economic Zone Dhabeji
• **Balochistan** Bostan Industrial Zone
• **Punjab** Punjab - China Economic Zone, Faisalabad.
• **AJK:** Mirpur Industrial Zone
• **FATA:** Mohmand Marble City
• **Federal Govt:** ICT Model Industrial Zone, Islamabad Development of Industrial Park on Pakistan Steel Mills Land at Port Qasim near Karachi
• **GB:** Moqpondas

Source: "CPEC Special Economic Zones (SEZs)," CPEC, *Government of Pakistan*, n.d., http://cpec.gov.pk/special-economic-zones-projects (accessed March 19, 2018).

Appendix H

Security Measures being employed for CPEC

- Physical deployment of Army and other Law Enforcement Agencies (LEA) troops on all static and roving projects.
- Deployment of covert security means (Hang around Security).
- Protected move of Chinese personnel from Airport to Project sites and vice versa.
- Coordination with civilian law enforcement agencies like local Police, Levies etc.
- Sensitization of Chinese Nationals working on various projects about prevailing security environment and measures taken for their protection.
- Fusion of Civil and Military intelligence agencies on sharing of intelligence.
- Intelligence based operations (IBOs) in the near vicinity of project sites.
- Employment of private security guards on less threatened sites.
- Clarity on rules of engagement for responding against miscreants.
- Approval of "Terms of Reference" for better cohesion amongst LEAs.

Quantum of Force (Raised or Being Raised) For Security of CPEC

Army   15000 (Raising completed and partially deployed)

Special Police Units (SPU)

Punjab   6000 (Raising completed and deployed)

Sind   3000 (Raising in process)

KPK   3000 (Recruitment of 600 individuals completed so far)

Balochistan Nil

Appendix I

Recommendations:

Road Infrastructure

Construction of the following roads is recommended as part of the proposed logical expansion of CPEC:

Sost-Misgar Valley-Kalam Darshi Fort-Mintaka Pass (GB) - The road should be linked further with Tashkurgan (China). This pass has 15,449 feet height and will provide an additional border crossing. Alternately, Kilik Pass route can also be used. The Mintaka route is also better suited for a railway line.

Sost-Chuparsan Valley-Chilinji Pass-Karambar Pass-Mastuj (GB & KP) - This would serve as an alternate to the Karakoram Highway. A tunnel with 8.5 km length can link Kozyaz and Chilinji Glaciers near Chilinji Pass. Also, a 3 km long tunnel can connect Chuparsan Valley with Misgar Valley and cut the distance to the Chinese border by about 20 km. A road spur should also link this road with the Baroghil Pass and the Wakhan corridor.

Ishkoman Valley-Chilinji Pass (GB) - This can provide a link between the proposed KKH Northern Bypass and its Shandur Pass offshoot which is presently under construction.

Chitral-Dorah Pass (KP) - This route has the potential of providing the shortest direct link with Afghan Badakhshan, Tajikistan, Kyrgyzstan and eastern Kazakhstan. In this way the Pamir Highway will be much better able to supplement the KKH.

Thakot-Buner-Karnal Sher M-1 Interchange (GB and KP) - This route can serve as a viable alternative to the Mansehra route.

Pasni-Hoshab (Baluchistan) - This can serve as alternative route linking Gwadar with the Eurasian hinterland.

Ormara-Hoshab (Baluchistan) - This would provide hinterland road connections to Ormara naval base.

Azad Railway Station (on Taftan Road)-Manzil-Afghan Border - This should be further linked with Herat (Afghanistan) and onwards to Turkmenistan via collective funding along the old, proposed Turkmenistan-Afghanistan-Pakistan (TAP) route which leads to the Makran coast. This would serve as the logical northern extension of the recently approved Panjgur-Nokundi Road. It also has the potential to serve as the shortest, perennial route leading to the CARs and Russia while also linking China (through Khorgas).

Railway Infrastructure

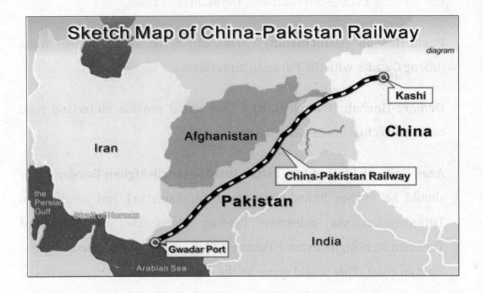

Figure A.1- Sketch Map of China-Pakistan Railway. "New railway tracks planned under CPEC," *Dawn News*, December 20, 2015, https://www.dawn.com/news/1227664 (accessed October 17, 2017).

Besides present proposals, it is recommended that Russia be encouraged to invest in linking Gwadar with Turkmenistan astride a north-south railway via Azad railway station, Herat, Torghundi, Aqina and Mazar Sharif with the Russian gauge.

i. In this way, Mazar e Sharif can be linked onwards with the Torkham crossing point along the Pak-Afghan border.

ii. Development of Makran Coastal ports including HorMiani, Somiani, Ormara, Kor Kalmat, Pasni and Jiwani.

Energy Pipelines

i. Energy pipelines linking the Indian Ocean Rim-land to China could help reduce its reliance on energy supplies via the Strait of Malacca.

ii. Turkmenistan-Afghanistan-Pakistan pipelines (TAP) can be incorporated as part of this project. For instance an outletopf the TAP can be developed at the Pasni port terminal, directly linking it with the CPEC's supply and transport infrastructure

iii. The Iran-Pakistan pipeline can also be linked further adding value to a robust energy supply chain. This would directly coincide with Chinese interests.

Appendix J

List of Countries along the Belt and Road

East Asia	South Asia	Central Asia	West Asia	CIS	Europe
Mongolia	Pakistan	Kazakhstan	Iran	Russia	Poland
Singapore	India	Uzbekistan	Iraq	Ukraine	Lithuania
Malaysia	Bangladesh	Turkmenistan	Turkey	Belarus	Estonia
Indonesia	Sri Lanka	Tajikistan	Syria	Georgia	Latvia
Myanmar	Maldives	Kyrgyzstan	Jordan	Azerbaijan	Czech Republic
Thailand	Bhutan		Lebanon	Armenia	Slovakia
Laos	Nepal		Israel	Moldova	Hungry
Cambodia	Afghanistan		Palestine		Slovenia
Vietnam			Saudi Arabia		Croatia
Brunei			Yemen		Bosnia & Herzegovina
Philippines			Oman		Montenegro
			UAE		Serbia
			Qatar		Albania
			Kuwait		Romania
			Bahrain		Bulgaria
			Greece		Macedonia
			Cyprus		
			Egypt		

Source: *Fung Business Intelligence Centre*
Helen Chin, Winnie He, *The Belt and Road Initiative: 65 Countries and Beyond*, Report by Fung Business Intelligence Centre, May 2016.
https://www.fbicgroup.com/sites/default/files/B%26R_Initiative_65_Countries_an d_Beyond.pdf (accessed October 2, 2018)

Appendix K

List of Agreements/MoUs Signed during visit of Chinese President

Agreements worth US $28 billion were signed to kick-start early harvest projects, while projects worth US $17 billion, which are in the pipeline, will follow as soon as the required studies, processes and formalities are completed. The groundbreaking and signing of financial agreements has demonstrated that there is a strong will on both sides to implement the portfolio of $45 billion agreed under the CPEC framework as early as possible to help Pakistan meet its energy needs. The agreements and MOUs signed are as under:

1. Economic and technical cooperation agreement between China and Pakistan.

2. Exchange of notes of feasibility study of the demonstration project of the DTMB.

3. Exchange of notes on provision of anti-narcotics equipment.

4. Exchange of notes on provision of law enforcement equipment.

5. Exchange of notes on feasibility study of Gwadar hospital

6. MoU on provision of Chinese governmental concessional loan for second phase up-gradation of the Karakorum Highway (Havelian to Thakot).

7. MOU on provision of Chinese governmental concessional loan for Karachi-Lahore Motorway (Multan to Sukkur).

8. MoU on provision of Chinese governmental concessional loan for Gwadar port East Bay Expressway Project.

9. MoU on provision of Chinese governmental concessional loan for Gwadar international airport.

10. Protocol on banking services to agreement on trade in services.

11. MoU on provision of material for tackling climate change.

12. Framework agreement on cooperation on major communications infrastructure project.

13. MoU on cooperation between NDRC of China and Ministry of Planning Development and Reform of Pakistan.

14. MoU on Pro Bono Projects in the Port of Gwadar Region.

15. MoU on establishment of China-Pakistan joint cotton bio-tech laboratory.

16. Framework agreement between the National Railway Administration, China and the Ministry of Railways, Pakistan on joint feasibility study for up-gradation of ML1 and establishment of Havelain dry port of Pakistan Railways.

17. Protocol on the establishment of China-Pakistan joint marine research center.

18. MoU on cooperation between the State Administration of Press, Publication, Radio, Films and Television of China and Ministry of Information, Broadcasting and National Heritage of Pakistan.

19. Triple party agreement between China Central Television and PTV and Pakistan Television Foundation on the re-broadcasting of CCTV-NEWS/CCTV -9 Documentary in Pakistan.

20. Protocol on establishment of sister cities relationship between Chengdu city Sichuan Province of PRC and Lahore city.

21. Protocol on establishment of sister cities Relationship between Zhuhai city, Guangdong province and Gwadar city.

22. Protocol on establishment of sister cities relationship between Karamay City, XianjianUgur, and Gwadar city.

23. Framework agreement between NEA and MoPNR on Gwadar-Nawabshah LNG terminal and pipeline project.

24. Commercial contract on Lahore Orange Line Metro Train Project.

25. Agreement on financing for Lahore Orange line Metro Train project.

26. MoU on financing for KKH up-gradation Phase-2 (Havelian to Takot), KLM, Gwadar east bay expressway, Gwadar international airport projects.

27. Financing agreement relating to the 870MW hydro-electric Suki Kinari hydropower project between EXIM Bank of China, Industrial and Commercial Bank of China Limited and SK Hydro (Private) Limited.

28. Financing cooperation agreement between the EXIM Bank of China and Port Qasim Electric Power Company (Private) Limited (on Port Qasim 2x660MW coal-fired power plant).

29. Framework facility agreement for 720MW Karot hydropower project between China Development Bank Corporation, EXIM Bank of China and Karot Power Company (Private) Limited.

30. Term sheet of the facility for Zonergy 9x100 MW solar project in Punjab between China Development Bank Corporation, EXIM Bank of China and Zonergy Company limited.

31. Drawdown agreement on Jhimpir wind power project between UEP Wind Power (Private) Limited as borrower and China Development Bank Corporation as lender.

32. Terms and conditions in favor of Sindh Engro Coal Mining Company for Thar Block II 3.8Mt/a mining Project, Sindh province, Pakistan arranged by China Development Bank Corporation.

33. Terms and conditions in favor of Engro Powergen Thar (Private) Limited, Sindh province, Pakistan for Thar Block II 2x330MW coal fired power project arranged by China Development Bank Corporation.

34. Framework agreement of Financing Cooperation in Implementing the China-Pakistan Economic Corridor between China Development Corporation and HBL.

35. MoU with respect to cooperation between Wapda and CTG.

36. MoU among PPIB, CTG, and Silk Road Fund on Development of Private Hydro Power Projects.

37. Facility operating agreement for Dawood Wind Power project between ICBC and PCC of China and HDPPL.

38. Framework agreement for promoting chinese investments and industrial parks development in Pakistan between ICBC and HBL on financial services corporation.

39. The financing term sheet agreement for Thar Block –I between ICBC, SSRL.

40. Energy strategic cooperation framework agreement between Punjab province and China Huaneng Group.

41. Framework agreement on the China Pakistan Economic Corridor Energy Project Cooperation.

42. Cooperation agreement between Sino-Sindh Resources (Pvt) Ltd and Shanghai Electric Group for Thar Coalfield Block I Coal-Power integrated Project in Pakistan.

43. Cooperation agreement for Matiyari-Lahore and Matyari (Port Qasim)-Faisalabad Transmission and Transformation Project between National Transmission Distribution Company (NTDC) and National Grid of China.

44. IA on Port Qasim Coal fired Power Plant between Power China and GoP.

45. Facility Agreement for the Sahiwal Coal-fired Power Plant Project between industrial and Commercial Bank of China Limited, Huaneng Shandong Electricity limited and Shandong Ruyi Group.

46. Cooperation agreement on Hubco Coal-fired Power Plant Project between CPIH and Hubco Power Company.

47. Facilitation Agreement on Salt Range Coal-fired Power Project between CMEC and Punjab Government.

48. MoU between NUML Pakistan and Xinjiang Normal University, Urumqi China for Cooperation on Higher Education.

49. Agreement on collaboration on establishment of NUML International Center of education (NICE) between NUML Pakistan and Xinjiang Normal University, Urumqi, China.

On this occasion the two leaders inaugurated the following projects by unveiling the plaques:

1. Industrial and Commercial Bank of China, Lahore Branch.

2. Energization of 100 MW solar power plants at Quad-i-Azam solar park, Bahawalpur.

3. FM 98 Dosti Channel studio PBC-CRI, Islamabad.

4. Demonstration project of DTMB Broadcasting in Pakistan.

5. China Cultural center Pakistan.

6. China-Pakistan Joint Research Center for small hydropower, Islamabad.

7. China-Pakistan cross-border optical fiber cable system project.

8. Metro rail transit system on the Orange Line in Lahore.

Ground breaking of following power projects was also jointly done by Prime Minister Muhammad Nawaz Sharif and President Xi Jinping via video link:

1- Karot 720 MW Hydropower project.

2- Dawood 50 MW Wind-power project.

3- Sachal 50 MW Wind-power project.

4- Zonergy 900 MW solar project.

5- Jhimpir 100 MW Wind-power project.

Source: "List of Pakistan-China MoUs", The Nation, (April 21, 2015).,
http://www.pcgv.org/April%2023%202015.pdf (accessed Nov 8, 2018).

Appendix L

Financing Run Down of 22 CPEC Projects

	Name of Project	Amount (Million USD)	Total Amoun (Million USD
I: Infrastructure Projects Funded by Chinese Concessional Loan	KKH Phase-II (Havelian-Thakot)	1315	5874
	Karachi-Lahore Motorway Sukkur- Multan Section (392KM)	2889	
	Metro Rail Transit System on the Orange Line in Lahore	1626	
	Laying of Optical Fiber Cable (OFC) from Rawapindi to Khunjrab	44	
Energy Projects Funded by Investment from Chinese Companies and Partners(includir g Companiesfr o Pakistan, Qata r and IFC of Warld Bank)	50MW Dawood Wind Power Project	115	12815*
	100MW Pakistan Jhimpir UEP Wind Power Phase I Project	252	
	Sachal 50MW Wind Power Project	134	
	Zonergy 300MW Solar Project in	460	

Punjab		
Port Qasim 2×660MW Coal-fired Power Project	2085	
Sahiwal 1320MW Coal-fired Power Plant	1800	
720MW Karot Hydro-Power Project	1698	
660MW HUBCO Coal Power Plant	1995	
Three Gorges Second and Third Wind Power Projects (100MW)	224	
Gwadar Port Operation and Development of Free Zone	250	
SUKI KINARI Hydro-Power Project	1802	
2×330MW Mine Mouth Coal Fired Power Plant and 3.8Mta Open Cast Lignite Mine	2000	

III : Projects Funded by Chinese Interest-free Loan	Expressway East Bay Gwadar	143	143
IV : Projects Funded by Chinese Grant	Gwadar Smart Port City Master Plan	4	29
	DTMB Demonstration Project	23	
	China-Pakistan Friendship School in Gwadar	0.4	
	CPEC Emergency Medical Center in Gwadar	1.6	
V : Projects Funded by Pakistan Government	Feasibility study for Upgradation of ML1 and Establishment of Havelian Dryport of Pakistan Railways	3	3
Total:		USD 18,864 Million	

* Including 3 Billion Equity from Chinese Companies and 9.8 Billion of Commercial Loan

Source: Mian Babar, "Chinese Debt Burden: Fact and Fiction", Pakistan Today, (December 29, 2018). https://www.pakistantoday.com.pk/2018/12/29/chinese-debt-burden-facts-and-fiction/#.XCfXLWE3xA8.twitter (accessed December 29, 2018).

List of Figures

List of Graphs

List of Tables

Author Profiles

Dr. Song Guoyou is a Professor at the Institute of International Studies at the Fudan University, China. He is also Director of the University's Center for Economic Diplomacy Studies and Deputy Director of its Center for American Studies. He focuses on China-U.S. relations, China's foreign economic policies and global governance. He also holds the posts of Senior Research Fellow at the International Economics and Finance Institute of the Ministry of Finance, and is also a member of the China National Committee for Pacific Economic Cooperation Council (PECC). He acquired his Ph.D in International Relations from Fudan University in 2006.

Lt Gen (Retired) Naeem Khalid Lodhi, HI (M), is the former caretaker Defence Minister, Ex Chief Executive and Managing Director of Fauji Fertilizer Company Limited. He was commissioned in the Army in 1972. He holds a Bachelor's degree in Engineering (Civil), graduate of the Command and Staff College Quetta and National Defence University, Islamabad. He has served on various command, staff and instructional assignments in his career in the Army including the important appointments of Directing Staff at National Defence College (now National Defence University) Islamabad. He has also served as Commander Corps Engineers, General Officer Commanding of an Infantry and an Engineers Division, Director General Staff Duties at General Headquarters Rawalpindi and Corps Commander Bahawalpur.

Ambassador (Retired) Syed Hasan Javed has been working as the Director of the Chinese Studies Centre of Excellence at the School of Social Sciences and Humanities (S3H) NUST, Islamabad since January 2016. He holds a Master's degree in Economics and joined the Civil Service of Pakistan in 1979. He has served as Pakistan's Ambassador in Germany, Singapore, and Mauritius. In the People's Republic of China he has served on two diplomatic assignments spanning over a decade He speaks fluent Chinese and is the author of several books on China including the Pakistani Best-Seller, Chinese Made Easy.

Dr. Liu Jun is an Associate Professor, Director South Asia Institute, Yunnan University, China. He has written extensively on the economic and financial impacts of China's rise as a global power, as well its far-reaching implications both for the region and the world. His work spans over the changing nature of international relations, politics and comparative economic systems with a key focus on China.

Dr. Vaqar Ahmed is Joint Executive Director at the Sustainable Development Policy Institute (SDPI). Earlier, he has served at the UNDP, and has undertaken assignments with Asian Development Bank, World Bank Group, and Ministries of Finance, Planning, and Commerce in Pakistan. He holds a PhD in Economics with a focus on public finance and international trade reforms. He has written extensively on macroeconomic modeling, inclusive growth and infrastructure reforms, trade and taxation policies, regional trade agreements, trade in services, energy governance, border-related trade infrastructure, youth employment, and social safety nets. He is a visiting faculty member and researcher in different international and local institutes.

Dr. Zafar Mahmood is Professor of Economics and Head of Research at the School of Social Sciences & Humanities, National University of Sciences and Technology (NUST), Islamabad. He has completed his MPhil and PhD degrees from Columbia University. He has served as a Senior Economist at the Kuwait Institute for Scientific Research and as Chief of Research at the Pakistan Institute of Development Economics. Dr. Mahmood has nine books to his credit and has widely published in peer reviewed international and national journals. He is the Managing Editor of NUST Journal of Social Sciences and Humanities and referee to many other journals. He has served as a consultant to the World Bank, UNDP, UN-ESCAP, International Development Center of Japan (Tokyo), Institute of Social Studies (Hague) and DRI/McGraw-Hill (USA).

Dr. Shabbir Ahmed Khan is Director of the Area Study Center for Russia, China and Central Asia at the University of Peshawar. He has acquired his PhD from the University of Peshawar and his Masters in Economics from Tashkent, Uzbekistan. He has also completed his Post - Doctoral training from the Diplomatic Academy in Moscow, operative under the Foreign Ministry of the Russian Federation.

Dr Shabana Fayyaz, is an Assistant Professor at the Defense & Strategic Studies Department, Quaid-I-Azam University, Islamabad. She holds a PhD from the University of Birmingham, UK. Her expertise is on the themes of non-traditional security; violent extremism; counter-terrorism; de-radicalization; Pakistan's foreign policy, role of women in conflict resolution and South Asian politics. She is an alumni of the "Women and Security Program" at Harvard Kennedy School and has also participated in the Annual Colloquium of Institute of Inclusive Security, Massachusetts (Harvard) and Washington D C. USA. She is the coordinator of the Pakistan chapter of Women without Borders and a member of the advisory board of the Peace and Collaborative Development Network. She serves on the editorial boards of Pakistan Institute of Peace Studies and the Institute of Strategic Studies Islamabad.

Brigadier (Retired) Abdul Rahman Bilal, SJ, was commissioned in the Pakistani Army in 1974 and later joined the Special Services Group. He has performed staff duties related to macro level planning. For his exemplary services as an officer he was decorated with the Sitara-e-Jurrat. After retirement, he has served as the Rector of the Fauji Foundation University, Islamabad. Presently, he is an international advisor on development, security and diplomacy, working with numerous private and public sector organizations.

Ms. S Sadia Kazmi is Director Academics, Policy & Program at the Strategic Vision Institute. She holds an MS degree in Political Science from University of Auckland, New Zealand and an MPhil in Defence and Strategic Studies from Quaid-i-Azam University, Islamabad. She is also pursuing her PhD research work in the Department of Strategic Studies at National Defence University, Islamabad. She has served as a Lecturer in the Department of Diplomatic Studies at Fatima Jinnah Women University, Rawalpindi; Department of Politics and International Relations at International Islamic University, Islamabad; and in the Department of Mass Communication at National University of Modern Languages, Islamabad. Ms. Sadia has also been conducting regular workshops with the Sustainable Development Policy Institute (SDPI) and Foreign Services Academy as a Resource Person in the areas of Peace, Conflict Analysis, Conflict Resolution and Conflict transformation.

Mr. Hassan Dawood Butt is Project Director and CPEC Coordinator at the CPEC Secretariat for the Ministry of Planning Development and Reforms, Government of Pakistan. He has served as a diplomat at the Embassy of Pakistan in Beijing, China. He has worked closely with both the Chinese government and various organizations for expanding bilateral ties in the realms of finance, investment and economic cooperation. He specializes in project oversight and management and has extensive experience working with the Pakistan Navy.

Mr. Waqas Jan is a Research Associate and Program Coordinator for the China Studies & Information Centre (CSIC) at the Strategic Vision Institute, Islamabad. He holds a Master's degree (with Distinction) in International Relations from the University of Nottingham. His Current research interests include, CPEC, Pak-China relations and Pakistan's role in the wider South Asian region's growth and development. He has written extensively on the discursive power of Super-Power politics and takes keen interest in examining the underlying nuances of 'Narrative' both within Regional and International Politics. These are drawn from his extensive experience as a Media, Communications and Advocacy professional, having worked across a broad range of public, private and non-governmental organizations, with a domestic as well as regional outlook.

Ms. Qurat-ul-Ain Hafeez is working as a Research Associate at Strategic Vision Institute, Islamabad. She holds an MPhil degree in International
297

Relations from the School of Politics and International Relations, Quaid-i-Azam University, Islamabad, and a Masters in Defence and Diplomatic Studies from Fatima Jinnah Women University, Rawalpindi, Pakistan. She has also worked as a Research Officer at the Inter Services Public Relations (ISPR), Rawalpindi,

INDEX

BIBLIOGRAPHY

Documents/Policy Papers/Reports

Ahmad, Azhar. "Gwadar Port: Potentials and Prospects." Report, *Pakistan Institute for Conflict and Security Studies*. Islamabad, 2015.

"Afghanistan: The Challenge of Relations with Pakistan." *Parliamentary Information and Research Service Publication PRB*. January 9, 2008. https://lop.parl.ca/content/lop/ResearchPublications/prb0733-e.pdf (accessed October 17, 2017).

Akinci, Gokhan, and James Crittle. "Special Economic Zone: Performance, Lessons Learned, and Implication for Zone Development. *Foreign Investment Advisory Service (FIAS) Occasional Paper*. 2008. http://documents.worldbank.org/curated/en/3439014683309 77533/Special-economic-zone-performance-lessons-learned-and-implication-for-zone-development (accessed August 10, 2018).

Albert, Eleanor. "Competition in the Indian Ocean." *Council on Foreign Relations*. May 19, 2016. https://www.cfr.org/backgrounder/competition-indian-ocean (accessed October 18, 2018).

Allworth, Edward. "Uzbekistan." *Encyclopedia Britannica*, n.d. https://www.britannica.com/place/Uzbekistan (accessed October 17, 2017).

Amadeo, Kimberly. "China's Economy Facts and Effect on the U.S. Economy How Much China Really Affects the U.S. Economy." August, 2018. https://www.thebalance.com/china-economy-facts-effect-on-us-economy-3306345 (accesses August 14, 2018).

Asey, Tamim. "The Other Drawdown -Why Donor Fatigue is Threatening to Derail Afghanistan." *Foreign Policy*. November 10, 2014. http://foreignpolicy.com/2014/11/10/the-other-drawdown-why-donor-fatigue-is-threatening-to-derail-afghanistan/ (accessed October 17, 2017).

" Briefing Notes on Some of the Main Issues of the Doha Round." *World Trade Organization*, n.d. https://www.wto.org/english/tratop_e/dda_e/status_e/brief00_e.htm (accessed September 14, 2018).

Betty, Huang and Le Xia. "China | ODI from the Middle Kingdom: What's next after the big turnaround?." *BBVA Research*. February 2018. https://www.bbvaresearch.com/wp-content/uploads/2018/02/201802_ChinaWatch_China-Outward-Investment_EDI.pdf (accessed September 24, 2018).

"Building the Belt and Road: Concept, Practice and China's Contribution." *Belt and Road Portal*. May 5, 2017. https://eng.yidaiyilu.gov.cn/zchj/qwfb/12731.htm (accessed May 10, 2017).

Calabrese, John. "The China-Pakistan Economic Corridor (CPEC): Underway and Under Threat." December 20, 2016. http://www.mei.edu/content/map/china-pakistan-economic-corridor-cpec-underway-and-under-threat (accessed July 29, 2017).

"Central Asia - Energy - International Cooperation and Development – European Commission." *International Cooperation and Development, European Union*. July 1, 2014. https://ec.europa.eu/europeaid/regions/central-asia/eu-central-asia-energy-cooperation_en (accessed October 20, 2018).

"China and the WTO." *World Trade Organization*. n.d. https://www.wto.org/english/thewto_e/countries_e/china_e.htm (accessed August 14, 2018).

Cooley, Alexander. "Kyrgyzstan on the Brink." *Current History*. October, 2010. http://www.currenthistory.com/Article.php?ID=828 (accessed August 14, 2018).

David, Dollar. "The AIIB and the 'One Belt, One Road." *Brookings Institute*, 2015. https://www.brookings.edu/opinions/the-aiib-and-the-one-belt-one-road/ (accessed July 05, 2017).

Denisenko, Mikhail. "Migration to Russia and the Current Economic Crisis." *E-International Relations*, May 5, 2017. http://www.e-ir.info/2017/05/05/migration-to-russia-and-the-current-economic-crisis/ (accessed October 17, 2017).

"Doing Business in Pakistan." *World Bank Group*, n.d. http://www.doingbusiness.org/data/exploreeconomies/pakistan (accessed October 11, 2018).

"Economic Data." *State Bank of Pakistan*, n.d. http://www.sbp.org.pk/ecodata/index2.asp (accessed September 10, 2018).

Ewalle, Laurence Vand. "In Depth Analysis Pakistan and China Iron Brothers Forever?." *European Union*, June, 2015. http://www.europarl.europa.eu/RegData/etudes/IDAN/2015/549052/EXPO_IDA(2015)549052_EN.pdf (accessed September 10, 2018).

Farole, Thomas and GokhanAkinci. "Special Economic Zones: Progress, Emerging Challenges, and future directions." *The World Bank*, August 1, 2011. http://documents.worldbank.org/curated/en/752011468203980987/Special-economic-zones-progress-emerging-challenges-and-future-directions (accessed September 10, 2018).

Farole, Thomas. "Special Economic Zones: Performance, Policy and Practice—with a Focus on Sub-Saharan Africa." *World Bank,* September 2010. http://siteresources.worldbank.org/INTRANETTRADE/Resources/Pubs/SpecialEconomicZones_Sep2010.pdf (accessed September 10, 2018).

Fedorenko, Vladimir. "The New Silk Road Initiative in Central Asia." *Rethink Institution*, November 2013. https://iias.asia/research/belt-road-initiative-electronic-library (accessed April 3, 2017).

"Fishery and Aquaculture Country Profile, the Islamic Republic of Pakistan." *Food and Agriculture Organization of the United Nations*, February 2009. http://www.fao.org/fishery/docs/DOCUMENT/fcp/en/FI_CP_P K.pdf (accessed October 23, 2018).

"GDP (current US$) China, United States, Germany, Japan and India. " *World Bank, n.d.* https://data.worldbank.org/indicator/NY.GDP.MKTP.CD?locatio ns=CN-US-DE-JP (accessed November 15, 2017).

Government of China, Ministry of Commerce. *The Belt and Road Initiative's Economic and Trade Cooperation to Achieve Positive Progress,* December 27, 2016. http://www.mofcom.gov.cn/article/difang/201612/201612023 88848.shtml (accessed December 27, 2016).

Government of China. Ministry of Culture. "*The Belt and Road Cultural Development Action Plan (2016-2020).*" *Government of China. Ministry of Culture*, December 28, 2016. http://zwgk.mcprc.gov.cn/auto255/201701/t20170113_47759 1.html (accessed December 28, 2016).

"*China Pakistan Economic Corridor, Cross Border Optical Fiber Cable.*" *Government of Pakistan- China Pakistan Economic Corridor*, n.d. http://cpec.gov.pk/project-details/40 (accessed February 1, 2018).

"CPEC Infrastructure Projects." *China Pakistan Economic Corridor*, n.d. http://cpec.gov.pk/infrastructure/ (accessed July 13, 2017).

"CPEC Infrastructure Projects." *China Pakistan Economic Corridor*, n.d. http://cpec.gov.pk/infrastructure (accessed February 19, 2018).

"CPEC Projects Update." *China Pakistan Economic Corridor*, n.d. http://cpec.gov.pk/progress-update/ (accessed July 13, 2017).

Grawert, Elke, Rabia Nusrat and Zulfiqar Ali Shah. "Afghanistan's Cross-Border Trade with Pakistan and Iran and the Responsibility for Conflict-Sensitive Employment." BICC Working Paper, *Bonn International Center for Conversion*, April, 2017,

https://www.bicc.de/uploads/tx_bicctools/bicc_workPaper_04_
2017.pdf. (accessed October 17, 2017).

Huang, Zheping. "All the Buzzwords Xi Jinping Added to the Chinese
Communist Party's Constitution." *Quartz*, October 25, 2017.
https://qz.com/1111474/chinas-19th-party-congress-all-the-
buzzwords-xi-jinping-added-to-the-chinese-communist-partys-
constitution/ (accessed 6 October, 2018).

Hussain, Muzaffar. "China Pakistan Economic Corridor (CPEC):
Challenges and the Way Forward." *Naval Postgraduate School
Monterey, California*, June 2017.
https://calhoun.nps.edu/bitstream/handle/10945/55626/17Ju
n_Hussain_Muzaffar.pdf?sequence=1 (accessed October 17,
2017).

Hussain, Zahid. "Sources of Tension in Afghanistan and Pakistan: A
Regional Perspective." *CIDOB Policy Research Project*, December
2011.

"Introduction." *Asian Infrastructure Investment Bank*, n.d.
https://www.aiib.org/en/about-aiib/ (accessed August 14,
2018).

Invest in Kazakhstan. "10 Reasons to Invest in Kazakhstan." *Embassy of
the Republic of Kazakhstan- Qatar*, n.d. http://www.kazakhstan-
bern.ch/en/?page_id=314 (accessed April 24, 2017).

Kamran, Sehar. "Pak-Gulf Defense and Security Cooperation." *Center for
Pakistan and Gulf Studies*, January 2013.
http://cpakgulf.org/documents/Pak-Gulf-Security-Ties-final.pdf
(accessed October 17, 2017).

Kang, Joong Shik, and Wei Liao ."Chinese Imports: What's Behind the
Slowdown?." *International Monetary Fund*, 2016.
https://www.imf.org/external/pubs/ft/wp/2016/wp16106.pdf
(accessed August 13, 2018).

Kanwal, Gurmeet. "Pakistan's Gwadar Port: A New Naval Base in China's
String of Pearls in the Indo-Pacific." *Center for Strategic and
International Studies (CSIS)*, Apr 2, 2018.

www.csis.org/analysis/pakistans-gwadar-port-new-naval-base-chinas-string-pearls-indo-pacific (accessed October 22, 2018).

"Long Term Plan for China-Pakistan Economic Corridor (2017-2030)." *Ministry of Planning Development and Reforms*, 2017. https://www.pc.gov.pk/uploads/cpec/LTP.pdf (accessed October 17, 2018).

Mahmood , Zafar. (2018) "Opportunities and Challenges of Special Economic Zones under CPEC for Pakistan." The International Academic Seminar on Industrial Cooperation and Construction of Industrial Zones, *CPEC: Center for Pakistan Studies of Peking University, and China Three Gorges International Corporation*, January 5-7, 2018.

Markey, Daniel S., and West James. "Behind China's Gambit in Pakistan." *Council on Foreign Relations (CFR)*, May 12, 2016. https://www.cfr.org/expert-brief/behind-chinas-gambit-pakistan. (accessed October 17, 2017).

"Meeting Asia's Infrastructure Needs." *Asian Development Bank , n.d.* https://www.adb.org/publications/asia-infrastructure-needs (accessed February 27, 2017).

"Ministerial Conference on Transport." *UNESCAP*, December, 2016. http://www.unescap.org/sites/default/files/Strengthening%20Connectivity%20South%20Asia%20new%20note.pdf (accessed October 17, 2017).

"National Development and Reform Commission with 13 Departments and Units to Establish the Belt and Road' PPP Work Mechanism." *National Development and Reform Commission of PRC*, January, 2017. http://tzs.ndrc.gov.cn/zttp/PPPxmk/gzdt/201701/t20170106_834560.html (accessed January 6, 2017).

Norris, Robert S M., and William Arkin. "Russian (C.I.S.) Strategic Nuclear Forces: End of 1994." *Bulletin of the Atomic Scientists,* March, 1995.

https://www.tandfonline.com/doi/abs/10.1080/00963402.199
5.11658057 (accessed January 18, 2017).

"Organization of the United Nations." February, 2009.
http://www.fao.org/fishery/docs/DOCUMENT/fcp/en/FI_CP_P
K.pdf (accessed October 23, 2018).

"Pakistan Economic Survey 2017-18." *Ministry of Finance Pakistan*, 2018.
http://www.finance.gov.pk/survey_1718.html (accessed August
10, 2018).

PBC. "Preliminary Study on Pakistan and China Trade Partnership Post
FTA." *Pakistan Business Council*, 2013.
https://www.pbc.org.pk/research/preliminary-study-on-
pakistan-and-china-trade-partnership-post-fta/ (accessed
August 10, 2018).

Peoples Republic of China. "China's Foreign Trade." *The State Council of
Peoples Republic of China,* December 11,
http://english.gov.cn/archive/white_paper/2014/08/23/conte
nt_281474983043184.htm (accessed August 13, 2018).

Putin, Vladimir. "New Integration Project for Eurasia: Future in Making
Today." *Izvestia*, October 3, 2011.
https://www.rusemb.org.uk/press/246 (accessed April 19,
2017).

"Presidential Executive Order on Buy American and Hire American."
White House, April 18, 2017.
https://www.whitehouse.gov/presidential-actions/presidential-
executive-order-buy-american-hire-american/ (accessed
October 5, 2018).

"Repaving the Ancient Silk Routes." *PWC Global*, n.d.
https://www.pwc.com/gx/en/issues/growth-markets-
centre/publications/repaving-the-ancient-silk-routes.html
(accessed August 17, 2018).

Rapoza, Kenneth. "China's 'Best and Brightest' Leaving U.S. Universities
and Returning Home." *Forbes*, Apr 17, 2017.
https://www.forbes.com/sites/kenrapoza/2017/04/17/chinas-

best-and-brightest-leaving-u-s-universities-and-returning-home/#5cd9a071d41e (accessed September 14, 2018).

Rick, Rowden. "Understanding Foreign Relations between India and Iran." *Sheffield Political Economy Research Institute (SPERI),* July 12, 2017. http://speri.dept.shef.ac.uk/2017/07/12/understanding-foreign-relations-between-india-and-iran/ (accessed October 17, 2017).

Schiavenza, Matt. "A Surprising Map of the World Shows Just How Big China's Population Is?." *The Atlantic,* August 14, 2013. https://www.theatlantic.com/china/archive/2013/08/a-surprising-map-of-the-world-shows-just-how-big-chinas-population-is/278691/ (accessed August 13, 2018).

Shepard, Wade. "China's Seaport Shopping Spree: What China Is Winning By Buying Up The World's Ports." *Forbes Magazine,* September 7, 2017. www.forbes.com/sites/wadeshepard/2017/09/06/chinas-seaport-shopping-spree-whats-happening-as-the-worlds-ports-keep-going-to-china/#4e66f9ae4e9d (accessed October 22, 2018).

Siddiqi, Sabena. "Reconnecting Central Asia." *Katehon,* February 21, 2017. http://katehon.com/article/reconnecting-central-asia (accessed April 27, 2017).

"Special Economic Zones Act, 2012." *Board of Investment,* December, 2015. http://boi.gov.pk/UploadedDocs/Downloads/Modified%20SEZ%20Act%202012.pdf (accessed August 2, 2018).

Sood, Vikram. "The New Great Game: an All Asian Game?." *Observer Research Foundation,* April 6, 2017. https://www.orfonline.org/expert-speak/new-great-game-all-asian/ (accessed August 2, 2018).

"Textile Division." *Textile industry Division Government of Pakistan,* n.d. http://www.textile.gov.pk/ (accessed October 19, 2018).

. "Vision and Actions on Jointly Building Silk Road Economic Belt and 21st-Century Maritime Silk Road." *National Development and Reform Commission, Ministry of Foreign Affairs, and Ministry of Commerce of the People's Republic of China*, n.d. https://eng.yidaiyilu.gov.cn/qwyw/qwfb/1084.htm (accessed March, 2015).

"Engine Selection for Very Large Container Vessels." *Winterthur Gas & Diesel Ltd.,* September, 2016. https://www.wingd.com/media/1756/wingdpaper_engine_sele ction_for_very_large_container_vessels_201609.pdf (accessed October 17, 2017).

"World Oil Transit Chokepoints." *U.S Energy Information Administration (EIA)*, July 25, 2017. https://www.eia.gov/beta/international/regions-topics.php?RegionTopicID=WOTC (accessed October 5, 2018).

Xia, Yafeng. "The Cold War and Chinese Foreign Policy." *E-International Relations*, July, 2008. https://www.e-ir.info/2008/07/16/the-cold-war-and-China/ (accessed October 15, 2015).

Yusuf, Shahid. "Can Chinese FDI Accelerate Pakistan's Growth?." *George Washington University, School of Business*, 2013. https://www.theigc.org/wp-content/uploads/2014/09/Yusuf-2013-Working-Paper1.pdf (accessed October 15, 2015).

Zhanbin, Zhang. "Six Characteristics and Ideas of New Normal of China's Economy." *Guangming Daily News*, January 11, 2016. http://economy.gmw.cn/2016-01/11/content_18447411.htm (accessed December 12, 2017).

Zhou, Yikun. Wei Yong and Xiangqun Zhang (eds.). "International Conference on SEZ Experience and Opportunities." Conference Proceedings: *World Special Economic Zone Development Forum*, Ha Long City, QuangNinh Province of Vietnam, March 18-22.

"4th Review of the China Pakistan Free Trade Agreement (CPFTA) & Recommendations for Phase II Negotiations."*Pakistan Business Council*, 2018. https://www.pbc.org.pk/wp-content/uploads/PBC-final-5.pdf (accessed october 17, 2018).

Books/Journal Articles

Abid, Massarrat, and Ayesha Ashfaq. "CPEC: Challenges and opportunities for Pakistan." *Journal of Pakistan Vision* 16, no. 2 (2015):142-169.

Ahmed, Vaqar, Abid. Q., Suleri, and Javed, A. "Strengthening South Asia Value Chain" *South Asia Economic Journal16*, no. 2 (2015):55-74.

Ahmed, Vaqar, Abid Q. Suleri, and Muhammad Adnan. "FDI in India: Prospects for Pakistan." in *India-Pakistan Trade*, 193-219. New Delhi : Springer, 2015.

Ahmed, Vaqar. *Pakistan's Agenda for Economic Reforms*. Oxford: Oxford University Press, 2017.

Akber, Ali. "China Pakistan Economic Corridor: Prospects and Challenges for Regional Integration." *Arts and Social Sciences Journal* 7, no. 4 (2016): 1-5.

Alexander , Cooley. *Great Games, Local Rules*. New York: Oxford University Press, 2012.

Amjad, Rashid, and Awais Namra. "Pakistan's Productivity Performance and TFP Trends 1980-2015: Cause for real concern." *Lahore Journal of Economics* 21, no. 21 (September 2016): 33-63.

Amjad, Rashid. *The Pakistani Diaspora: Corridors of Opportunity and Uncertainty*. Lahore: Lahore School of Economics: 2017.

Anwar, Zahid. "Gwadar Deep Sea Port's Emergence as Regional Trade and Transportation Hub: Prospects and Problems." *Journal of Political Studies* 1, no. 2 (2011):97.

Bhatia, NK. "India, Chabahar, and the Changing Regional Dynamics." *CLAWS Journal* (Winter 2016): 103.

Blank, Stephen. "The Intellectual Origin of the Eurasian Union." in *Putin's Grand Strategy: Eurasia and its Discontents*, ed. S. Frederick Starr and Svante E. Cornell, 14-28. Washington: Central Asia-Caucasia Institute, 2014.

Botsford, George W. *A History of the Ancient World*. London: The MacMillan Company,1913.

Brzezinski ,Zbigniev. *The Grand Chess Board*. New York: Basic Books, 1998.

Butt, Khalid Manzoor, Anam Abid But. "Impact of CPEC on Regional and Extra Regional Actors." *Journal of Political Science* 33 (January 2015): 23-44.

Buzan, Barry. "A Framework for Regional Security Analysis." in *South Asian Insecurity and the Great Powers*. London: Palgrave Macmillan, 1986.

Changhe, Su. "Governance and Order in the World of Connectivity." *World Economics and Politics*, no. 438 (February 2017): 32.

Erika, Weinthal and Luong Pauline Jones."Energy Wealth and Tax Reform in Russia and Kazakhstan." *Resources Policy* 27, no. 4 (2001)): 215-223.

Guo, Huijun. "Investment Cooperation between China and Central Asia in the Context of 'the Belt and Road' - Based on the Perspective of Transportation Infrastructure Investment." *International Economic Cooperation*, no. 2 (2017): 74.

Gupta, Eshita. "Oil Vulnerability Index of Oil-Importing Countries." *Energy Policy*, 36, no. 3 (March 2008): 1195–1211.

Haasheng, Zhao. "Central Asia in Chinese Strategic Thinking." in, *The New Great Game: China and South and Central Asia in the Era of Reforms*, ed. Thomas Fingar, 181. USA: Stanford University Press, 2016.

Halford , J. Mackinder. "The Geographical Pivot of history (1904)." *The Geographical Journal* 170, no. 4 (December 2004): 298 321.

Bin, Hu, and Zheng Liansheng."Asia Connectivity: China's Strategy, Policy and Action." *Frontiers*, no. 23 (2015): 76

Ikenberry, G. John. "The Rise of China and the Future of the West." Foreign Affairs 87, no. 1 (January/February 2008): 23-37.

Jacques, Martin. When China Rules the World: The End of the Western World and the Birth of a New Global Order, Second Edition. Penguin Books: August, 2012.

Javaid, Umbreen, and Asifa Jahangir. "Pakistan-China Strategic Relationship: A Glorious Journey of 55 Years." *Journal of the Research Society of Pakistan* 52, no. 1 (2015): 157-183

Kataria, Jafar Riaz, and Anum Naveed. "Pakistan China Social and Economic Relations." *South Asian Studies* 29, no. 2 (2014): 395-410

Kayani, Farrukh, & et al. "China-Pakistan Economic Relations: Lessons for Pakistan." *Pakistan Journal of Commerce and Social Sciences* 7, no. 3 (2013): 454- 462.

Khan ,Shabir Ahmad. "Dynamics of Trade Corridors and Energy Pipeline Politics." in *Pakistan's Strategic Environment; Post 2014*, ed. Mushir Anwar, 71-90. Islamabad: Islamabad Policy Research Institute, 2014.

Khan, Shabir Ahmad. "Tashkent in November 2005." *Central Asia*, no. 58 (Summer 2006)

Khan, Shabir Ahmad. "Tashkent in November 2005", *Central Asia*, no. 58 (Summer 2006): 167-176.

Khan, Hafeez-ur-Rahman."Pakistan's Relations with the People's Republic of China." *Pakistan Horizon* 14, no. 3 (1961): 212-232.

Khan, Muhammad Khurshid, Sana Asma and Kiran Afifa. "Balochistan Unrest Internal and External Dimensions." *NDU Journal* (2012): 104.

Khan, Raja M, and M. Saif ur Rehman Khan. "Gwadar Port: An Economic Hub or a Military Outpost." *Journal of Contemporary Studies*, 2, no. 1(2013): 51.

Khan, Shabir Ahmad, and Saima Kyani. "Pipeline Politics in Central Asia: Paradox of Competitive/Cooperative Relations between the United States, Russia and China." *Central Asia*, no. 73 (Winter 2013): 57-83.

Khan, Shabir Ahmad."Geo-Economic Imperatives of Gwadar Sea Port and Kashgar Economic Zone for Pakistan and China." *IPRI Journal* 13, no. 2 (Summer 2013): 87-100.

Khan, Shazia Mehmood."Turkmenistan-Pakistan Bilateral Relations: From Strength to Strength."*Defence Journal* 20, no. 10 (2017): 37.

Kissinger, Henry. *Diplomacy*. New York: Simon & Schuster, 1994.

Liaqat, Zara. "The End of Multi-Fibre Arrangement and Firm Performance in the Textile Industry: New Evidence." *The Pakistan Development Review* 52, no. 2 (Summer 2013): 97-126.

Lo, Bobo. *Axis of Convenience*. London: Chatam House, 2008.

Malik, Ahmed Rashid. "The Pakistan-China Bilateral Trade: The Future Trajectory." *Strategic Studies* 37, no. 1 (2017): 66-89.

Malik, Hasan Yaser. "Strategic importance of Gwadar Port" Journal of Political Studies, 19, no.2 (2012): 57.

Manzoor, R., Shehryar Khan Torub and Vaqar Ahmed, "Health Services Trade between India and Pakistan." *The Pakistan, Journal of Social Sciences* 8 (2017): 112-122.

Mearsheimer, John J. *the Tragedy of Great Power Politics*. USA: W. W. Norton & Company, 2014.

Moberg, Lotta. "The Political Economy of Special Economic Zones." *Journal of Institutional Economics* 11, no. 1 (2015): 167-190.

Nona, Mikhelidze. "After the 2008 Russia-Georgia War: Implications for the Wider Caucasus." *The International Spectator* 44, no. 3 (2009): 27-42.

P. J Schafer. "The Concept of Security." Human and Water Security in Israel and Jordan Springer Briefs in *Environment, Security, Development and Peace* 3 (2013): 113.

Parag Khanna, *Connectography: Mapping the Future of Global Civilization*. Random House: 2016.

Peyrouse, Sebastien, and Raballand Gael. "Central Asia: the New Silk Road Initiative's questionable economic rationality." *Eurasian Geography and Economics*, 56, no. 4 (2015):405-420.

Rahman, Saif Ur, and Shurong Zhao. "Analysis of Chinese Economic and National Security Interests in China-Pakistan Economic Corridor (CPEC) under the Framework of One Belt One Road (OBOR) Initiative." *Arts Social Science Journal* 8, no. 284 (2017).

Ran, Xie, and ZhouJun. "Environmental Protection is the Best Background Color of the Belt and Road." *Environmental Economy, no.*198 (2017): 24-34.

Richard Pomfret. "Trade and Transport in Central Asia." *Global Journal of Emerging Market Economies* 2, no. 3 (2010): 237-256.

Rodrigue, Jean-Paul. "Straits, Passages and Chokepoints: A Maritime Geostrategy of Petroleum Distribution." Cahiers De Géographie Du Québec, 48, no. 135 (Dec 2004): 364.

Shanmin, Yan. *Global Action Report of the Belt and Road Initiative*. Beijing: Social Sciences Academic Press, 2015.

Shirk, Susan L. *China: Fragile Superpower: How China's Internal Politics Could Derail Its Peaceful Rise*. Oxford: Oxford University Press, 2007.

Slobodchiko, Michael O. *Strategic Cooperation: Overcoming the Barriers of Global Anarchy*. UK: Lexington Books, 2013.

Song, Guoyou. "The Strategic Conception of 'the Belt and Road' and the New Development of China 's Economic Diplomacy." *International Review* 46 (2015): 29-30.

Stein, Aurel. "On Alexander's Route into Gedrosia: An Archaeological Tour in Las Bela." The Geographical Journal102, no. 5/6 (Nov - Dec 1943): 193-227.

Thomas, Zimmerman. *The New Silk Roads: China, the US and Future of Central Asia*. New York University: Centre on International Cooperation, October, 2015.

Tisdell, Clem. "Economic Reform and Openness in China: China's Development Policies in the Last 30 Years." Economic Analysis and Policy 39, no. 2 (September 2009): 271-294.

Torbakov, Igor. "Managing Imperial Peripheries: Russia and China in Central Asia." in *The New Great Game*, ed. Thomas Fingar, 251. USA: Stanford University Press, 2016.

Vinokurov, Evgeny. "Eurasian Economic Union: Current State and Preliminary Results." *Russian Journal of Economics* 3, no.1 (March 2017): 54-70.

Wei, Lim Tai. "China's Pivot to Central and South Asia." in *China's One Belt One Road*, ed. LIM Tai Wei, Henry Chan Hong Lee and others, 272. London: Imperial College Press, 2016.

Wei, Shang-Jin. "Foreign Direct Investment in China: Sources and Consequences." In *Financial Deregulation and Integration in East Asia*, ed. Takatoshi Ito and Anne O. Krueger, 77-105. US: University of Chicago Press, 1996.

Woolfrey, Sean Woolfrey. "Special Economic Zones and Regional Integration in Africa." *Journal of Trade and Law Center* (July 2013): 108.

Xin, Lim Wen. "China's Belt and Road Initiative: A Literature Review." in *China's One Belt One Road*, ed. LIM Tai Wei, Henry Chan King Lee and others, 115. London: Imperial College Press, 2016.

Yao , Shujie. "Economic Development and Poverty Reduction in China Over 20 Years of Reforms." *Economic Development and Cultural Change* 48, no. 3 (April 2000): 447- 474.

Yuzhu, Wang. "The Connectivity Economics in Regional Integration." *Frontiers* 77, (May 2015): 21.

Zelin, Wu. "Connectivity of Regional Cooperation in Asia: A Preliminary Analytical Framework." *World Economics and Politics*, no. 430 (2016): 83.

Zhao, Huasheng. "Central Asia in Chinese Strategic Thinking." in *the New Great Game: China and South and Central Asia in the Era of Reform*, ed. Thomas Fingar, 181. USA: Stanford University Press, 2016.

Newspapers /Magazines

Abi-habib, Maria. "How China Got Sri Lanka to Cough Up a Port." *The New York Times*, June 25, 2018, https://www.nytimes.com/2018/06/25/world/asia/china-sri-lanka-port.html (accessed October 8th, 2018).

Ahmad, Mansoor. "CPEC to Benefit Pakistan in both Short- And Long-Term." *The News*, February 4, 2017, https://www.thenews.com.pk/print/183809-CPEC-to-benefit-Pakistan-in-both-short-and-long-term (accessed August 17, 2018).

Ahmad, Manzoor. "China's Role and Interests in Central Asia." *Dawn*, October 6, 2016.

Ahmad, Naveed. "Gwadar, Chabahar and Dubai." *The Express Tribune*, March 14, 2017, https://tribune.com.pk/story/1354422/gwadar-chabahar-dubai/ (accessed October. 17, 2017).

Ahmed Amin. "Blue Revolution' To Enhance Fisheries Production." *Dawn*, July 02, 2018, https://www.dawn.com/news/1417342 (accessed October 23, 2018).

Ashraf, Junaid. "CPEC Key to Economic Success of China's Belt and Road Initiative." *Asia Times*, August 25, 2017, http://www.atimes.com/cpec-key-economic-ripening-belt-road-initiative/ (accessed August 17, 2018).

Aziz, Faisal. "Singapore's PSA Takes over Pakistan's Gwadar Port." *Reuters*, February 6, 2007, https://uk.reuters.com/article/singapore-pakistan/update-1-singapores-psa-takes-over-pakistans-gwadar-port-idUKISL16944320070206 (accessed October 5th, 2018).

Biswas, Ashis. "Can Pakistan Handle CPEC Impact?." *Dhaka Tribune*, October 07, 2017, http://www.dhakatribune.com/world/south-asia/2017/10/07/can-pakistan-handle-cpec-impact/ (accessed October 17, 2017).

Butt, Naveed. "Special Economic Zones: Chinese Seek New Trade Avenues." *Business Recorder*, October 17, 2017, https://fp.brecorder.com/2017/10/20171017226751/ (accessed February, 2018).

Chapman, Ben. "Donald Trump Blasts General Motors for Making Cars in Mexico Temporarily Damaging the Company's Stock." *The Independent*, January 3, 2017, https://www.independent.co.uk/news/business/news/donald-trump-general-motors-gm-twitter-blast-making-cars-mexico-stock-value-president-elect-a7507356.html (accessed December 12, 2017).

Chen, Weihua. "BRI 'Fruitful', But Debt Risk an Issue." *China Daily*, April 19, 2018, http://www.chinadaily.com.cn/a/201804/19/WS5ad8293da3105cdcf6519467.html (accessed September 19, 2018).

Chowdhury, Debasish R. "Pakistan Happy to Aid in China's Quest for Land Route to the West; India, Not so Much." *South China Morning Post*, 19 Nov. 2013, www.scmp.com/business/commodities/article/1359761/pakistan-happy-aid-chinas-quest-land-route-west-india-not-so (accessed October 18th, 2018).

"China 2008: The Global Financial Crisis." *China Digital Times*, December 8, 2008, https://chinadigitaltimes.net/2008/12/2008-financial-crisis-and-china/ (accessed September 20, 2018).

"Eastern, Western Routes of CPEC to Be Completed by 2019." Mattis Global Link News, June 29, 2017, https://mettisglobal.news/eastern-western-routes-of-cpec-to-be-completed-by-2019-hassan-daud/ (accessed February 19, 2018).

Griffiths, James. "Just What is This One Belt, One Road Thing Anyway?." May 12, 2017, https://edition.cnn.com/2017/05/11/asia/china-one-belt-one-road-explainer/index.html (accessed July 13, 2017).

Gul, Ayaz. "Pakistan: Saudi Arabia to Join China-Funded Development Project." *Voice of America,* September 20, 2018, https://www.voanews.com/a/pakistan-saudi-arabia-to-join-china-funded-development-project/4580299.html (accessed October 15, 2018).

"Gwadar Port handed over to China." *Express Tribune*, February 18, 2013, https://tribune.com.pk/story/509028/gwadar-port-handed-over-to-china/ (accessed September 11, 2018).

Hart, Michael. "Central Asia's Oil and Gas Now Flows to the East." *The Diplomat*, Aug 19, 2016, https://thediplomat.com/2016/08/central-asias-oil-and-gas-now-flows-to-the-east/ (accessed October 20, 2018).

"Highlights of China's Central Economic Work Conference 2014." *China Daily*, December 15, 2014, http://www.chinadaily.com.cn/bizchina/2014-12/15/content_19086822.htm (accessed May 12, 2017).

Hernandez, Marco, et al. "China's Super Link to Gwadar Port - A Visual Explainer." South China Morning Post, May 12, 2017, https://multimedia.scmp.com/news/china/article/One-Belt-One-Road/pakistan.html (accessed October 19th, 2018).

Iqbal, Shahid. "Trade Gap with China Rises to $9.7bn in FY18." Dawn, July 29, 2018, https://www.dawn.com/news/1423551 (accessed october 17, 2018).

Jaspal, Zafar Nawaz. "CPEC's Potential to Revolutionize Regional Cooperation and Make Pakistan Pivotal." *Global village Space*, March 17, 2017, https://www.globalvillagespace.com/cpecs-potential-to-revolutionize-regional-cooperation/ (accessed July 29, 2017).

Johnson, Kay. "Pakistani PM Welcomes First Large Chinese Shipment to Gwadar Port." *Reuters*, 13 Nov. 2016, https://www.reuters.com/article/us-pakistan-china-port/pakistani-pm-welcomes-first-large-chinese-shipment-to-gwadar-port-idUSKBN1380LU (accessed October 20th, 2018).

Kakar, Rafiullah. "Making Sense of the CPEC Controversy." *The Express Tribune*, January 21, 2016, https://tribune.com.pk/story/1031850/making-sense-of-the-cpec-controversy/ (accessed September 11, 2018).

Khan, Sharif, "Gwadar Launches CPEC Trade Today." *The Nation*, November 13, 2016, https://nation.com.pk/13-Nov-2016/gwadar-launches-cpec-trade-today (accessed March 19, 2018).

Khan, Wajahat S. "Gwadar Port Project Reveals China's Regional Power Play," *NBC News*, April 30, 2016, https://www.nbcnews.com/news/world/gwadar-port-project-reveals-chinas-regional-power-play-n558236 (accessed September 11, 2018).

Kiani, Khaleeq. "Special Economic Zones Take Centre Stage as CPEC Talks Advance." November 21, 2017, https://www.dawn.com/news/1371792 (accessed February 23, 2018).

Kotoky, Anurag, and A Anantha Lakshmi. "India 'Concerned' by China Role in Pakistan Port." *Reuters*, February 6, 2013, https://www.reuters.com/article/us-india-airshow-china-idUSBRE9150BX20130206 (accessed October 18, 2018).

"Keynote Address by President Xi Jinping at the Opening Ceremony of the World Economic Forum's." *Xinhua News*, January 18, 2017, http://cpc.people.com.cn/n1/2017/0118/c64094-29031339.html (accessed January 12, 2018).

Macfie, Nick. "Li Keqiang Urges Development of 'China-Pakistan Economic Corridor'." South China Morning Post, May 23, 2013, www.scmp.com/news/china/article/1244267/li-keqiang-urges-development-china-pakistan-economic-corridor (accessed October 19, 2018).

Malik, Rashid, "Route Alignment Controversy." *The Nation*, February 20, 2015, https://nation.com.pk/20-Feb-2015/route-alignment-controversy?show=blocks?version=amp. (accessed November 29, 2017).

Mardell, Jacob. "The 'Community of Common Destiny' in Xi Jinping's New Era." *The Diplomat*, October 25, 2017, https://thediplomat.com/2017/10/the-community-of-common-destiny-in-xi-jinpings-new-era/ (accessed October 6, 2018).

Mearsheimer, John J. "Can China Rise Peacefully?." *The National Interest*, October 25, 2014, http://nationalinterest.org/commentary/can-china-rise-peacefully-10204?page=show (accessed November 23, 2014).

Menon, Rhea. "Thailand's Kra Canal: China's Way around the Malacca Strait." *The Diplomat*, April 6, 2018, https://thediplomat.com/2018/04/thailands-kra-canal-chinas-way-around-the-malacca-strait/ (accessed December 05, 2018).

Michał, Romanowski. "Decoding Central Asia: What's next for the US Administration?." *The Diplomat*, February 28, 2017, https://thediplomat.com/2017/02/decoding-central-asia-whats-next-for-the-us-administration/ (accessed April 19, 2017).

"Ministry of Transport Will Promote The 'Silk Road' Traffic Construction From Six Aspects." *Xinhua News*, March 27, 2014, http://news.xinhuanet.com/politics/2014-03/27/c_119981612.htm (accessed March 27, 2014).

Muneer, S.M. "Economic Relations between Pakistan and China." *Business Recorder*, December 15, 2016, https://fp.brecorder.com/2016/12/20161215113672/ (accessed July 7, 2018).

Nikki, Sun. "China Development Bank Commits $250bn to Belt and Road." *Asian Review*, January 15, 2018, https://asia.nikkei.com/Economy/China-Development-Bank-commits-250bn-to-Belt-and-Road (accessed September 19, 2018).

Nodirbek. "How Serious Is the Islamic State Threat to China?." *The Diplomat*, March 14, 2017, https://thediplomat.com/2017/03/how-serious-is-the-islamic-state-threat-to-china/ (accessed September 12, 2018).

Noor, Muhammad Asif, and Farhat Asif. "20 Years of Diplomatic Relations between Kazakhstan & Pakistan." *The Diplomatic Insight*, 2012, http://ipd.org.pk/wp-content/uploads/Book-Kazakhstan-Pakistan-20-Years-of-Diplomatic-Relations.-Final.pdf (accessed October 17, 2017).

"Opinion Polls: More Than 70% of Americans Support Trump "Executive Order to buy U.S. Goods and Hire Americans"." *Sputnik News*, April 24, 2017, http://sputniknews.cn/politics/201704241022443387/ (accessed November 11, 2017).

"Pak-China Friendship is Higher than Mountains, Deeper than Ocean and Sweeter than Honey: PM." *The Nation*, December 9, 2010, https://nation.com.pk/19-Dec-2010/pakchina-friendship-is-higher-than-mountains-deeper-than-ocean-and-sweeter-than-honey-pm (accessed July 7, 2018).

Rehman, Abdur, and Vaqar Ahmed. "CPEC and regional integration." *The News on Sunday*, October 2, 2016, http://tns.thenews.com.pk/cpec-regional-integration/#.W9FfJ3szbIU (accessed October 10, 2018).

Shahid, Aleem. "Gateways along Border Planned." *Dawn*, December 14, 2006, https://www.dawn.com/news/223351/gateways-along-border-planned (accessed July 13, 2017).

Shahid, Saleem. "Gwadar Project Launched: Musharraf Lauds China's Assistance." *Dawn*, March 23, 2002, www.dawn.com/news/27285 (accessed October 22, 2018).

Shaikh, Ayesha. "In Search of Greener Pastures."*Aurora.com*, September 25, 2018, https://aurora.dawn.com/news/1143181 (accessed October 19, 2018).

Shao, Xiaoyi, & Umesh Desai. "China Challenge: Getting Poor Migrant Workers to Buy Vacant Homes." *Reuters*, January 4, 2016, https://www.reuters.com/article/china-property-idUSKBN0UI08220160104 (accessed August 14, 2018).

Stevens, Andrew. "Pakistan Lands $46 Billion Investment from China." *CNN Money*, April 20, 2015, https://money.cnn.com/2015/04/20/news/economy/pakistan-china-aid-infrastucture/ (accessed October 22, 2018).

Stuart, Elizabeth. "China has Almost Wiped out Urban Poverty, Now it Must Tackle Inequality." *The Guardian*, August 19, 2015, https://www.theguardian.com/business/economics-blog/2015/aug/19/china-poverty-inequality-development-goals (accessed August 14, 2018).

Soliev, ZahidGishkor. "Economic Corridor: 12,000-Strong Force to Guard Chinese Workers." *Express Tribune.* March 30, 2015. https://tribune.com.pk/story/861078/economic-corridor-12000-strong-force-to-guard-chinese-workers/ (accessed August 31, 2018).

Sudha, Ramachandran. "CPEC Takes a Step Forward as Violence Surges in Baluchistan." *Asia Times,* November 16, 2016, http://www.atimes.com/cpec-takes-step-forward-violence-surges-balochistan/ (accessed November 29, 2017,).

Raza, Syed Irfan. "15000 Military Personnel Protecting CPEC." *Dawn,* February 21, 2017, https://www.dawn.com/news/1316040/ (accessed August 31, 2018).

"TF-88: Pakistan Navy Special Task Force for CPEC Security Inaugurated." *Times of Islamabad,* December 13, 2016. http://timesofislamabad.com/tf-88-pakistan-navy-special-task-force-cpec-security-inaugurated/2016/12/13/ (accessed on January 29, 2016).

Tarar, Nadeem Omar. "Cementing the Friendship Bond: Pak-China Cultural Ties." *Hilal Magazine,* October, 2015, http://hilal.gov.pk/index.php/layouts/item/1672-cementing-the-friendship-bond-pak-china-cultural-ties (September 13, 2017).

"U.S. Support for the New Silk Road." *US Department of State,* 2017, https://2009-2017.state.gov/p/sca/ci/af/newsilkroad/index.htm (accessed April 23, 2017).

Walsh, Declan. "Chinese Firm Will Run Strategic Pakistani Port at Gwadar." *The New York Times,* Jan 13, 2013, https://www.nytimes.com/2013/02/01/world/asia/chinese-firm-will-run-strategic-pakistani-port-at-gwadar.html?_r=0 (accessed October 5th, 2018).

Wang, Jian. "One Belt One Road": A Vision for the Future of China-Middle East Relations." *Al Jazeera Centre for Studies,* May 9, 2017, http://studies.aljazeera.net/mritems/Documents/2017/5/10/9034672c6c8945d1b52014fe6dbcb7c4_100.pdf (accessed October 17, 2017).

Wang, Tao, and Yampolsky Rachel. "Will China and Russia's Partnership in Central Asia Last?." *The Diplomat,* September 21, 2015 https://thediplomat.com/2015/09/will-china-and-russias-partnership-in-central-asia-last/ (accessed April 11, 2017).

Wei, Hao Yin. "German Media: China Contributes Far More to the World Economic Growth than Europe and the United States." *China News*, December 30, 2016, http://www.chinanews.com/cj/2016/12-30/8109467.shtml (accessed November 12, 2017).

"Xi Jinping Presided Over Non-Party Forums and Democratic." *Xinhua News Agency*, March 03, 2013, http://news.xinhuanet.com/politics/2013-03/20/c 124478704 7.htm (accessed November 13, 2016).

Y, P. Pant. "Nepal-India Trade Relations Some Recent Trends." *The Economic Weekly*, February 24, 1962, https://www.epw.in/journal/1962/8/special-articles/nepal-india-trade-relations-some-recent-trends.html (accessed November 13, 2017).

Yousafzai, Fawad. "CDWP Approves 31 Projects of Rs 713b." *The Nation*, May 3, 2018, https://nation.com.pk/03-May-2018/cdwp-approves-31-projects-of-rs713b (accessed July 23, 2018).

Zhaoli, Wu. "Economic Corridor Will Be Lever for All of South Asia." *Global Times*, May 30, 2013, http://www.globaltimes.cn/content/800223.shtml (accessed November 29, 2017).

"6th JCC on CPEC Held in Beijing." *China Daily*, December 30, 2016, http://www.chinadaily.com.cn/world/2016-12/30/content 27820740.htm (accessed July 13, 2017).

"7th Meeting of Joint Coordination Committee (JCC) Of Pakistan China Economic Corridor (CPEC)." *China Pakistan Economic Corridor*, November 1, 2017, http://cpec.gov.pk/news/74 (accessed November 29, 2017).